Wanamaker

THE

MAKING

OF A

POEM

A Norton Anthology of
Poetic Forms

THE
MAKING
OF A
POEM

A Norton Anthology of
Poetic Forms

EDITED BY

Mark Strand

AND

Eavan Boland

W. W. NORTON & COMPANY

NEW YORK · LONDON

The text of this book is composed in Granjon with the display set in Granjon
Composition by Allentown Digital Services Division of
R.R. Donnelley & Sons Company
Manufacturing by the Haddon Craftsmen
Book design by BTD NYC

LIBRARY OF CONGRESS CATALOGING-IN-PUBLICATION DATA
The making of a poem : a Norton anthology of poetic forms / edited by Mark Strand
and Eavan Boland.
p.   cm.
Includes bibliographical references (p.) and index.
ISBN 0-393-04916-7
1. English poetry   2. American poetry.   3. Literary form.   I. Strand, Mark, 1934–
II. Boland, Eavan.
PR1175.M275 2000
821.008—dc21
99-055233

W. W. Norton & Company, Inc., 500 Fifth Avenue, New York, N.Y. 10110
www.wwnorton.com

W. W. Norton & Company Ltd., 10 Coptic Street, London WC1A 1PU

3   4   5   6   7   8   9   0

Table of Contents

THE BALLAD

THE STANZA

II METER

III SHAPING FORMS

THE ELEGY

The Pastoral

THE ODE

Introductory Statement

This book looks squarely at some of the headaches and mysteries of poetic form. To start with, it is intended to help with down-to-earth queries. How does a sonnet work? What are the rules of a sestina, and who established them? What gets repeated in a villanelle? And where?

In order to provide some answers, we have gone back to the exuberant history of forms, have drawn them out of their shadows in French harvest fields and small Italian courts and have laid out as clearly as possible their often turbulent passage across centuries. We hope the reader will be enchanted, as we have been, by the compelling witness of poet after poet discovering and unfolding their inner world through outward customs and cadences. We hope the reader will agree that these forms are—as we believe—not locks, but keys.

The fascination of poetic form, however, goes well beyond the answer to questions about structure and origin. Once these are answered, another door opens, another labyrinth waits. This book is also intended as a small map of the journey through corridors where history, society, solitude, and power are all traceable from a single poetic form.

The journey is not a smooth one. And so a note on our method and our choices: Perhaps the chief problem is that form is a powerful filter, but not an inclusive one. Women were often underrepresented in poetry in the sixteenth, seventeenth, and eighteenth centuries. They were absent—whether in retrospect or reality—more often than not, from the festival of form that poetry became in those centuries. This would be much more the case had the scholarship of poets and critics like Sandra Gilbert and Susan Gubar not placed the work of poets such as Mary Wroth, Anne Finch, and Charlotte Smith in a more visible formal context. Our inclusion of them here owes much to that placing. Wherever other women from these centuries can be heard in their sometimes inhospitable moment—from Bradstreet to Dickinson—we have included them.

But there were other difficulties, of another sort. The poems of a number of poets we admired were often not suitable for this book. This put us in an awkward, often regrettable position as editors. Despite the fact that we might have included those poems in any collection of our favorites, the fact that they did not illustrate or add to our purposes here kept them out.

In the same way, and for some of these reasons, minority visions and popular voices are not as present as we wanted them to be in the formal poems we chose from earlier centuries. There are reasons for this, and the reasons make a further subtle and important argument about the sociology of poetic form: In the societies that produced the sonnet, the villanelle, the sestina, poetic form was not just an expression of art, it was also a register of power. The society, and its rulers, which provided protection for the poet, had real expectations for the product. Wit, learning, and flattery were all factors of form. The shadow of power lay across it, and therefore poetic form became a visible part of high civilization; often an ambiguous jewel in the crown of a dominant culture.

But the true and final power of form is not societal: poetic form, when it comes from deep feeling as it does in the poems we have chosen, is also deeply human. We have done our best with the outward signs. The real story here is the inward grace: The subtlety, elegance, and hunger of the human spirit is obvious everywhere in this book, neither constrained by nor separable from the cadences, rhymes, lines, and structures that shelter it. Increasingly, toward the mid and late twentieth century those voices which form—as a consequence of power and erudition—had excluded in earlier centuries now entered the fray and added, changed, subverted, and gloriously radicalized poetry. In our section on open forms we have tried to give a sense of these revisions.

There is no denying that anyone editing a book on poetic form in the late twentieth century also finds themselves, by chance or choice, in a charged space made up of narratives that keep bumping into one another. We could not solve or even address these arguments in their entirety. Nor could we walk away from them. And so we have done what editors have done throughout history: We have acknowledged them by elaborating on them.

In the section on closed forms we show the often complicated workings of historic poetic models. We explain that history as clearly as we can. We trace these models in the contemporary moment, and see them renewed in daring and surprising contexts. In doing this, we have wanted to show that a radical in poetry may be someone using conventional form, as well as challenging it. In the section on open forms we suggest that the great changes to poetic form that happened in this century should be seen, not as a disruption, but as a dialogue with those earlier models. And that any real understanding of poetic form, in its widest sense, involves an understanding of that dialogue. The section on open forms also emphasizes our view that form and formalism are associated, but not interchangeable terms. That to consider them as such diminishes the continuity and enrichment of poetry, especially in this century.

We have traced this dialogue through the superb new voices that came into poetry in this century. These voices, from the poets of the Harlem Renaissance to the first modernists to the radical statements of Adrienne Rich, have destabilized our sense of poetic form only to add to it. They have done this by initiating a powerful dialogue with the poetic forms of the past, often changing and widening some of the animating ideas behind poetic form: who the poet is, for instance, and why the poem is written. The section on open forms is intended to show that new ideas of poetic form often emerge in the process of negotiating the charged space between what is inherited and what is known.

When poetic form is seen as a dialogue, the arguments for or against modernism, for or against formalism, for or against tradition enter a more coherent context. Poetry is shown to be, as it always has been, a process, as well as a product. A great part of that process is the poet's interior conversation with a possessed and dispossessed formal past, and also with a great exterior discourse. When the poem is finished, the dialogue continues—enriched by that poem, but still restless and incomplete.

The selection of the poems has been both rewarding and difficult. How to measure, choose, allocate space, and balance the argument with the example? This has been the challenge. With the reader in mind, we have hit on an unusual but workable compromise. From the work of poets whose poems in other centuries defined the possibilities of these forms, we offer several examples. But in the case of twentieth-century poets, and for the sake of variety and equity, we have used one poem from each poet. This we felt, gave the best working model of the wonderful, unpredictable contemporary theater of practice and experiment. Occasionally this has been a painful discipline. It forced us to choose, for instance, between Elizabeth Bishop's villanelle or her sestina. (We chose the former.) But it also has, we believe, surprising rewards for the reader. Form, in history and society, is not just a series of masterpieces. It is also the reflex, the song, the choice, the backhand practice, and the joyous enterprise of all poets at all times.

The editors of this book are both working poets. There is plenty here that is idiosyncratic—a witness to our advocacy as well as our enthusiasm. We make no claims to have been comprehensive. However, our attempts to include the dialogue as well as the poem in our overview of poetic form will, we hope, give both readers and writers a clearer view of the passionate conversation that is, and always has been, at the center of this art.

—Mark Strand
Eavan Boland

On Becoming a Poet by Mark Strand

"You, Andrew Marvell" by Archibald MacLeish

And here face down beneath the sun
And here upon earth's noonward height
To feel the always coming on
The always rising of the night:

To feel creep up the curving east
The earthy chill of dusk and slow
Upon those under lands the vast
And ever climbing shadow grow

And strange at Ecbatan the trees
Take leaf by leaf the evening strange
The flooding dark about their knees
The mountains over Persia change

And now at Kermanshah the gate
Dark empty and the withered grass
And through the twilight now the late
Few travelers in the westward pass

And Baghdad darken and the bridge
Across the silent river gone
And through Arabia the edge
Of evening widen and steal on

And deepen on Palmyra's street
The wheel rut in the ruined stone
And Lebanon fade out and Crete
High through the clouds and overblown

And over Sicily the air
Still flashing with the landward gulls
And loom and slowly disappear
The sails above the shadowy hulls

And Spain go under and the shore
Of Africa the gilded sand
And evening vanish and no more
The low pale light across that land

Nor now the long light on the sea:

And here face downward in the sun
To feel how swift how secretly
The shadow of the night comes on . . .

I

"You, Andrew Marvell" by Archibald MacLeish was the first poem
about which I felt passionate, the first that I thought I understood, the
first that I actually wished I had written. My own poems—the few
that I wrote in my adolescence—were feverish attempts to put "my
feelings" on paper, and little more. Their importance, at least for me,
their only reader, was exhausted by the time they were written. In
those days my life was one of constantly shifting weather, and the
world within was rarely in sync with the world without. No wonder
the linearity, the cool emotional order of "You, Andrew Marvell"
appealed to me.

The poem was saying things that I wished I could say. The same
feelings that had troubled me, and whose victim I was, now seemed,
coming from the poem, sources of pleasure. When I read it for the
first time, I knew little about poetry. I didn't know who Andrew
Marvell was, nor did I know where half of the places were that
MacLeish mentions. I only knew—what was most important for me
then—that I was the figure "face down beneath the sun." I was the
one whose consciousness was connected to the nearing of the night,
to its shadow creeping always closer. This description of the distant
night's inevitable approach, even as it reflected my own increasing
awareness of mortality, was calming. I now felt located in a vastness,
which, in my real life, had made me feel lost. The emotions that
overwhelmed my solitude took on a shape, one that I found pleasing
no matter how often I returned to it. I had no idea of how the poem
accomplished its magic, and somehow, despite my many readings of
it, I was never moved to inquire.

It wasn't until years later, after I had written and published my poems, that I took a close look at it. I remember the mesmerizing power its list of places had over me, how it gave grandiose definition to my vague and fugitive thoughts about death and time passing. But what I had experienced this time was something else. I was aware, as I had been in the past, that the poem seemed suspended between times. Only now that suspension seemed to feature a strange circularity, each event marked by a newness but eerily resembling the events that had come before. The trees at Ecbatan shared something with the grasses at Kermanshah and the gulls over Sicily. Beginning with "And" and ending inconclusively with an ellipsis, the poem as a whole hints at this suspended circularity. Not only does the first line begin with an "and," but the second line does as well, so that the poem seems to insist on its own connective character and, moreover, to allude to something that is ongoing, that won't stop: "And here face down beneath the sun / And here upon earth's noonward height." In other words, "You, Andrew Marvell" is both about time and in time, about motion and in motion. It is both linear and circular, and what it suggests is not just the simple diurnal round of night and day, but the more tragic rise and fall of civilizations.

And yet, the poem's speaker seems oddly removed from what he describes—not just because he is situated temporally at precisely noon ("earth's noonward height"), but because his feeling is unattached to tense or to personhood. It exists in an overriding infinitive, out of time but responsive to time: "To feel the always coming on /The always rising of the night://To feel creep up the curving east /The earthly chill of dusk." Just as "and" is used in the first two lines to underscore the additive elements of the poem, so "always" is used in the next two lines to characterize with reasonable insistence what the infinitive "to feel" can embrace, which is to say "everything."

In another significant gesture of encompassment, the poem's first rhyme of "sun" and "on" is also its last rhyme, not only marking the duration of the speaker's attention, but bringing the poem around to what feels like an ending, except that here the ending is a reenactment of the beginning. And it is not only the repeated rhyme that accomplishes the poem's circularity, but its minimal punctuation as well. A colon is used twice, once four lines from the beginning and again four lines from the end. In each symmetrical instance it signals a pause, which will be followed by the additional pause of the stanza break. The lengthening and doubling of the pause helps to emphasize in yet another way the centrality of the infinitive "to feel."

But somehow the urgency that usually attends feeling is missing. What is suggested, instead, is that "to feel" embodies a temporal character and though different from the circular, suspended temporality it responds to, it nevertheless appears related to it. Moreover, because of the ambiguous and, I believe, elaborate way "to feel" is presented, the poem appears to be acknowledging a response that we've already had while at the same time urging us to participate in an extended reconstruction of it. To feel the night come, its advent in various and ravishing manifestations, to be swept up in the vastness of time, to feel it all inwardly, face downward in the sun, is what the poem seems to insist on, but with a languor that is in direct contrast to the heated urgency implicit in the speech of the lover in Marvell's "To His Coy Mistress." In that poem, to which this one obviously responds, no dispassionate view of time's devastating power can be reenacted. Love, the act of love, the pleasure it seeks might offer the illusion of sidestepping the inevitable; but the lovers cannot stop the sun, all they can do is make it run, that is, make time pass more quickly, join their heat to the sun's heat. In MacLeish's poem, there is definitely "world enough and time." Its serenity, the casual way it ticks off exotic places, carries with it the implication that there is something beautiful about bending to what is inexorable, and that meditating on one's immortality can seem a form of transcendence.

Another aspect of MacLeish's use of "to feel" is how it internalizes the huge impersonality of time, and how it makes the visual record of ascending night into a private matter instead of simply a geographic one. We are asked to feel the reach of the poem's vision for as long as we can. And this is probably why it appealed to me as a teenager. The experience the poem offered was that of an immense privacy at the center of which was a figure whose imagination provided the purest and most far-reaching provocation for feeling.

I also undoubtedly liked it for its apparent simplicity. I had no idea that a highly sophisticated craftsmanship was responsible for its easeful disclosures, that the virtual absence of punctuation gave it an added fluency, lending its geographical accretions a hypnotic inevitability. I knew that meter was involved in the enchantment I felt, but I didn't know how important its strict maintenance was to the poem's meaning, that keeping time was the surest way the poem had of adhering to its subject, that the pause and stress of its iambic tetrameter line was as sobering and as steady as nightfall.

The poem's lack of punctuation is one of its most pronounced formal features, the one most responsible for its fluency and the casual way its modifiers shift, clinging momentarily to one noun or verb, then joining forces with another, sometimes following, sometimes preceding. This happens most obviously and most strikingly in the second and third stanzas, first with the rhyme word "slow" and then with the oddly reiterated "strange": "To feel creep up the curving east /The earthly chill of dusk and slow / Upon those under lands the vast /And ever climbing shadow grow//And strange at Ecbatan the trees /Take leaf by leaf the evening strange."

"Slow" in stanza two is how "the ever climbing shadow grow[s]," but in stanza three it is also how "leaf by leaf" the trees at Ecbatan absorb the evening. The effortless way "and slow" is coupled with "and strange" three lines later might have been compromised into syntactical fussiness had commas been used. And in an equally understated way, "strange" at the end of the second line of stanza three enacts a doubleness that suits its meaning. It seems at first, in a graceful inversion, like a modifier of "evening." But that's only if we place a comma after it. If the comma is placed before it, then it modifies "the flooding dark" in the subsequent line. Not only that, but the "knees" belong to the "trees," as if rhyme, in compensation for the missing punctuation, were assigning meaning. This works if we place a period after "knees," but doing so only forces the next three lines into an implied sentence of disturbing flatness: "The mountains over Persia change //And now at Kermanshah the gate /Dark empty and the withered grass." With a comma after "knees," however, the line would be subordinated to line four of the third stanza, which could end in either a comma or a period.

And one could go on from there, endlessly changing an imaginary punctuation, creating new shades of meaning, new emphases, but it would be fruitless, since the poem works best just as it is. Its ambiguities are essential not only to its fluidity, but to its vast suggestiveness as well. The poem urges us to read its lines one after another without stopping, yet insisting, it seems to me, on the integrity of each. The line, after all, and not the sentence, is its basic unit. It has no sentences other than the ones our playfulness or, more likely, our insecurity, would have us invent for it.

II

One might think that my ability to analyze and comment on the technique by which "You, Andrew Marvell" asserts its particular hold on the reader would alter my response to the poem. But my response now is pretty much what it was then. I am still that figure face down beneath the sun. The experience of the poem has paradoxically overcome the poem's message of mutability. And the sense that I am still myself—myself essentially as I was—is as present as the knowledge of how swiftly, how secretly the shadow of the night comes on. It is as if the poem's power to enchant carried with it an obligation to reassure.

Something beyond knowledge compels our interest and our ability to be moved by a poem. As an adolescent I may not have known anything about the intricacies of poetry, but I was beginning to think about mortal matters the way an adult does. And that more than anything made it possible for me to respond to "You, Andrew Marvell," and, thereafter, to other lyric poems. When I say "lyric poems" I mean poems that manifest musical properties, but are intended to be read or spoken, not sung. They are usually brief, rarely exceeding a page or two, and have about them a degree of emotional intensity, or an urgency that would account for their having been written at all. At their best, they represent the shadowy, often ephemeral motions of thought and feeling, and do so in ways that are clear and comprehensible. Not only do they fix in language what is often most elusive about our experience, but they convince us of its importance, its truth even. Of all literary genres, the lyric is the least changeable. Its themes are rooted in the continuity of human subjectivity and from antiquity have assumed a connection between privacy and universality. There are countless poems from the past that speak to us with an immediacy time has not diminished, that gauge our humanness as accurately and as passionately as any poem written today.

It is not difficult to imagine that most people who have lived on this planet have felt in considering the coming of night the advent of their own mortality. And what they felt did not seem bound by the particular century in which they lived. It is clear that Archibald

Macleish was bound—at least when he was writing this poem—by a notion of time having more to do with the passing of events, human life being one of them, than he was in a theoretical, abstract, or strictly twentieth-century vision of time. For in "You, Andrew Marvell" the earth does not turn. It is darkness that is active. It is darkness that happens to the world just as surely as death will happen to the one face downward in the sun. The poem is bound by a schema that is no less true for standing apart from what science tells us is true. Like most lyrics, it reminds us that we live in time and allows us to feel a certain joy in that knowledge. The losses that are inseparable from experience take on a certain sweetness and resonance.

It is likely that the lyric, either by its formal appeal to memory when rhyme and meter are used, or simply by its being an artifact, provides a redress to its message of human evanescence. "You, Andrew Marvell" is about loss, but the naming of places, even as they fall under the cloak of dark, is an act of restoration. Cities and civilizations are taken away but new ones appear. The ellipsis at the poem's end seems to imply that another cycle of replenishment is on its way; just as the word "always," used with such emphasis at the start of the poem, implies the superabundance and availability of time.

III

It is hard for me to separate my development as a reader of poems from my career as a poet. If my readings have any acuity or sensitivity, it is probably because I have paid close attention to how my own poems worked, and to which ways and to what extent I might improve them. This mutual dependency is always reflected in the work. A poem will make continual reference to an experience while at the same time call attention to itself as a vehicle for meaning.

Although I no longer wish I had written "You, Andrew Marvell," I wish, however, that I could write something like it, something with its sweep, its sensuousness, its sad crepuscular beauty, something capable of carving out such a large psychic space for itself. It is one of the poems that I read and reread, and that reinforces my belief in poetry, and that makes me want to write. There is something about it that moves me in ways that I don't quite understand, as it were communicating more than what it actually says. This is often the case with good poems—they have a lyric identity that goes beyond whatever their subject happens to be. They have a voice, and the formation of that voice, the gathering up of imagined sound into utterance, may be the true occasion for their existence. A poem may be the residue of an inner urgency, one through which the self wishes to register itself, write itself into being, and, finally, to charm another self, the reader, into belief. It may also be something equally elusive—the ghost within every experience that wishes it could be seen or felt, acknowledged as a kind of meaning.

It could be a truth so forgiving that it offers up, a humanness in which we are able to imagine ourselves. A poem is a place where the conditions of beyondness and withinness are made palpable, where to imagine is to feel what it is like to be. It allows us to have the life we are denied because we are too busy living. Even more paradoxically, a poem permits us to live in ourselves as if we were just out of reach of ourselves.

Poetic Form: A Personal Encounter
by Eavan Boland

A child is standing in a room in a winter dusk. The light fil-
tering through the glass is thick and foggy and strange.
The child is about six years of age. Here also, with his back
to the window, is the child's father. He is reading aloud the first lines
from William Blake's poem about a tiger. It is a poem he likes and he
reads it with emphasis. "Tyger! Tyger! burning bright: / In the
forests of the night." The rhythms are strong and commanding. The
father's voice sounds exactly as it does when he is angry. The child is
interested, struck, awed. She stands listening to the rhythms. She
catches some of the sense. She is enchanted and oppressed, all at the
same moment.

Is that all? After all, this is how a lot of children come across po-
etry, standing in front of a parent, hearing their voice change out of
its everyday tone. But there are some other factors here. They are just
at the edge of the scenario, almost out of sight, and now they need to
be considered.

The previous summer the same child had gone to the zoo in
Dublin with the same father. The light was vivid, the colors were gar-
ish. The whole place was crisscrossed with confusing signs and clus-
ters of people in front of cages. Somehow she got lost in the lion
house. For some minutes—maybe only five or ten—she ran up and
down in the gloomy, frightening interior. The lions paced and the

tigers turned swiftly around and around behind their bars. She was confused and fascinated and lost. Then her father called her name, in that angry voice. Then she was found.

And now back to the winter dusk. The lines of the poem do not quite enter a clear space. There is something waiting for them. As their music and emphasis enters the strange, foggy room through a human voice they are met by the memory of summer light and fear. And so even as the words of the poem happen, they are already arranging, in the most subtle and powerful way, experiences that have already happened. They are cutting across time and completed experience to show that, after all, it was incomplete.

That child was me. The encounter with Blake's poem was indeed in a wintry room full of the grit and smoke of London fog. No question about that. The real question is where the encounter with form began. And this is where the first touch of the mystery of form begins. I can return now to the room, to the child, to the sounds my father is making of the tiger burning ominously in the forest.

I could return and argue persuasively that the form was already there. That it inhered not in sounds, or words, or sense but in wordless, vivid fear. That made me ready to reformalize the dangerous beasts of those few terrified moments, the angry sound of my name being called by this very voice. But then I could go to the other side and say, no, not so. Form waited for me: waited for more than a hundred years on that page. Waited in cold print and cool and changing paper shapes. Waited to find the child, rather than the other way around.

The child is gone. I am nineteen years of age and beginning to write and publish poems. I live outside the center of Dublin in a flat overlooking a narrow garden. At the kitchen window is a table. On the table is a notebook. And there, at night when I come back from University, I encounter poetic form. Or what I think is poetic form. I live in a small city with an intense, old-fashioned poetic life. Modernism has passed through it and has gone again. These are the early nineteen-sixties but the poem that is most admired is not the fractured narrative of modernist example. It is a hybrid throwback to the nineteenth century: a mixture of the Irish and British lyric. It has moving parts. Cogs and wheels and bearings. And since this is the poem in the air around me, this is the one I try to become accomplished in. I try to write in stanzas, with rhymes. I think respectfully of a poem as moving through cadences, as being disrupted by rhyme at the end of the line, as being reconnected by music to the next line even while the connection has been broken by sense. Although poets had almost nothing to do with the academic world in Ireland at that time, there was a surprisingly solemn and official view of poetics in the world in which I lived. Meters had names. Poems were dissected according to those names. The names were hard and bleak and Latinate. Nevertheless I learned what an iamb was and a trochee. I called them by their names as if this would give me access to a closed and important circle of understanding, through which I would become more a poet.

I can still see myself, tapping my little finger on the tablecloth and counting back in drum taps toward my thumb. I can see myself trying to judge what a trochee with its long, harsh crowlike noise might look like at the start of one of my poems. I think about how to compensate for its dissonance with nursery rhyme foot stamps. Not all of it seems like schoolwork. Occasionally I see a glitter of movement, like the top edge of a waterfall in the distance. But mostly it seems hard, useless, at a tangent from what I really want to express in poetry. Sometimes to console myself, I tell myself that I am no different from any young musician, reading sheet music in a conservatory. Or any young painter, squiggling paint out onto a palette, learning to call red carmine and orange ochre.

And yet by midnight depression would settle in. What was I doing there in a flat, closed away from language in this futile dissection of it? I was nearly twenty years of age. I was Irish. I was a woman. Beyond my window was a city of shadows and echoes. Beyond that again was a space full of voices, whispers, agitations which I could hardly hear and yet needed to. Out there somewhere was the orchestra of excitement and exchange about the nature of poetry in our century. It was a place where letters, journals, lectures, and good old-fashioned quarrels were all stating the obvious: that poetry had changed. That we were part of the change. That we needed, as poets, to define it for ourselves in order to avail of it.

This broad, democratic uproar would come to seem to me one of the most exciting and enabling dimensions of being a contemporary poet. But I was not yet a citizen of the democracy. Instead I was aware of many rules and all my failures. I was aware of a stern past offering harsh definitions of the act of poetry, some of which I would have to challenge in order to survive. But none of these realities ever entered the poem. Nor did the color of the shirt I was wearing, nor the sound of a telephone ringing downstairs. Where was the poem that I had once heard, with a tiger snarl and a perfect music, through which I understood my life even as I listened to it? I couldn't write it. I was not even sure anymore than I could read it. I had learned a line. And it had silenced me.

And now it is a few miles away and fifteen years later. The summer night is just setting in, hardly an hour before midnight. Everything is fresh, dark, alive. Earlier, after the rain, there were water drops and wasps under the fuchsia. The hills disappeared and the August constellations rose, only to disappear in the humid skies of south Dublin.

Again the table. Again the notebook. But this time everything is different. The poem that is on the page is in stanzas. There is a line. It is broken in certain places. But there the resemblance ends with the earlier flat and the nighttime struggle with form when I was nineteen.

What exactly has changed? To start with, if I get up from the table, walk out of my room, I can hear the breathing and stirring of my small children. All day I will have been with them: lifting them, talking to them, drying their tears, setting their clothes aside at the end of the day. Through all these tasks and pleasures I have begun to hear my voice. It is the entirely natural, sometimes exasperated and always human voice of someone living in the middle of their life, from task to task, full of love and intense perceptions.

Is that all? That question again. Yes it is, but strangely, this time, it is enough. That voice I hear every day, which is my own voice, which is emerging from the deepest origins of my self—which is never practised, rehearsed, or made artificial by self-consciousness—has begun to invade my lyric sense of the poem.

Now when I sit down to write a poem I am determined that this voice will be integral to it. That I will hear it in the poem, just as I have heard it an hour earlier as I lifted a bicycle and said good night to a neighbour. Just as I heard it when I opened the window of a child's room and put out the large brown moth that was fluttering behind the curtain.

And it is that voice that now begins to shift the interior of the poem, with its granite weights of custom and diffidence. It is that voice that complies with a life rather than the other way around. Without realizing it, I have come upon one of the shaping formal energies: the relation of the voice to the line. That simple discovery begins to dissolve all the borrowed voices of my apprenticeship. I begin to see how it would be to be able to work with the line by working against it, pushing the music of dailyness against the customary shapes of the centuries. Suddenly I see how these contrary forces make language plastic. And how exciting it is to find that a poetic language will liberate and not constrain.

And suddenly also, that crackle and static of voices debating the century in terms of its poetry is able to be heard in my starlit suburb. I can listen to it because I have joined it. What I have learned to do, in fact—which is simply, in technical terms to use the voice *against* the line, rather than with it as the nineteenth-century poets did—is only a fraction, although to me a vital one, of the enormous treasure of technical innovation that the poets of the twentieth century have engaged in.

And so, almost without knowing it, I have joined up with the journey of poets in my time: one of the most demanding, poignant, and adventurous journeys that poets have ever undertaken. Its destination is never quite certain. The static messages, in that sense, are continuing. But its point of departure remains clear. It is the form of the poem. That form which comes as a truth teller and intercessor from history itself, making structures of language, making music of feeling. This book is about the point of departure. And its intention is simply to allow the reader and the writer of poetry, wherever they are, to travel hopefully.

Acknowledgments

This book, and its editors, owe a great debt to our editor Jill Bialosky's tact, patience, and faith. Sandra Gilbert, Franklin Burroughs, Kevin Casey were all helpful readers. Drake Bennett's assistance was invaluable. In terms of the actual assembling of the various pieces, we would like to thank Nan Cohen, a Jones Lecturer in Poetry at Stanford, who worked on the permissions, and Joanie Mackowski, a Stegner Fellow in Poetry at Stanford. Indeed, the resources of Stanford University, from its library to the help and advice of colleagues, were greatly valued.

I

Verse Forms

Overview

Verse forms do not define poetic form: they simply express it. It is an important distinction. For many people what is off-putting about poetic form is the belief, sometimes based on an unlucky class or exam, that these are cold and arbitrary rules, imposed to close out readers rather than include them.

The various poems and histories that follow will contradict that. They show that poetic form is not abstract, but human. Nor is it a monolith. The villanelle is different from the sonnet. To understand them fully it is necessary to see how distinct their histories are, how separate their purposes. And the distinction, in turn, is the reason that each poetic form has been rediscovered—or indeed rejected—in such a different way in the twentieth century. The sonnet, for instance, whose octave and sestet, or quatrains and couplet, were once the lock and key of Renaissance wit, has not attracted contemporary poets in the way the villanelle has. It does not offer the same chance to be both bleak and redemptive that the circular refrain of the villanelle gives.

This is the charm and power of poetic form. It is not imposed; it is rooted. Those roots may reach deep into the harvests of Italy, where the villanelle may once have been sung as a round song. Or they may feed in the small treacherous courts where the troubadours vied with each other, and the sestina became a masterwork of one of them, Arnaut Daniel. But whatever the circumstance, they are lodging deep into human history. We have tried to clarify some of this for the reader.

Even more exciting—and we have allowed as much space as possible for this—is the sight of contemporary poets, in completely different circumstances, bringing new voices to old forms. The way in which a twentieth-century poet like Elizabeth Bishop or Dylan Thomas can rediscover the villanelle, and entrust it with their deepest dreams and feelings, is a proof of how these forms reinscribe themselves over and over again. This thrilling relation, between a time and a form, is at the heart of this section.

The Villanelle at a Glance

1) It is a poem of nineteen lines.

2) It has five stanzas, each of three lines, with a final one of four lines.

3) The first line of the first stanza is repeated as the last line of the second and fourth stanzas.

4) The third line of the first stanza is repeated as the last line of the third and fifth stanzas.

5) These two refrain lines follow each other to become the second-to-last and last lines of the poem.

6) The rhyme scheme is *aba*. The rhymes are repeated according to the refrains.

The History of the Form

I t hardly seems likely that a form so sparkling and complicated as the villanelle could have had its origin in an Italian harvest field. In fact it came from an Italian rustic song, the term itself *villanella* thought to derive from *villano,* an Italian word for "peasant," or even *villa* the Latin word for "country house" or "farm."

If it was a round song—something sung with repetitive words and refrains—it may have taken its first, long-lost shape as an accompaniment to the different stages of an agricultural task. Binding sheaves perhaps, or even scything. No actual trace of this early origin remains. By the time the villanelle emerges into poetic history, it does so as a French poem with pastoral themes.

The form we know today began with the work of a French poet called Jean Passerat. He was a popular, politically engaged writer in sixteenth-century France. When he died in 1602, he left behind him several poems that had entered popular affection and memory.

One of these was his villanelle about a lost turtledove: a disguised love song. Even through a fraction of Passerat's poems on his lost turtledove, the twentieth-century villanelle can be seen clearly:

> *J'ai perdu my tourterelle:*
> Est-ce point celle que j'oy?

Je veux aller apres elle.
Tu regretes ta femelle?
Helas! aussi fais je-moy:
J'ai perdu ma tourterelle.

With the publication of this villanelle and because of its immedi-ate popularity—amounting almost to popular-song status in its day—the form defined itself through contact with an audience: a striking but not uncommon way for poetic form to find itself.

This poem established the pattern for all future villanelles, both in French and English. The actual structure is as follows. Five stanzas occur of three lines each. They are followed by a stanza, a quatrain, of four lines. This is common to all villanelles. The first line of the first stanza serves as the last line of the second and fourth stanzas. The third line of the first stanza serves as the last line of the third and fifth stanzas. And these two refrain lines reappear to constitute the last two lines of the closing quatrain. This intricate metrical pattern is set off by intricate rhyming. The rhyme scheme is *aba,* for the first three lines of the poem. And these rhymes reappear to match and catch the refrains, throughout the villanelle. The third line of the first stanza rhymes with the third line of the fourth stanza. And so on.

In the 1870s in England, French poetry became an object of in-terest and admiration. Swinburne, for instance, wrote an elegy for Baudelaire. This was followed by an interest in the forms of French verse and several poets of the time, including Henley and Oscar Wilde, took it up. Oscar Wilde's villanelle was written in 1891 and, though stiff and ornamental, shows the form ready to be launched into the twentieth century.

The Contemporary Context

Over the course of this century some of the finest poets have turned to the villanelle. And this in an age when artifice in poetry has been distrusted. What does the villanelle do that other poems cannot?

Perhaps the single feature of the villanelle that twentieth-century poets most made their own is the absence of narrative possibility. Figural development is possible in a villanelle. But the form refuses to tell a story. It circles around and around, refusing to go forward in any kind of linear development, and so suggesting at the deepest level, powerful recurrences of mood and emotion and memory.

Unlike most other rhymed poems, where the sound of single syllables is repeated once or twice, the villanelle repeats one sound thirteen times and another six. And two entire lines are each repeated four times. It is this last feature that sets the form aside from other poems. The villanelle cannot really establish a conversational tone. It leans toward song, toward lyric poetry. And while the subject of most lyric poems is loss, the formal properties of the villanelle address the idea of loss directly.

Its repeated lines, the circularity of its stanzas, become, as the reader listens, a repudiation of forward motion, of temporality and therefore, finally, of dissolution. Each stanza of a villanelle, with its refrains, becomes a series of retrievals.

ERNEST DOWSON

Villanelle of His Lady's Treasures

I took her dainty eyes, as well
    As silken tendrils of her hair:
And so I made a Villanelle!

I took her voice, a silver bell,
    As clear as song, as soft as prayer;
I took her dainty eyes as well.

It may be, said I, who can tell,
    These things shall be my less despair?
And so I made a Villanelle!

I took her whiteness virginal
    And from her cheeks two roses rare:
I took her dainty eyes as well.

I said: "It may be possible
    Her image from my heart to tear!"
And so I made a Villanelle.

I stole her laugh, most musical:
    I wrought it in with artful care;
I took her dainty eyes as well;
And so I made a Villanelle.

EDWIN ARLINGTON ROBINSON

The House on the Hill

They are all gone away,
    The House is shut and still,
There is nothing more to say.

Through broken walls and gray
    The winds blow bleak and shrill:
They are all gone away.

Nor is there one to-day
    To speak them good or ill:
There is nothing more to say.

Why is it then we stray
   Around the sunken sill?
They are all gone away,

And our poor fancy-play
   For them is wasted skill:
There is nothing more to say.

There is ruin and decay
   In the House on the Hill:
They are all gone away.
There is nothing more to say.

WILLIAM EMPSON

Missing Dates

Slowly the poison the whole blood stream fills.
It is not the effort nor the failure tires.
The waste remains, the waste remains and kills.

It is not your system or clear sight that mills
Down small to the consequence a life requires;
Slowly the poison the whole blood stream fills.

They bled an old dog dry yet the exchange rills
Of young dog blood gave but a month's desires;
The waste remains, the waste remains and kills.

It is the Chinese tombs and the slag hills
Usurp the soil, and not the soil retires.
Slowly the poison the whole blood stream fills.

Not to have fire is to be a skin that shrills.
The complete fire is death. From partial fires
The waste remains, the waste remains and kills.

It is the poems you have lost, the ills
From missing dates, at which the heart expires.
Slowly the poison the whole blood stream fills.
The waste remains, the waste remains and kills.

THEODORE ROETHKE

The Waking

I wake to sleep, and take my waking slow.
I feel my fate in what I cannot fear.
I learn by going where I have to go.

We think by feeling. What is there to know?
I hear my being dance from ear to ear.
I wake to sleep, and take my waking slow.

Of those so close beside me, which are you?
God bless the Ground! I shall walk softly there,
And learn by going where I have to go.

Light takes the Tree; but who can tell us how?
The lowly worm climbs up a winding stair;
I wake to sleep, and take my waking slow.

Great Nature has another thing to do
To you and me; so take the lively air,
And, lovely, learn by going where to go.

This shaking keeps me steady. I should know.
What falls away is always. And is near.
I wake to sleep, and take my waking slow.
I learn by going where I have to go.

ELIZABETH BISHOP

One Art

The art of losing isn't hard to master;
so many things seem filled with the intent
to be lost that their loss is no disaster.

Lose something every day. Accept the fluster
of lost door keys, the hour badly spent.
The art of losing isn't hard to master.

Then practice losing farther, losing faster:
places, and names and where it was you meant
to travel. None of these will bring disaster.

I lost my mother's watch. And look! my last, or
next-to-last, of three loved houses went.
The art of losing isn't hard to master.

I lost two cities, lovely ones. And, vaster,
some realms I owned, two rivers, a continent.
I miss them, but it wasn't a disaster.

—Even losing you (the joking voice, a gesture
I love) I shan't have lied. It's evident
the art of losing's not too hard to master
though it may look like (*Write* it!) like disaster.

DYLAN THOMAS

Do Not Go Gentle into That Good Night

Do not go gentle into that good night,
Old age should burn and rave at close of day;
Rage, rage against the dying of the light.

Though wise men at their end know dark is right,
Because their words had forked no lightning they
Do not go gentle into that good night.

Good men, the last wave by, crying how bright
Their frail deeds might have danced in a green bay,
Rage, rage against the dying of the light.

Wild men who caught and sang the sun in flight,
And learn, too late, they grieved it on its way,
Do not go gentle into that good night.

Grave men, near death, who see with blinding sight
Blind eyes could blaze like meteors and be gay,
Rage, rage against the dying of the light.

And you, my father, there on the sad height,
Curse, bless, me now with your fierce tears, I pray.
Do not go gentle into that good night.
Rage, rage against the dying of the light.

JAMES MERRILL

The World and the Child

Letting his wisdom be the whole of love,
The father tiptoes out, backwards. A gleam
Falls on the child awake and wearied of,

Then, as the door clicks shut, is snuffed. The glove-
Gray afterglow appalls him. It would seem
That letting wisdom be the whole of love

Were pastime even for the bitter grove
Outside, whose owl's white hoot of disesteem
Falls on the child awake and wearied of.

He lies awake in pain, he does not move,
He will not call. The women, hearing him,
Would let their wisdom be the whole of love.

People have filled the room he lies above.
Their talk, mild variation, chilling theme,
Falls on the child. Awake and wearied of

Mere pain, mere wisdom also, he would have
All the world waking from its winter dream,
Letting its wisdom be. The whole of love
Falls on the child awake and wearied of.

MONA VAN DUYN

Condemned Site

Peter, Tom, David, Jim and Howard are gone.
Down hallways, in long-kept rooms, four others are in danger.
In Love's old boardinghouse the shades of five rooms are drawn.

At table their places are set, their tea-time kettle is on,
no space has been aired and emptied for the needy stranger,
though Peter, Tom, David, Jim and Howard are gone.

No one answers the ring of phone, the knocks from dusk to dawn
of Sorrow's cost-accountant, the would-be rearranger
of Love's old boardinghouse. The shades of five rooms are drawn

on the Heart's unlicensed embalming. Soon, fenced from the lawn,
only the watching world, privacy's dog-in-the-manger,
can say Peter, Tom, David, Jim and Howard are gone,

and even the world, turning, will glimpse them alive in a spawn
of unchanging images they tore from Time, the changer.
In Love's old boardinghouse the shades of five rooms are drawn,

but those rooms are bright and warm. Four other guests are in
    danger
in Love's old boardinghouse. The shades of five rooms are drawn
as if Peter, Tom, David, Jim and Howard were gone.
A house of shades is crumpled by Life, the great Stock Exchanger.

JOHN HOLLANDER

By the Sound

Dawn rolled up slowly what the night unwound
And gulls shrieked violently just out of sight.
That was when I was living by the sound.

The silent water heard the light resound
From all its wriggling mirrors, as the bright
Dawn rolled up slowly what the night unwound.

Each morning had a riddle to expound;
The wrong winds would blow leftward to the right,
In those days I was living by the sound:

The dinghies sank, the large craft ran aground,
Desire leapt overboard, perhaps in fright.
Dawn rolled up slowly what the night unwound.

But seldom, in the morning's lost-and-found
Would something turn up that was free of blight.
In those days I was living by the sound

The sky contrived, whose water lay around
The place that I was dreaming by the light
(Dawn rolled up slowly) what the night unwound
In those days. I was living by the sound.

HAYDEN CARRUTH

Saturday at the Border

Here I am writing my first villanelle
At seventy-one, and feeling old and tired—
"Hey, pops, why dontcha just give us the old death-knell?"—

And writing it what's more on the rim of hell
In blazing Arizona when all I desired
Was north and solitude and not a villanelle,

Working from memory and not remembering well
How many stanzas and in what order, wired
On Mexican coffee, seeing the death-knell

Of sun's salvos upon these hills that yell
Bloody murder silently to the much admired
Dead-blue sky. One wonders if a villanelle

Can do the job. Yes, old men now must tell
Our young world how these bigots and these retired
Bankers of Arizona are ringing the death-knell

For all of us, how ideologies compel
Children to violence. Artifice acquired
For its own sake is war. Frail Villanelle,

Have you this power? And must I go and sell
Myself? "Wow," they say, and "cool"—this hired
Old poetry guy with his spaced out death-knell.

Ah, far from home and God knows not much fired
By thoughts of when he thought he was inspired,
He writes by writing what he must. Death-knell
Is what he's found in his first villanelle.

DARYL HINE

Under the Hill

The gates fly open with a pretty sound,
Nor offer opposition to the knight.
A sensual world, remote, extinct, is found.

In walls that like luxurious thorns surround
The exquisite lewdness of the sybarite,
The gates fly open with a pretty sound.

Where venery goes hunting like a hound,
And all the many mouths of pleasure bite,
A sensual world, remote, extinct, is found.

The passionate pilgrim strayed beneath the ground
Meets only death, until, to his delight,
The gates fly open with a pretty sound.

In Venus' clutches, under Venus' mound,
He whiles away the long venereal night.
A sensual world, remote, extinct, is found.

The single function on which Venus frowned
Was birth; and, maybe, life has proved her right.
The gates fly open with a pretty sound.
A sensual world, remote, extinct, is found.

MARILYN HACKER

Villanelle

Every day our bodies separate,
explode torn and dazed.
Not understanding what we celebrate

we grope through languages and hesitate
and touch each other, speechless and amazed;
and every day our bodies separate

us further from our planned, deliberate
ironic lives. I am afraid, disphased,
not understanding what we celebrate

when our fused limbs and lips communicate
the unlettered power we have raised.
Every day our bodies' separate

routines are harder to perpetuate.
In wordless darkness we learn wordless praise,
not understanding what we celebrate;

wake to ourselves, exhausted, in the late
morning as the wind tears off the haze,
not understanding how we celebrate
our bodies. Every day we separate.

WENDY COPE

Reading Scheme

Here is Peter. Here is Jane. They like fun.
Jane has a big doll. Peter has a ball.
Look, Jane, look! Look at the dog! See him run!

Here is Mummy. She has baked a bun.
Here is the milkman. He has come to call.
Here is Peter. Here is Jane. They like fun.

Go Peter! Go Jane! Come, milkman, come!
The milkman likes Mummy. She likes them all.
Look, Jane, look! Look at the dog! See him run!

Here are the curtains. They shut out the sun.
Let us peep! On tiptoe Jane! You are small!
Here is Peter. Here is Jane. They like fun.

I hear a car, Jane. The milkman looks glum.
Here is Daddy in his car. Daddy is tall.
Look, Jane, look! Look at the dog! See him run!

Daddy looks very cross. Has he a gun?
Up milkman! Up milkman! Over the wall!
Here is Peter. Here is Jane. They like fun.
Look, Jane, look! Look at the dog! See him run!

JACQUELINE OSHEROW

Villanelle for the Middle of the Night

Call it the refrigerator's hum at night,
The even breathing of a sleeping house
As a halo drifts in from a corner streetlight.

Awake, you train an ear to single out
A music jangling just beneath the noise.
Call it the refrigerator's hum at night.

Since you have no real hope of being accurate,
But what you mean is usually as diffuse
As a halo drifting from a corner streetlight.

Tonight, though, it is concentrated, intimate,
Luring you to store up what it says
(Call it the refrigerator's hum at night;

That, at least, accommodates the feel of it)
To try to temper yearning into praise,
As a halo drifting from a corner streetlight

Tempts an unsuspecting city street
With its otherworldly armory of shadows.
Call it the refrigerator hums at night,
Call it back. It's drifting mourns the streetlight.

Close-Up of a Villanelle

"ONE ART"

by Elizabeth Bishop

PHOTO BY JAMES LAUGHLIN; COURTESY FARRAR, STRAUS & GIROUX

Elizabeth Bishop was born in 1911. In October of that year, just eight months after her birth, her father died. She went to live with her maternal grandparents for five years in Great Village, Nova Scotia. What began as a childhood sanctuary became a landscape of meaning.

In June 1916, when Bishop was five, her mother suffered a breakdown and was institutionalized in Nova Scotia Hospital. She died when Bishop was eighteen. Her mother's frailty and death remained a powerful, oblique theme and enters the villanelle here.

One Art plays with the strictness of the villanelle in subtle, heatbreaking ways. The tone of the poem—throwaway, brave, resilient—is at odds with the dark voice of the form, whose refrains suggest the finality of all these losses, from small to great: a bunch of keys, a watch, a city, a human love.

Bishop's choice of the villanelle to formalize this heartbreaking catalogue of losses emphasizes the form's power for twentieth-century poets. It allows no easy narrative resolution, it turns around and around, building an acoustic chamber for the words, the lines, the meanings: *The art of losing isn't hard to master.* As the villanelle gathers strength and speed, this coda—*the art of losing*—moves in and out of irony, grief, self-accusation, regret. The repetition of the lines allows them to take on new meanings each time they're repeated. Each time *the art of losing* is heard, repeated, readdressed, it takes on a new layer, a different force. The words of loss become louder, different, more ominous and yet at the same time more human. This effect of the villanelle—to make an acoustic chamber for single words—was particularly well understood by Bishop.

The Sestina

The Sestina at a Glance

1) It is a poem of thirty-nine lines.

2) It has six stanzas of six lines each.

3) This is followed by an envoi of three lines.

4) All of these are unrhymed.

5) The same six end-words must occur in every stanza but in a changing order that follow a set pattern.

6) This recurrent pattern of end-words is known as "lexical repetition."

7) Each stanza must follow on the last by taking a reversed pairing of the previous lines.

8) The first line of the second stanza must pair its end-words with the last line of the first. The second line of the second stanza must do this with the first line of the first and so on.

9) The envoi or last three lines must gather up and deploy the six end-words.

The History of the Form

The inventor of the sestina, Arnaut Daniel, belonged to a group of twelfth-century poets—the troubadours—who needed, for their fame and fortune, to shock, delight, and entertain.

The sestina has thirty-nine lines and six stanzas. The stanzas have six lines each. There is an envoi of three lines at the end. Unusually, there are no rhymes. The repetitions stand in for rhyme and are of the words at the end of each line. The same six end-words are used throughout.

But there is a fixed distance for these repetitions. In the first stanza for instance, the word at the end of the sixth line must begin the first line of the second stanza. The second line of the second stanza repeats the end-word of the first line of the first stanza. And so on.

Elaborate repetitions build up over thirty-nine lines: This is the way the sestina operates. These patterns of repetition are constructed across a selected number of key words, so that in the end the sestina becomes a game of meaning, played with sounds and sense.

The sestina, then is very much a troubadour form.

The wit and ambition of its inventors have shaped it right up to our own day. But who were the troubadours?

The troubadours first appear in southern France in the twelfth century. Their name is almost certainly extracted from the verb *trobar*—meaning "to invent or compose verse." They were famous, celebrated, much in fashion, and eventually very influential on the European poetry of the next few centuries.

But here any real comparison with the contemporary folksinger has to end. The folksinger is often a dissident, a protester against social and political conditions. The troubadours were not. They were court poets. They sang—their poems were always accompanied by music—for French nobles like the Duke of Aquitaine or the Count of Poitiers. They competed with one another to produce the wittiest, most elaborate, most difficult styles. This difficult, complex style was called the *trobar clus*. The easier, more open one was called the *trobar leu*. The sestina was part of the *trobar clus*. It was the form for a master troubadour.

The Contemporary Context

The sestina's popularity with contemporary poets has a great deal to do with how easily it accommodates itself to conversation or plain style discourse. Ordinary speech tends to repeat certain words, in fact, this is a salient feature of how people talk: Repetition becomes a form of affirmation, a way of establishing fixity. An example might be: "Did you really go to the store?" "Yes, I'm telling you I went to the store." "Well, then, what kind of store was it?" "A furniture store, you dumb ass." "Are you calling me an ass?" "I am because you simply won't believe I went to the store."

Besides the adaptability of the sestina to common speech, it often provides the formal groundwork for a circular narrative, often of questionable meaning and amounting to little more than variations on a theme—a theme dependent upon and perhaps developed around the six words chosen for repetition.

Because of the character of the sestina's envoi, it is often dropped. This avoidance of absolute closure amounts to a revision of the form. But there are other revisions possible. One of the more common of these is variation in line length. This creates an element of surprise since the repeated words come at intervals that are unpredictable.

EDMUND SPENSER

Ye wastefull woodes, bear witness of my woe
from *The Shepheardes Calender* (August, lines 151–189)

Ye wastefull woodes bear witness of my woe,
Wherein my plaints did oftentimes resound:
Ye carelesse byrds are privie to my cryes,
Which in your songs were wont to make a part:
Thou pleasaunt spring hast luld me oft a sleepe,
Whose streames my tricklinge teares did ofte augment.

Resort of people doth my greefs augment,
The walled townes do worke my greater woe:
The forest wide is fitter to resound
The hollow Echo of my carefull cryes,
I hate the house, since thence my love did part,
Whose waylefull want debarres myne eyes from sleepe.

Let stremes of teares supply the place of sleepe:
Let all that sweete is, voyd: and all that may augment
My doole, drawe neare. More meete to wayle my woe,
Bene the wild woodes my sorrowes to resound,
Then bedde or bowre, both which I fill with cryes,
When I them see so waist, and fynd no part
Of pleasure past. Here will I dwell apart
In gastfull grove therefore, till my last sleepe
Doe close mine eyes: so shall I not augment
With sight of such a chaunge my restlesse woe:
Helpe me, ye banefull byrds, whose shrieking sound
Ys signe of dreery death, my deadly cryes

Most ruthfully to tune. And as my cryes
(Which of my woe cannot bewray least part)
You heare all night, when nature craveth sleep,
Increase, so let your yrksome yells augment.
Thus all the night in plaints, the daye in woe
I vowed have to wayst till safe and sound

She home returne whose voyces silver sound
To cheerefull songs can chaunge my cheerelesse cryes.

Hence with the Nightingale will I take part,
That blessed byrd, that spends her time of sleepe
In songs and plaintive pleas, the more taugment
The memory of hys misdeede that bred her woe:

And you that feele no woe, when as the sound
Of these my nightly cryes ye heare apart,
Let breake your sounder sleepe and pitie augment.

PHILIP SIDNEY

from *Old Arcadia* (**IV. ii** [**Agelastus**])

Since wailing is a bud of causeful sorrow,
   Since sorrow is the follower of ill fortune,
   Since no ill fortune equals public damage,
   Now prince's loss hath made our damage public,
   Sorrow pay we unto the rights of Nature,
   And inward grief seal up with outward wailing.

Why should we spare our voice from endless wailing,
   Who justly make our hearts the seats of sorrow,
   In such a case where it appears that Nature
   Doth add her force unto the sting of fortune,
   Choosing alas, this our theatre public,
   Where they would leave trophies of cruel damage?

Then since such pow'rs conspire unto our damage
   (Which may be known, but never helped with wailing)
   Yet let us leave a monument in public,
   Of willing tears, torn hair, and cries of sorrow.
   For lost, lost is by blow of cruel fortune
   Arcadia's gem, the noblest child of Nature.

O Nature doting old, O blinded Nature,
   How hast thou torn thyself, sought thine own damage,
   In granting such a scope to filthy fortune,
   By thy imp's loss to fill the world with wailing!
   Cast thy stepmother eyes upon our sorrow,
   Public our loss: so, see, thy shame is public.

O that we had, to make our woes more public,
   Seas in our eyes, and brazen tongues by nature,
   A yelling voice, and hearts composed of sorrow,
   Breath made of flames, wits knowing naught but damage,
   Our sports murd'ring ourselves, our musics wailing,
   Our studies fixed upon the falls of fortune.

No, no, our mischief grows in this vile fortune,
   That private pangs cannot breathe out in public
   The furious inward griefs with hellish wailing;
   But forced are to burden feeble Nature
   With secret sense of our eternal damage,
   And sorrow feed, feeding our souls with sorrow.

Since sorrow then concludeth all our fortune,
   With all our deaths show we this damage public.
   His nature fears to die who lives still wailing.

BARNABE BARNES

Sestine 4 from *Parthenophil and Parthenophe*

Eccho, what shall I do to my Nymphe, when I goe to behold her?
                   Eccho, hold her.
So dare I not, least she should thinke that I make her a pray then?
                   Eccho, pray then.
Yea, but at me she will take scorne, proceeded of honor?
                   Eccho, on her.
Me beare will she (with her to deale so saucilie) neuer?
                   Eccho, euer.
Yea but I greatly feare, she will haue pure thoughts to refuse such?
                   Eccho, fewe such.
Then will I venture againe more bold, if you warne me to do so?
                   Eccho, do so.
I must write with teares, and sighes, before that I do so?
                   Eccho, do so.
But what if my teares, and sighes be to weake to remoue her?
                   Eccho, moue her.
So shall yee moue huge Alpes with teares, and sighes, if you may
  such.
                   Eccho, you may such.

If any that shall affirme for a truth, I shall hold that they lye then?
    Eccho, lye then.
If I studie to death (in kinde) shall I lye neuer?
    Eccho, euer.
Oh what is it to lye, is't not dishonor?
    Eccho, tis honor.
Then to flatter a while her, is't not dishonor?
    Eccho, honor.
Then will I wrest out sighes, and wring forth teares when I do so?
    Eccho, do so.
Least she finde my craft, with her I may toye neuer?
    Eccho, euer.
Then if you iest in kinde with her you winne her?
    Eccho, you winne her.
Then (what time she laughes from her hart) shall I smile then?
    Eccho, ey smile then.
They that like my toyes, is it harme if I kisse such?
    Eccho, ey kisse such.
Yea but most Ladyes haue disdainefull mindes, to refuse such?
    Eccho, fewe such.
In what space shall I know, whether her loue resteth in honour?
    Eccho, in one hower.
Oh for such a sweet hower my life of howers will I pray then?
    Eccho, ay then!
Then if I finde as I would, more bold to vrge her I may be so?
    Eccho, be so.
But if she do refuse, then woe to th'atempter?
    Eccho, attempt her.
She will proudly refuse, and speakes in iest neuer?
    Eccho, euer.
So though still she refuse, she speakes in iest euer?
    Eccho, euer.
Then such (as these) bee the true best signes to seeke out such?
    Eccho, seeke out such.
Such will I seeke but what shall I do when I first shall attempt her?
    Eccho, tempt her.
How shall I tempt her-eare she stand on termes of her honor?
    Eccho, on her.

Oh might I come to that! I thinke it is euen so
          Eccho, tis euen so.
Strongly to tempt, and moue (at first) is surely the best then?
          Eccho, the best then.
What (when they do repugne, yet cry not forth) will they do then?
          Eccho, do then.
With such a blunt proeme, Ladies shall I moue neuer
          Eccho, euer.
I must waite at an inche on such Nymphes whom I regard so
          Eccho, guarde so.
Those whom in hart I loue, my faith doth firmely deserue such
          Eccho, serue such.
Then (to become their slaues) is no great dishonor?
          Eccho, honor.
But to the muses (first) I will recommend her
          Eccho, commende her.
They that pittie louers i'st good if I prayse such?
          Eccho, ey prayse such.
If that I write their prayse, by my verse shall they liue neuer?
          Eccho, euer.
If thy wordes be true, with thankes take adew then.
          Eccho, adew then.

DANTE GABRIEL ROSSETTI

Sestina: Of the Lady Pietra degli Scrovigni (translation)

To the dim light and the large circle of shade
I have clomb, and to the whitening of the hills,
There where we see no colour in the grass.
Nathless my longing loses not its green,
It has so taken root in the hard stone
Which talks and hears as though it were a lady.

Utterly frozen is this youthful lady,
Even as the snow that lies within the shade;
For she is no more moved than is the stone
By the sweet season which makes warm the hills
And alters them afresh from white to green,
Covering their sides again with flowers and grass.

When on her hair she sets a crown of grass
The thought has no more room for other lady;
Because she weaves the yellow with the green
So well that Love sits down there in the shade,—
Love who has shut me in among low hills
Faster than between walls of granite-stone.

She is more bright than is a precious stone;
The wound she gives may not be healed with grass:
I therefore have fled far o'er plains and hills
For refuge from so dangerous a lady;
But from her sunshine nothing can give shade,—
Not any hill, nor wall, nor summer-green.

A while ago, I saw her dressed in green,—
So fair, she might have wakened in a stone
This love which I do feel even for her shade;
And therefore, as one woos a graceful lady,
I wooed her in a field that was all grass
Girdled about with very lofty hills.

Yet shall the streams turn back and climb the hills
Before Love's flame in this damp wood and green
Burn, as it burns within a youthful lady,
For my sake, who would sleep away in stone
My life, or feed like beasts upon the grass,
Only to see her garments cast a shade.

How dark soe'er the hills throw out their shade,
Under her summer-green the beautiful lady
Covers it, like a stone covered in grass.

ALGERNON CHARLES SWINBURNE
Sestina

I saw my soul at rest upon a day
As a bird sleeping in the nest of night,
Among soft leaves that give the starlight way
To touch its wings but not its eyes with light;

So that it knew as one in visions may,
And knew not as men waking, of delight.

This was the measure of my soul's delight;
It had no power of joy to fly by day,
Nor part in the large lordship of the light;
But in a secret moon-beholden way
Had all its will of dreams and pleasant night,
And all the love and life that sleepers may.

But such life's triumph as men waking may
It might not have to feed its faint delight
Between the stars by night and sun by day,
Shut up with green leaves and a little light;
Because its way was as a lost star's way,
A world's not wholly known of day or night.

All loves and dreams and sounds and gleams of night
Made it all music that such minstrels may,
And all they had they gave it of delight;
But in the full face of the fire of day
What place shall be for any starry light,
What part of heaven in all the wide sun's way?

Yet the soul woke not, sleeping by the way,
Watched as a nursling of the large-eyed night,
And sought no strength nor knowledge of the day,
Nor closer touch conclusive of delight,
Nor mightier joy nor truer than dreamers may,
Nor more of song than they, nor more of light.

For who sleeps once and sees the secret light
Whereby sleep shows the soul a fairer way
Between the rise and rest of day and night,
Shall care no more to fare as all men may,
But be his place of pain or of delight,
There shall he dwell, beholding night as day.

Song, have thy day and take thy fill of light
Before the night be fallen across thy way;
Sing while he may, man hath no long delight.

SIR EDMUND GOSSE

Sestina

Fra tutti il primo Arnaldo Daniello
Gran maestro d'amor.
—*Petrarch*

In fair Provence, the land of lute and rose,
Arnaut, great master of the lore of love,
First wrought sestines to win his lady's heart,
Since she was deaf when simpler staves he sang,
And for her sake he broke the bonds of rhyme,
And in this subtler measure hid his woe.

'Harsh be my lines,' cried Arnaut, 'harsh the woe
My lady, that enthorn'd and cruel rose,
Inflicts on him that made her live in rhyme!'
But through the meter spake the voice of Love,
And like a wild-wood nightingale he sang
Who thought in crabbed lays to ease his heart.

It is not told if her untoward heart
Was melted by her poet's lyric woe,
Or if in vain so amorously he sang;
Perchance through cloud of dark conceits he rose
To nobler heights of philosophic song,
And crowned his later years with sterner rhyme.

This thing alone we know: the triple rhyme
Of him who bared his vast and passionate heart
To all the crossing flames of hate and love,
Wears in the midst of all its storm of woe,—
As some loud morn of March may bear a rose,—
The impress of a song that Arnaut sang.

'Smith of his mother-tongue,' the Frenchman sang
Of Lancelot and of Galahad, the rhyme
That beat so bloodlike at its core of rose,
It stirred the sweet Francesca's gentle heart
To take that kiss that brought her so much woe
And sealed in fire her martyrdom of love.

And Dante, full of her immortal love,
Stayed his drear song, and softly, fondly sang
As though his voice broke with that weight of woe;
And to this day we think of Arnaut's rhyme
Whenever pity at the labouring heart
On fair Francesca's memory drops the rose.

Ah! sovereign Love, forgive this weaker rhyme!
The men of old who sang were great at heart,
Yet have we too known woe, and worn thy rose.

RUDYARD KIPLING

Sestina of the Tramp-Royal

Speakin' in general, I 'ave tried 'em all—
The 'appy roads that take you o'er the world.
Speakin' in general, I 'ave found them good
For such as cannot use one bed too long,
But must get 'ence, the same as I 'ave done,
An' go observin' matters till they die.

What do it matter where or 'ow we die,
So long as we've our 'ealth to watch it all—
The different ways that different things are done,
An' men an' women lovin' in this world;
Takin' our chances as they come along,
An' when they ain't, pretendin' they are good?

In cash or credit—sno, it aren't no good;
You 'ave to 'ave the 'abit or you'd die,
Unless you lived your life but one day long,
Nor didn't prophesy nor fret at all,
But drew your tucker some'ow from the world,
An' never bothered what you might ha' done.

But, Gawd, what things are they I 'aven't done?
I've turned my 'and to most, an' turned it good,
In various situations round the world—
For 'im that doth not work must surely die;
But that's no reason man should labour all
'Is life on one same shift—life's none so long.

Therefore, from job to job I've moved along.
Pay couldn't 'old me when my time was done,
For something in my 'ead upset it all,
Till I 'ad dropped whatever 'twas for good,
An', out at sea, be'eld the dock-lights die,
An' met my mate—the wind that tramps the world!

It's like a book, I think, this bloomin' world,
Which you can read and care for just so long,
But presently you feel that you will die
Unless you get the page you're readin' done,
An' turn another—likely not so good;
But what you're after is to turn 'em all.

Gawd bless this world! Whatever she 'ath done—
Excep' when awful long—I've found it good.
So write, before I die, "'E liked it all!"

EZRA POUND

Sestina: Altaforte

Loquitur: *En* Bertrans de Born. Dante Alighieri put this man in hell for that he was a
stirrer-up of strife. Eccovi! Judge ye! Have I dug him up again? The scene is at his
castle, Altaforte. "Papiols" is his jongleur. "The Leopard," the *device* of Richard
(Coeur de Lion).

I

Damn it all! all this our South stinks peace.
You whoreson dog, Papiols, come! Let's to music!
I have no life save when the swords clash.
But ah! when I see the standards gold, vair, purple, opposing
And the broad fields beneath them turn crimson,
Then howl I my heart nigh mad with rejoicing.

II

In hot summer have I great rejoicing
When the tempests kill the earth's foul peace,
And the light'nings from black heav'n flash crimson,
And the fierce thunders roar me their music
And the winds shriek through the clouds mad, opposing,
And through all the riven skies God's swords clash.

III

Hell grant soon we hear again the swords clash!
And the shrill neighs of destriers in battle rejoicing,
Spiked breast to spiked breast opposing!
Better one hour's stour than a year's peace
With fat boards, bawds, wine and frail music!
Bah! there's no wine like the blood's crimson!

IV

And I love to see the sun rise blood-crimson.
And I watch his spears through the dark clash
And it fills all my heart with rejoicing
And pries wide my mouth with fast music
When I see him so scorn and defy peace,
His lone might 'gainst all darkness opposing.

V

The man who fears war and squats opposing
My words for stour, hath no blood of crimson
But is fit only to rot in womanish peace
Far from where worth's won and the swords clash
For the death of such sluts I go rejoicing;
Yea, I fill all the air with my music.

VI

Papiols, Papiols, to the music!
There's no sound like to swords swords opposing,
No cry like the battle's rejoicing
When our elbows and swords drip the crimson
And our charges 'gainst "The Leopard's" rush clash.
May God damn for ever all who cry "Peace!"

VII

And let the music of the swords make them crimson!
Hell grant soon we hear again the swords clash!
Hell blot black for alway the thought "Peace"!

WELDON KEES

After the Trial

Hearing the judges' well-considered sentence,
The prisoner saw long plateaus of guilt,
And thought of all the dismal furnished rooms
The past assembled, the eyes of parents
Staring through walls as though forever
To condemn and wound his innocence.

And if I raise my voice, protest my innocence,
The judges won't revoke their sentence.
I could stand screaming in this box forever,
Leaving them deaf to everything but guilt;
All the machinery of law devised by parents
Could not be stopped though fire swept the rooms.

Whenever my thoughts move to all those rooms
I sat alone in, capable of innocence,
I know now I was not alone, that parents
Always were there to speak the hideous sentence:
"You are our son; be good; we know your guilt;
We stare through walls and see your thoughts forever."

Sometimes I wished to go away forever;
I dreamt of strangers and of stranger rooms
Where every corner held the light of guilt.
Why do the judges stare? I saw no innocence
In them when they pronounced the sentence;
I heard instead the believing voice of parents.

I can remember evenings when my parents,
Settling my future happily forever,
Would frown before they spoke the sentence:
"Someday the time will come to leave these rooms
Where, under our watchful eyes, you have been innocent;
Remember us before you seize the world of guilt."

Their eyes burn. How can I deny my guilt
When I am guilty in the sight of parents?
I cannot think that even they were innocent.

At least I shall not have to wait forever
To be escorted to the silent rooms
Where darkness promises a final sentence.

We walk forever to the doors of guilt,
Pursued by our own sentences and eyes of parents,
Never to enter innocent and quiet rooms.

ANTHONY HECHT

The Book of Yolek

Wir haben ein Gesetz,
Und nach dem Gesetz soll er sterben.

The dowsed coals fume and hiss after your meal
Of grilled brook trout, and you saunter off for a walk
Down the fern trail, it doesn't matter where to,
Just so you're weeks and worlds away from home,
And among midsummer hills have set up camp
In the deep bronze glories of declining day.

You remember, peacefully, an earlier day
In childhood, remember a quite specific meal:
A corn roast and bonfire in summer camp.
That summer you got lost on a Nature Walk;
More than you dared admit, you thought of home;
No one else knows where the mind wanders to.

The fifth of August, 1942.
It was morning and very hot. It was the day
They came at dawn with rifles to The Home
For Jewish Children, cutting short the meal
Of bread and soup, lining them up to walk
In close formation off to a special camp.

How often you have thought about that camp,
As though in some strange way you were driven to,
And about the children, and how they were made to walk,
Yolek who had bad lungs, who wasn't a day
Over five years old, commanded to leave his meal
And shamble between armed guards to his long home.

We're approaching August again. It will drive home
The regulation torments of that camp
Yolek was sent to, his small, unfinished meal,
The electric fences, the numeral tattoo,
The quite extraordinary heat of the day
They all were forced to take that terrible walk.

Whether on a silent, solitary walk
Or among crowds, far off or safe at home,
You will remember, helplessly, that day,
And the smell of smoke, and the loudspeakers of the camp.
Wherever you are, Yolek will be there, too.
His unuttered name will interrupt your meal.

Prepare to receive him in your home some day.
Though they killed him in the camp they sent him to,
He will walk in as you're sitting down to a meal.

MILLER WILLIAMS

The Shrinking Lonesome Sestina

Somewhere in everyone's head something points toward home,
a dashboard's floating compass, turning all the time
to keep from turning. It doesn't matter how we come
to be wherever we are, someplace where nothing goes
the way it went once, where nothing holds fast
to where it belongs, or what you've risen or fallen to.

What the bubble always points to,
whether we notice it or not, is home.
It may be true that if you move fast
everything fades away, that given time
and noise enough, every memory goes
into the blackness, and if new ones come—

small, mole-like memories that come
to live in the furry dark—they, too,
curl up and die. But Carol goes
to high school now. John works at home

what days he can to spend some time
with Sue and the kids. He drives too fast.

Ellen won't eat her breakfast.
Your sister was going to come
but didn't have the time.
Some mornings at one or two
or three I want you home
a lot, but then it goes.

It all goes.
Hold on fast
to thoughts of home
when they come.
They're going to
less with time.

Time
goes
too
fast.
Come
home.

Forgive me that. One time it wasn't fast.
A myth goes that when the quick years come
then you will, too. Me, I'll still be home.

ALBERTO RÍOS

Nani

Sitting at her table, she serves
the sopa de arroz to me
instinctively, and I watch her,
the absolute *mamá,* and eat words
I might have had to say more
out of embarrassment. To speak,
now-foreign words I used to speak,
too, dribble down her mouth as she serves
me albondigas. No more

than a third are easy to me.
By the stove she does something with words
And looks at me only with her
back. I am full. I tell her
I taste the mint, and watch her speak
smiles at the stove. All my words
make her smile. Nani never serves
herself, she only watches me
with her skin, her hair. I ask for more.

I watch the *mamá* warming more
tortillas for me. I watch her
fingers in the flame for me.
Near her mouth, I see a wrinkle speak
of a man whose body serves
the ants like she serves me, then more words
from more wrinkles about children, words
about this and that, flowing more
easily from these other mouths. Each serves
as a tremendous string around her,
holding her together. They speak
nani was this and that to me
and I wonder just how much of me
will die with her, what were the words
I could have been, was. Her insides speak
through a hundred wrinkles, now, more
than she can bear, steel around her,
shouting, then, What is this thing she serves?

She asks me if I want more.
I own no words to stop her.
Even before I speak, she serves.

Close-Up of a Sestina

"SESTINA: ALTAFORTE"

by Ezra Pound

PHOTO BY BORIS DE RACHEWILTZ; COURTESY OF NEW DIRECTIONS PUBLISHING CORP.

Ezra Pound, born in 1885, was a master of paradox and invention. Through his skills as editor and his witness as poet, he was to prove a rare and powerful catalyst for many of the tensions and renewals of poetic form in his time. In 1912 he helped to found the Imagist group, which was committed to formal experimentation. A short while later he proposed a different movement called Vorticism. Behind many of his arguments was a forceful and original sense that poetry had come to a crossroads. He constantly advocated renewal of language, a clearing out of modes of expression and perception about poetry. "Every literaryism, every book word, fritters away a scrap of the reader's patience."

But Pound was paradoxically tender-hearted about the writers and movements of the past, from the troubadours to Sextus Propertius. He returned frequently to their forms. The sestina here—likely to appeal to Pound precisely because it was Arnaut Daniel's invention—is a case in point. It is part pastiche, part modernist recreation. There is a blustering, loud-mouthed anger in the voice and this gives a clue to Pound's purposes and achievement with the form. The sestina is a poem that through design and requirement can blunt the voice. But here the voice is privileged by Pound. The sestina's regulations are observed, the repetitions are consistent, but the human bluster and anger is heard as a powerful, poignant counterpoint to them. This is a sestina that is exceptional in its insistence that the voice be heard clearly through the demanding requirements of a closed form.

The Pantoum

The Pantoum at a Glance

1) Each pantoum stanza must be four lines long.

2) The length is unspecified but the pantoum must begin and end with the same line.

3) The second and fourth lines of the first quatrain become the first and third lines of the next, and so on with succeeding quatrains.

4) The rhyming of each quatrain is *abab*.

5) The final quatrain changes this pattern.

6) In the final quatrain the unrepeated first and third lines are used in reverse as second and fourth lines.

The History of the Form

The pantoum is Malayan in origin and came into English language poetry, as so many other strict forms have, through France. It is derived from the Malayan word *pantun* and French references to it early in the nineteenth century are to the *malais pantun*. Victor Hugo was not the first to use the form there—this was done by Ernest Fouinet before him in the nineteenth century—but he gave it fashion and popularity in his book *Orientales*. Charles Baudelaire did the same with a pantoum called "Harmonie du soir."

The pantoum is unusual among strict forms in that it is not of a specified length. It works by quatrains. The quatrains are repeated and the patterns within them are required. But the length of the pantoum is left to the individual poet.

Of all verse forms the pantoum is the slowest: The reader takes four steps forward, then two back. It is the perfect form for the evocation of a past time. Like the villanelle, like the sestina, these forms attract poets because, within the requirements and demands and repetitions, there are possibilities for the making and evoking of time past that are not to be found in straightforward narrative and not entirely in lyric either.

The Contemporary Context

Donald Justice's "pantoum of the Great Depression" shows what a contemporary poet might do with a pantoum, as does Carolyn Kizer's dark and witty pantoum on parenthood. Since the pantoum easily enchants, the close repetition of lines sets up a tight, mesmerizing chain of echoes. It is also a form that allows its listener to relax since all of the lines make a second appearance—what was missed the first time can be picked up on the second.

It also demands less from the poet, since he or she is forced to invent only half the number of lines that they would for any other poem of similar length. And yet the form is certainly demanding for both reader and poet, with its strange twists of antinarrative time and its unexpectedly hypnotic repetitions.

AUSTIN DOBSON

In Town

"The blue fly sung in the pane."
—*Tennyson.*

Toiling in Town now is "horrid,"
(There is that woman again!)

June in the zenith is torrid,
Thought gets dry in the brain.

There is that woman again:
"Strawberries! fourpence a pottle!"
Thought gets dry in the brain;
Ink gets dry in the bottle.

"Strawberries! fourpence a pottle!"
Oh for the green of a lane!
Ink gets dry in the bottle;
"Buzz" goes a fly in the pane!

Oh for the green of a lane,
Where one might lie and be lazy!
"Buzz" goes a fly in the pane;
Bluebottles drive me crazy!

Where one might lie and be lazy,
Careless of Town and all in it!
Bluebottles drive me crazy:
I shall go mad in a minute!

Careless of Town and all in it,
With some one to soothe and to still you;
I shall go mad in a minute;
Bluebottle, then I shall kill you!

With some one to soothe and to still you,
As only one's feminine kin do,
Bluebottle, then I shall kill you:
There now! I've broken the window!

As only one's feminine kin do,
Some muslin-clad Mabel or May!
There now! I've broken the window!
Bluebottle's off and away!

Some muslin-clad Mabel or May,
To dash one with eau de Cologne;
Bluebottle's off and away;
And why should I stay here alone!

To dash one with eau de Cologne,
All over one's eminent forehead;
And why should I stay here alone!
Toiling in Town now is "horrid."

DONALD JUSTICE

Pantoum of the Great Depression

Our lives avoided tragedy
Simply by going on and on,
Without end and with little apparent meaning.
Oh, there were storms and small catastrophes.

Simply by going on and on
We managed. No need for the heroic.
Oh, there were storms and small catastrophes.
I don't remember all the particulars.

We managed. No need for the heroic.
There were the usual celebrations, the usual sorrows.
I don't remember all the particulars.
Across the fence, the neighbors were our chorus.

There were the usual celebrations, the usual sorrows
Thank god no one said anything in verse.
The neighbors were our only chorus,
And if we suffered we kept quiet about it.

At no time did anyone say anything in verse.
It was the ordinary pities and fears consumed us,
And if we suffered we kept quiet about it.
No audience would ever know our story.

It was the ordinary pities and fears consumed us.
We gathered on porches; the moon rose; we were poor.
What audience would ever know our story?
Beyond our windows shone the actual world.

We gathered on porches; the moon rose; we were poor.
And time went by, drawn by slow horses.

Somewhere beyond our windows shone the world.
The Great Depression had entered our souls like fog.

And time went by, drawn by slow horses.
We did not ourselves know what the end was.
The Great Depression had entered our souls like fog.
We had our flaws, perhaps a few private virtues.

But we did not ourselves know what the end was.
People like us simply go on.
We have our flaws, perhaps a few private virtues,
But it is by blind chance only that we escape tragedy.

And there is no plot in that; it is devoid of poetry.

CAROLYN KIZER

Parents' Pantoum

For Maxine Kumin

Where did these enormous children come from,
More ladylike than we have ever been?
Some of ours look older than we feel.
How did they appear in their long dresses

More ladylike than we have ever been?
But they moan about their aging more than we do,
In their fragile heels and long black dresses.
They say they admire our youthful spontaneity.

They moan about their aging more than we do,
A somber group—why don't they brighten up?
Though they say they admire our youthful spontaneity
They beg us to be dignified like them

As they ignore our pleas to brighten up.
Someday perhaps we'll capture their attention
Then we won't try to be dignified like them
Nor they to be so gently patronizing.

Someday perhaps we'll capture their attention.
Don't they know that we're supposed to be the stars?

Instead they are so gently patronizing.
It makes us feel like children—second-childish?

Perhaps we're too accustomed to be stars,
The famous flowers glowing in the garden,
So now we pout like children. Second-childish?
Quaint fragments of forgotten history?

Our daughters stroll together in the garden,
Chatting of news we've chosen to ignore,
Pausing to toss us morsels of their history,
Not questions to which only we know answers.

Eyes closed to news we've chosen to ignore,
We'd rather excavate old memories,
Disdaining age, ignoring pain, avoiding mirrors.
Why do they never listen to our stories?

Because they hate to excavate old memories
They don't believe our stories have an end.
They don't ask questions because they dread the answers.
They don't see that we've become their mirrors,

We offspring of our enormous children.

JOHN ASHBERY

Pantoum

Eyes shining without mystery,
Footprints eager for the past
Through the vague snow of many clay pipes,
And what is in store?

Footprints eager for the past,
The usual obtuse blanket.
and what is in store
For those dearest to the king?

The usual obtuse blanket
Of legless regrets and amplifications
For those dearest to the king.
Yes, sirs, connoisseurs of oblivion,

Of legless regrets and amplifications,
That is why a watchdog is shy.
Yes, sirs, connoisseurs of oblivion,
These days are short, brittle; there is only one night.

That is why a watchdog is shy,
Why the court, trapped in a silver storm, is dying.
These days are short, brittle; there is only one night
And that soon gotten over.

Why, the court, trapped in a silver storm, is dying!
Some blunt pretense to safety we have
And that soon gotten over
For they must have motion.

Some blunt pretense to safety we have:
Eyes shining without mystery
For they must have motion
Through the vague snow of many clay pipes.

NELLIE WONG

Grandmothers's Song

Grandmothers sing their song
Blinded by the suns' rays
Grandchildren for whom they long
For pomelo-golden days

Blinded by the sun's rays
Gold bracelets, opal rings
For pomelo-golden days
Tiny fingers, ancient things

Gold bracelets, opal rings
Sprinkled with Peking dust
Tiny fingers, ancient things
So young they'll never rust

Sprinkled with Peking dust
To dance in fields of mud
So young they'll never rust
Proud as if of royal blood

To dance in fields of mud
Or peel shrimp for pennies a day
Proud as if of royal blood
Coins and jade to put away

Or peel shrimp for pennies a day
Seaweed washes up the shore
Coins and jade to put away
A camphor chest is home no more

Seaweed washes up the shore
Bound feet struggle to loosen free
A camphor chest is home no more
A foreign tongue is learned at three

Bound feet struggle to loosen free
Grandchildren for whom they long
A foreign tongue is learned at three
Grandmothers sing their song

J. D. McCLATCHY

The Method

When you're away I sleep a lot,
Seem to pee more often, eat
Small meals (no salad), listen
To German symphonies and . . . listen.

Sympathy, more often than not,
Is self-pity refined to Fire
And German Symphonies. *Nun lesen.*
Read a book. Write "The Method."

Or is self-pity, refined, two fires
Seen as one? Instructions collapse:
Write the book. (Read: a method.)
The hearth's easy, embered expense,

Seen as one instruction, collapses
In the blue intensity of a match.
The heart's lazy: remembrance spent
Forgetting. Love, break a stick.

In the blue intensity of as much
It is bound to catch—the far away—
Forgetting love. Break a stick.
The flames are a reward, of sorts.

They're bound to reach that far away.
The book says so. And who can't say
The flames are his reward? Of course
They are dying. Still, they scorch

The book. Say so, and—two can play—
Fires kindle *(smack!)* their own display.
They are dying, still. How they scorched
When I put this light to time.

Kindled fires smack of their own display.
Of smaller denials, no saying. Listen:
Where I put this light, it's time,
When you're away, asleep, or lost.

Close-Up of a Pantoum
"PANTOUM OF THE GREAT DEPRESSION"

by Donald Justice

onald Justice was born in Miami, Florida, in 1925. A graduate of the University of Miami, he attended the universities of North Carolina, Stanford, and Iowa. His books include *New and Selected Poems* (Alfred A. Knopf, 1995); *A Donald Justice Reader* (1991); *The Sunset Maker* (1987), a collection of poems, stories, and a memoir; *Selected Poems* (1979), for which he won the Pulitzer Prize; *Departures* (1973).

Like Frost, Donald Justice has an acute sense of the pessimistic lyric—the poem that turns meter and music to a darker use. Like Bishop, he also has a sense of the ironic juxtaposition between a powerful and menacing event and the game-like forms that circle in on themselves, changing the event as they narrate it, such as the villanelle, sestina, and pantoum.

His "Pantoum of the Great Depression" accomplishes this by placing an ironic speaker within the demanding repetitions, so that the tone sets off the horror of the memory. The incantation, nevertheless, takes on a quality of revisited grief. And finally the grief of memory defeats the voice of irony.

The Sonnet

The Sonnet at a Glance

1) It is a poem of fourteen lines, usually iambic.

2) There are two kinds of sonnet, with very different histories behind their different forms: the Petrarchan and the Shakespearean.

3) The Petrarchan sonnet is Italian in origin, has an octave of eight lines and a sestet of six. The rhyme scheme of the octave is *ababcdcd* and of the sestet *cdecde*.

4) The Shakespearean sonnet was developed in England and has far more than just surface differences from the Petrarchan.

5) The rhyme scheme of the Shakespearean sonnet is *ababcdcdefefgg*. There is no octave/sestet structure to it. The final couplet is a defining feature.

The History of the Form

The sonnet's origins are in the small, sunlit courts of Sicily. It lingered there for two hundred years before it made the journey into English poetry.

The wildfire and historic development of the form began when Francesco Petrarca, who lived in Tuscany and was born in 1304, published his *Canzoniere,* a sequence of 366 poems, 317 of which were sonnets to an idealized lover, called Laura. Petrarch had been influenced by Dante.

With their wit, their yearning, and their ability to make a narrative out of a necklace of short poems, *Canzoniere* became a European bestseller. By the time of Petrarch's death in 1374, his circle of influence included Chaucer and Boccaccio.

It was the Italian originators who developed one of the features of the sonnet that survives to the present day, the octave and sestet division: One strong opening statement of eight lines is followed by a resolution to the emotional or intellectual question of the first part of the poem. This shape made the sonnet a self-sufficient form, open to shades of mood and tone. They also established the rhyme scheme *abbaabba* in the octave and *cdecde* in the sestet. This degree of close and repetitive rhyme, in turn, reflected the rich resources of Italian rhyme.

The sonnet took time to come to England. When it did it fell into the hands of Thomas Wyatt a doomed master and one of its first champions there, who adapted it to his own uses and talents: He used the Petrarchan octave but introduced a rhyming couplet at the end. His contemporary and friend the Earl of Surrey also introduced more rhymes into it. In Italian there were only five rhymes. After Wyatt and Surrey the sonnet could have seven—a change that benefited practitioners in a language with less abundant rhymes than Italian.

Wyatt and Surrey, by shifting the English sonnet away from the slightly more intellectual and argumentative Petrarchan form, gave a new resonance to the ending, through the often declamatory couplet. By Shakespeare's time, this couplet was often the loudest, most powerful part of the sonnet.

The powerful and enriching development of the sonnet in the English language certainly owes something to the fact that it presented poets with this choice. On the one hand, there was the Shakespearean sonnet, with its three quatrains and final couplet, which allowed a fairly free association of images to develop lyrically toward a conclusion. Or there was the Petrarchan sonnet as Milton used it in "On His Blindness," with all the dignity of proposal and response.

The Contemporary Context

On one level, the sonnet suits our world. Despite the fact that its origins are in the formality and decorum of Italian court poetry, it has kept pace with some of the most important developments in modern poetry.

To start with it is short, easily comprehended and its historic structure still opens the way for living debate and subtle argument. One of the characteristics of recent poetic history, on both sides of the Atlantic, has been a tension between lyric and narrative. The sonnet is able to take its place in the debate: to suggest narrative progress through its sequence structure, while, in single units, it is capable of the essential lyric qualities of being musical, brief, and memorable.

Contemporary poets, for over two hundred years, have continued to be drawn to the sonnet. But few modern poets have been willing to commit themselves to the major, architectural sequences of a Petrarch or a Shakespeare. Instead the sonnet—with either the couplet at the end or the octave/sestet structure—has become a part of speech. Many poets have used it at one time or another. Some of the finest sonnets in the language have been written by poets who were only occasional sonneteers, such as Yeats.

It might be argued that an occasional form is what it has become: a fossil of its former life. Its imagistic compression of argument remains a major influence on the course of the stanza. It is one of the copingstones of poetic form. And it endures.

WILLIAM SHAKESPEARE

Shall I compare thee to a summer's day?
Sonnet 18

Shall I compare thee to a summer's day?
Thou art more lovely and more temperate:
Rough winds do shake the darling buds of May,
And summer's lease hath all too short a date;
Sometimes too hot the eye of heaven shines,
And often is his gold complexion dimmed;
And every fair from fair sometime declines,
By chance or nature's changing course untrimmed;
But thy eternal summer shall not fade,
Nor lose possession of that fair thou ow'st;
Nor shall death brag thou wand'rest in his shade,
When in eternal lines to Time thou grow'st:
    So long as men can breathe, or eyes can see,
    So long lives this, and this gives life to thee.

MICHAEL DRAYTON

Farewell to Love

Since there's no help, come, let us kiss and part;
Nay, I have done, you get no more of me,
And I am glad, yea glad with all my heart
That thus so cleanly I myself can free.
Shake hands forever, cancel all our vows,
And when we meet at any time again,
Be it not seen in either of our brows
That we one jot of former love retain.
Now at the last gasp of love's latest breath,
When, his pulse failing, passion speechless lies,
When faith is kneeling by his bed of death,
And innocence is closing up his eyes;
Now if thou wouldst, when all have given him over,
From death to life thou mightst him yet recover.

MARY WROTH

from Pamphilia to Amphilanthus
I

When night's black mantle could most darkness prove,
    And sleep, death's image, did my senses hire
    From knowledge of myself, then thoughts did move
    Swifter than those most swiftness need require.
In sleep, a chariot drawn by winged desire
    I saw, where sat bright Venus, Queen of Love,
    And at her feet, her son, still adding fire
    To burning hearts, which she did hold above.
But one heart flaming more than all the rest
    The goddess held, and put it to my breast.
    "Dear son, now shut," said she: "thus must we win."
He her obeyed, and martyred my poor heart.
    I, waking, hoped as dreams it would depart:
    Yet since, O me, a lover I have been.

JOHN MILTON

Sonnet XXIII: Methought I saw my late espousèd saint

Methought I saw my late espousèd saint
    Brought to me like Alcestis from the grave,
    Whom Jove's great son to her glad husband gave,
    Rescued from Death by force, though pale and faint.
Mine, as whom washed from spot of child-bed taint
    Purification in the Old Law did save,
    And such, as yet once more I trust to have
    Full sight of her in heaven without restraint,
Came vested all in white, pure as her mind.
    Her face was veiled; yet to my fancied sight
    Love, sweetness, goodness, in her person shined
So clear as in no face with more delight.
    But O, as to embrace me she inclined,
    I waked, she fled, and day brought back my night.

JOHN DONNE

Holy Sonnet: At the round earth's imagined corners

At the round earth's imagined corners, blow
Your trumpets, angels; and arise, arise
From death, you numberless infinities
Of souls, and to your scattered bodies go;
All whom the flood did, and fire shall, o'erthrow,
All whom war, dearth, age, agues, tyrannies,
Despair, law, chance, hath slain, and you whose eyes
Shall behold God, and never taste death's woe.
But let them sleep, Lord, and me mourn a space;
For, if above all these, my sins abound,
'Tis late to ask abundance of thy grace
When we are there. Here on this lowly ground,
Teach me how to repent; for that's as good
As if thou'hadst sealed my pardon with thy blood.

WILLIAM WORDSWORTH

Composed upon Westminster Bridge, September 3, 1802

Earth has not anything to show more fair:
Dull would he be of soul who could pass by
A sight so touching in its majesty;
This City now doth, like a garment, wear
The beauty of the morning; silent, bare,
Ships, towers, domes, theaters, and temples lie
Open unto the fields, and to the sky;
All bright and glittering in the smokeless air.
Never did sun more beautifully steep
In his first splendor, valley, rock, or hill;
Ne'er saw I, never felt, a calm so deep!
The river glideth at his own sweet will:
Dear God! the very houses seem asleep;
And all that mighty heart is lying still!

PERCY BYSSHE SHELLEY

Ozymandias

I met a traveler from an antique land
Who said: Two vast and trunkless legs of stone
Stand in the desert . . . Near them, on the sand,
Half sunk, a shattered visage lies, whose frown,
And wrinkled lip, and sneer of cold command,
Tell that its sculptor well those passions read
Which yet survive, stamped on these lifeless things,
The hand that mocked them, and the heart that fed:
And on the pedestal these words appear:
"My name is Ozymandias, king of kings:
Look on my works, ye Mighty, and despair!"
Nothing beside remains. Round the decay
Of that colossal wreck, boundless and bare
The lone and level sands stretch far away.

JOHN KEATS

Bright Star

Bright star, would I were steadfast as thou art—
    Not in lone splendor hung aloft the night
And watching, with eternal lids apart,
    Like nature's patient, sleepless Eremite,
The moving waters at their priestlike task
    Of pure ablution round earth's human shores,
Or gazing on the new soft fallen mask
    Of snow upon the mountains and the moors—
No—yet still steadfast, still unchangeable,
    Pillowed upon my fair love's ripening breast,
To feel forever its soft fall and swell,
    Awake forever in a sweet unrest,
Still, still to hear her tender-taken breath,
And so live ever—or else swoon to death.

CHRISTINA ROSSETTI

From *Monna Innominata*
II

Many in aftertimes will say of you
    "He lov'd her"—while of me what will they say?
    Not that I lov'd you more than just in play,
For fashion's sake as idle women do.
Even let them prate; who know not what we knew
    Of love and parting in exceeding pain,
    Of parting hopeless here to meet again,
Hopeless on earth, and heaven is out of view.
But by my heart of love laid bare to you,
    My love that you can make not void nor vain,
Love that foregoes you but to claim anew
      Beyond this passage of the gate of death,
    I charge you at the Judgment make it plain
      My love of you was life and not a breath.

ELIZABETH BARRETT BROWNING

from *Sonnets from the Portuguese*
XLIII

How do I love thee? Let me count the ways.
I love thee to the depth and breadth and height
My soul can reach, when feeling out of sight
For the ends of Being and ideal Grace.
I love thee to the level of everyday's
Most quiet need, by sun and candle-light.
I love thee freely, as men strive for Right;
I love thee purely, as they turn from Praise.
I love thee with the passion put to use
In my old griefs, and with my childhood's faith.
I love thee with a love I seemed to lose
With my lost saints—I love thee with the breath,
Smiles, tears, of all my life!—and, if God choose,
I shall but love thee better after death.

GERARD MANLEY HOPKINS

Carrion Comfort

Not, I'll not, carrion comfort, Despair, not feast on thee;
   Not untwist—slack they may be—these last strands of man
In me ór, most weary, cry *I can no more.* I can;
Can something, hope, wish day come, not choose not to be.
But ah, but O thou terrible, why wouldst thou rude on me
Thy wring-world right foot rock? lay a lionlimb against me? scan
With darksome devouring eyes my bruisèd bones? and fan,
O in turns of tempest, me heaped there; me frantic to avoid thee
   and flee?

     Why? That my chaff might fly; my grain lie, sheer and clear.
Nay in all that toil, that coil, since (seems) I kissed the rod,
Hand rather, my heart lo! lapped strength, stole joy, would laugh,
   chéer.
Cheer whom though? the hero whose heaven-handling flung me,
   fóot tród
Me? or me that fought him? O which one? is it each one? That
   night, that year
Of now done darkness I wretch lay wrestling with (my God!) my
   God.

EDNA ST. VINCENT MILLAY

What lips my lips have kissed, and where, and why

What lips my lips have kissed, and where, and why,
I have forgotten, and what arms have lain
Under my head till morning; but the rain
Is full of ghosts tonight, that tap and sigh
Upon the glass and listen for reply,
And in my heart there stirs a quiet pain
For unremembered lads that not again
Will turn to me at midnight with a cry.
Thus in the winter stands the lonely tree,
Nor knows what birds have vanished one by one,
Yet knows its boughs more silent than before:
I cannot say what loves have come and gone,

I only know that summer sang in me
A little while, that in me sings no more.

COUNTEE CULLEN

From the Dark Tower

(To Charles S. Johnson)

We shall not always plant while others reap
The golden increment of bursting fruit,
Not always countenance, abject and mute,
That lesser men should hold their brothers cheap;
Not everlastingly while others sleep
Shall we beguile their limbs with mellow flute,
Not always bend to some more subtle brute;
We were not made eternally to weep.

The night whose sable breast relieves the stark,
White stars is no less lovely being dark,
And there are buds that cannot bloom at all
In light, but crumple, piteous, and fall;
So in the dark we hide the heart that bleeds,
And wait, and tend our agonizing seeds.

PATRICK KAVANAGH

Epic

I have lived in important places, times
When great events were decided, who owned
That half a rood of rock, a no-man's land
Surrounded by our pitchfork-armed claims.
I heard the Duffys shouting 'Damn your soul'
And old McCabe stripped to the waist, seen
Step the plot defying blue cast-steel—
'Here is the march along these iron stones'
That was the year of the Munich bother. Which
Was more important? I inclined
To lose my faith in Ballyrush and Gortin

Till Homer's ghost came whispering to my mind
He said: I made the Iliad from such
A local row. Gods make their own importance.

E. E. CUMMINGS

from "Tulips and Chimneys"
I

the Cambridge ladies who live in furnished souls
are unbeautiful and have comfortable minds
(also, with the church's protestant blessings
daughters, unscented shapeless spirited)
they believe in Christ and Longfellow, both dead,
are, invariably interested in so many things—
at the present writing one still finds
delighted fingers knitting for the is it Poles?
perhaps.   While permanent faces coyly bandy
scandal of Mrs. N and Professor D
. . . . the Cambridge ladies do not care, above
Cambridge if sometimes in its box of
sky lavender and cornerless, the
moon rattles like a fragment of angry candy.

GEORGE BARKER

To My Mother

Most near, most dear, most loved and most far,
Under the window where I often found her
Sitting as huge as Asia, seismic with laughter,
Gin and chicken helpless in her Irish hand,
Irresistible as Rabelais, but most tender for
The lame dogs and hurt birds that surround her,—
She is a procession no one can follow after
But be like a little dog following a brass band.

She will not glance up at the bomber, or condescend
To drop her gin and scuttle to a cellar,
But lean on the mahogany table like a mountain

Whom only faith can move, and so I send
O all my faith, and all my love to tell her
That she will move from mourning into morning.

JANE COOPER

After the Bomb Tests
I

The atom bellies like a cauliflower,
Expands, expands, shoots up again, expands
Into ecclesiastical curves and towers
We pray to with our cupped and empty hands.
This is the old Hebraic-featured fear
We nursed before humility began,
Our crown-on-crown or phallic parody
Begat by man on the original sea.

The sea's delivered. Galvanized and smooth
She kills a tired ship left in her lap
—Transfiguration—with a half-breath
Settling like an animal in sleep.
So godhead takes the difficult form of love.
Where is the little myth we used to have?

GWEN HARWOOD

A Game of Chess

To John Brodie

Nightfall: the town's chromatic nocturne wakes
dark brilliance on the river; colours drift
and tremble as enormous shadows lift
Orion to his place. The heart remakes
that peace torn in the blaze of day. Inside
your room are music, warmth and wine, the board
with chessmen set for play. The harpsichord
begins a fugue; delight is multiplied.

A game: the heart's impossible ideal—
to choose among a host of paths, and know

that if the kingdom crumbles one can yield
and have the choice again. Abstract and real
joined in their trance of thought, two players show
the calm of gods above a troubled field.

SEAMUS HEANEY

The Haw Lantern

The wintry haw is burning out of season,
crab of the thorn, a small light for small people,
wanting no more from them but that they keep
the wick of self-respect from dying out,
not having to blind them with illumination.

But sometimes when your breath plumes in the frost
it takes the roaming shape of Diogenes
with his lantern, seeking one just man;
so you end up scrutinized from behind the haw
he holds up at eye-level on its twig,
and you flinch before its bonded pith and stone,
its blood-prick that you wish would test and clear you,
its pecked-at ripeness that scans you, then moves on.

DENIS JOHNSON

Heat

Here in the electric dusk your naked lover
tips the glass high and the ice cubes fall against her teeth.
It's beautiful Susan, her hair sticky with gin,
Our Lady of Wet Glass-Rings on the Album Cover,
streaming with hatred in the heat
as the record falls and the snake-band chords begin
to break like terrible news from the Rolling Stones,
and such a last light—full of spheres and zones.
August,
          you're just an erotic hallucination,
just so much feverishly produced kazoo music,
are you serious?—this large oven impersonating night,
this exhaustion mutilated to resemble passion,

the bogus moon of tenderness and magic
you hold out to each prisoner like a cup of light?

HENRI COLE

The Roman Baths at Nîmes

In the hall of mirrors nobody speaks.
An ember smolders before hollowed cheeks.
Someone empties pockets, loose change and keys,
into a locker. My god, forgive me.
Some say love, disclosed, repels what it sees,
yet if I touch the darkness, it touches me.
In the steamroom, inconsolable tears
fall against us. In the whirlpool, my arms,
rowing through little green crests, help to steer
the body, riding against death. Yet what harm
is there in us? I swear to you, my friend,
crossarmed in a bright beach towel, turning round
to see my face in lamplight, that eye, ear
and tongue, good things, make something sweet of fear.

MARY JO SALTER

Half a Double Sonnet

for Ben

Their ordeal over, now the only trouble
was conveying somehow to a boy of three
that for a week or two he'd be seeing double.
Surely he wouldn't recall the surgery
years later, but what about the psychic scars?
And so, when the patch came off, they bought the toy
he'd wanted most. He held it high. "Two cars!"
he cried; and drove himself from joy to joy.
Two baby sisters . . . One was enough of Clare,
but who could complain?—considering that another
woman had stepped forward to take care
of the girls, which left him all alone with Mother.
Victory! Even when he went to pee,
he was seconded in his virility.

MICHAEL PALMER

Sonnet
Now I see them

Now I see them sitting me before a mirror.
There's noise and laughter. Somebody
mentions that hearing is silver
before we move on to Table One
with the random numbers. I look down
a long street containing numbers.
A white four leans against the fence
and disappears. In the doorway
is the seven, then the x
painted red, so you can find it
more easily. Five goes by
without its cap. My father wears
the second x. He has a grey cloud
for a face, and dark lines for arms.

Close-Up of a Sonnet
"WHAT LIPS MY LIPS HAVE KISSED, AND WHERE, AND WHY"

by Edna St. Vincent Millay

COURTESY HARPERCOLLINS PUBLISHERS

E dna St. Vincent Millay was born in 1892. She was the first woman to win the Pulitzer Prize for poetry, in 1923 with her fourth book of poetry. Her first book, *Renascence,* was written when she was very young—the title poem when she was nineteen.

Millay's command of the sonnet was distinctive and unusual. Instead of taking the more leisurely pace of the public sonnet that had been the nineteenth-century model, she drove her sonnets forward with a powerful lyric music and personal emphasis. Her sonnets rely heavily on sibilance and assonance and alliteration. They are pieces of music to such an extent that they almost destabilize the tradition of the sonnet as a measured argument. Here she uses her distinctive music and high diction to produce an unusually quick-paced poem in the first octave and then a slower, more reflective sestet where the abandoned lover becomes a winter tree. This ability of the sonnet, to accomodate both lyric and reflective time, made it a perfect vehicle for twentieth-century poets like Millay.

The Ballad

The Ballad at a Glance

1) It is a short narrative, which is usually—but not always—arranged in four-line stanzas with a distinctive and memorable meter.

2) The usual ballad meter is a first and third line with four stresses—iambic tetrameter—and then a second and fourth with three stresses—iambic trimeter.

3) The rhyme scheme is *abab* or *abcb*.

4) The subject matter is distinctive: almost always communal stories of lost love, supernatural happenings, or recent events.

5) The ballad maker uses popular and local speech and dialogue often and vividly to convey the story. This is especially a feature of early ballads.

The History of the Form

The balladeer remains one of the most interesting and least-defined makers of form. His (rarely her) identity, appearance, ability, and standing changed from country to country. In Ireland he was often a village citizen, a bystander at political events and natural disasters: a storyteller with an ominous errand. In England he stood outside the court, outside history, reminding the populace of their passage through an imperial history, and their exclusion from it: In pursuit of this, he composed ballads on shipwrecks and uprisings and harvest romances. In America, where poetry developed at the same time as literacy, and where there was therefore less need for a division between the oral and written, the ballad became part of the vocabulary of the ordinary accomplishments of the American poet. And so the anonymous balladeer gradually vanished from the landscape.

Despite this, it seems obvious that the ballad came to poetry from song. It is a form found in every language, every country, every culture. Its shape, structure, and rhetoric are all defined by its roots in the oral tradition. As a form it is simple, direct—almost always a short narrative—and subtly left open for the next user, so that details, names, and events can be added on if necessary.

The ballad keeps an audience awake. Its subject matter is tabloid:

death, murder, suicide, disgrace, mystery. It is lurid, musical, communal. It leaps from event to event.

One of the signature traits of the ballad is the way that vernacular dialogue breaks into the narrative, turning it into a living, vivid theater of the speech of its particular moment. In the anonymous fifteenth-century ballad "Sir Patrick Spens," a knight has been sent by the Scottish king to sail out on dangerous seas. He drowns before the ballad is finished. This is a beautiful, economical telling of a story. In these two stanzas, as his voice and the voice of one of his sailors is heard, the immediacy, music, and fatalism of the ballad can be seen in all their raw power:

> "Mak haste, mak haste, my mirry men all,
>   Our guid ship sails the morn."
> "O say na sae, my master dear,
>   For I fear a deadly storm.
>
> "Late, late yestre'en I saw the new moon
>   Wi' the auld moon in hir arm,
> And I fear, I fear my dear master,
>   That we will come to harm."

The earliest ballad in manuscript form, called Judas, is in a collection in a Cambridge library. The ballad, as we know it, probably dates from the fourteenth and fifteenth centuries; but maybe earlier. The majority of ballads were not transcribed until the eighteenth century, and so a great deal of information about them has been lost. Not until the end of the nineteenth century did an English scholar, F. J. Child, produce a five-volume archive of ballad versions and alternatives called *The English and Scottish Ballads*. Nevertheless, there have been intense disagreements between scholars about their origins. During the earlier part of this century there was "a ballad war," with one set of scholars arguing that ballads were communal, that they grew out of dances and rituals. Others argued that they were individual, made by one balladeer, informed by communal concerns.

In the same way, no one can quite agree about ballad meter. All varieties of the ballad are based on four lines. Some critics have said that the meter is accentual. Some that it is accentual-syllabic. And some others in this century that it is foot-verse, with metrical pauses, but not confined by them.

In fact, whatever its name, the early ballad meter is recognizable as a series of small, intense sound-snapshots. Each line has four stresses, or alternately four and three. The rhyme scheme is *abcb* or *abab*. The music builds from verse to verse often making a hypnotic narrative. The form is designed so that the ballad maker's voice is clearly heard. It is a human, downright voice. It chooses plain words and short lines, vivid images and musical rhymes. And more than any other poetic form, except the dramatic monologue, the ballad insists on ordinary, day-to-day speech and vernacular and includes it in its verses.

The Contemporary Context

The idea of a poem written so close to a community that it is almost coauthored by it is very far from the concept of that tremendous loner—the modern poet. But this is what the ballad is.

And so the contemporary poet's ballad makes a fascinating contrast in this section to the ballad of the tradition. Because not only does this contemporary ballad, written by a contemporary poet, come from a different concept of the poet, it also seeks out a different audience. The audience for the traditional ballad was conscious of its identity as a community and aware that the balladeer spoke to and of that, with the powerful and transient ballad of local concern. The newer ballad is putting a subtly individual shape on the ballad impulse. By individualizing the poet's concerns—love or loss or self-realization—it inevitably breaks the old communal links with audience.

This might seem to show that the historical moment of the ballad may well be over. But the ballad comes out of deep sources of language and storytelling. In recent times new media continue to suggest the early origins and customs of the ballads. Country-and-western is one, and rap also is clear, narrative, and communal. It does not keep to the old quatrain or the old rhyme scheme. But its immediacy, music, and spontaneous methods of composition shed real light on the true nature of the ballad.

ANONYMOUS

The Cherry-tree Carol

Joseph was an old man,
    And an old man was he,
When he wedded Mary
    In the land of Galilee.

Joseph and Mary walked
    Through an orchard good,
Where was cherries and berries
    So red as any blood.

Joseph and Mary walked
    Through an orchard green,
Where was berries and cherries
    As thick as might be seen.

O then bespoke Mary
    So meek and so mild:
'Pluck me one cherry, Joseph,
    For I am with child.'

O then bespoke Joseph
    With words most unkind:
'Let him pluck thee a cherry
    That brought thee with child.'

O then bespoke the Babe
    Within his Mother's womb:
'Bow down then the tallest tree
    For my Mother to have some.'

Then bowed down the highest tree
    Unto his Mother's hand;
Then she cried 'See, Joseph,
    I have cherries at command.'

O then bespake Joseph
   'I have done Mary wrong;
But cheer up, my dearest,
   And be not cast down.'

Then Mary plucked a cherry
   As red as the blood,
Then Mary went home
   With her heavy load.

Then Mary took her Babe
   And sat him on her knee,
Saying, 'My dear Son, tell me
   What this world will be.'

'O I shall be as dead, Mother,
   As the stones in the wall;
O the stones in the streets, Mother,
   Shall mourn for me all.

Upon Easter-day, Mother,
   My uprising shall be;
O the sun and the moon, Mother,
   Shall both rise with me.'

ANONYMOUS

Sir Patrick Spens

The king sits in Dumferling town,
   Drinking the blude-reid wine:
"O whar will I get guid sailor,
   To sail this ship of mine?"

Up and spak an eldern knicht,
   Sat at the king's richt knee:
"Sir Patrick Spens is the best sailor
   That sails upon the sea."

The king has written a braid letter
   And signed it wi' his hand,

And sent it to Sir Patrick Spens,
    Was walking on the sand.

The first line that Sir Patrick read,
    A loud lauch lauched he;
The next line that Sir Patrick read,
    The tear blinded his ee.

"O wha is this has done this deed,
    This ill deed done to me,
To send me out this time o' the year,
    To sail upon the sea?

"Mak haste, mak haste, my mirry men all,
    Our guid ship sails the morn."
"O say na sae, my master dear,
    For I fear a deadly storm.

"Late, late yestre'en I saw the new moon,
    Wi' the auld moon in hir arm,
And I fear, I fear my dear master,
    That we will come to harm."

O our Scots nobles were richt laith
    To weet their cork-heeled shoon,
But lang or a' the play were played
    Their hats they swam aboon.

O lang, lang may their ladies sit,
    Wi' their fans into their hand,
Or ere they see Sir Patrick Spens
    Come sailing to the land.

O lang, lang may the ladies stand
    Wi' their gold kems in their hair,
Waiting for their ain dear lords,
    For they'll see them na mair.

Half o'er, half o'er to Aberdour
    It's fifty fadom deep,
And there lies guid Sir Patrick Spens
    Wi' the Scots lords at his feet.

ANONYMOUS

The Wife of Usher's Well

There lived a wife at Usher's Well,
   And a wealthy wife was she;
She had three stout and stalwart sons,
   And sent them o'er the sea.

They hadna been a week from her,
   A week but barely ane,
Whan word came to the carlin wife
   That her three sons were gane.

They hadna been a week from her,
   A week but barely three,
Whan word came to the carlin wife
   That her sons she'd never see.

"I wish the wind may never cease,
   Nor fashes in the flood,
Till my three sons come hame to me,
   In earthly flesh and blood."

It fell about the Martinmass,
   When nights are lang and mirk,
The carlin wife's three sons came hame,
   And their hats were o' the birk.

It neither grew in syke nor ditch,
   Nor yet in any sheugh;
But at the gates o' Paradise,
   That birk grew fair eneugh.

"Blow up the fire, my maidens,
   Bring water from the well;
For a' my house shall feast this night,
   Since my three sons are well."

And she has made to them a bed,
   She's made it large and wide,
And she's ta'en her mantle her about,
   Sat down at the bed-side.

Up then crew the red, red cock,
    And up and crew the gray;
The eldest to the youngest said,
    "'T is time we were away."

The cock he hadna crawed but once,
    And clapped his wings at a',
When the youngest to the eldest said,
    "Brother, we must awa'.

"The cock doth craw, the day doth daw,
    The channerin' worm doth chide;
Gin we be missed out o' our place,
    A sair pain we maun bide.

"Fare ye weel, my mother dear!
    Fareweel to barn and byre!
And fare ye weel, the bonny lass,
    That kindles my mother's fire!"

ANONYMOUS

My Boy Willie

It was early, early all in the Spring
    That my boy Willie went to serve the king
The night was dark and the wind blew high.
    It was then I lost my dear sailor boy.

Tha night is long and I can find no rest,
    The thought of Willie runs in my breast,
I'll search the green woods and village wide
    Still hoping my true love to find.

"Oh, father, father, give me a boat,
    Out on the ocean that I may float,
To watch the big boats as they pass by,
    That I might enquire for my sailor boy."

She was not long out upon the deep,
    When a man o'war vessel she chanced to meet,
Saying, "Captain, captain, now tell me true,
    If my boy Willie is on board with you."

"What sort of a boy is your Willie dear,
   Or what sort of a suit does your Willie wear?"
"He wears a suit of the royal blue,
   And you'll easy know him for his heart is true."

"Oh, then your boy Willie, I am sorry to say,
   Has just been drowned the other day,
On yon green island that we pass by,
   'Twas there we laid your poor sailor boy."

She wrung her hands and she tore her hair,
   And she sobbed and sighed in her despair,
And with every sob she let fall a tear,
   And every sigh was for her Willie dear.

"O, father, make my grave both wide and deep,
   With a fine tombstone at my head and feet;
And in the middle a turtle dove
   That the world may know that I died of love."

Come all you sailors who sail along
   And all you boatmen who follow on.
From the cabin-boy to the mainmast high
   Ye must mourn in black for my sailor boy.

JOHN GREENLEAF WHITTIER

The Changeling

For the fairest maid in Hampton
   They needed not to search,
Who saw young Anna Favor
   Come walking into church,—

Or bringing from the meadows,
   At set of harvest-day,
The frolic of the blackbirds,
   The sweetness of the hay.

Now the weariest of all mothers,
   The saddest two-years bride,
She scowls in the face of her husband,
   And spurns her child aside.

"Rake out the red coals, goodman,—
    For there the child shall lie,
Till the black witch comes to fetch her,
    And both up chimney fly.

"It's never my own little daughter,
    It's never my own," she said;
"The witches have stolen my Anna,
    And left me an imp instead.

"Oh, fair and sweet was my baby,
    Blue eyes, and hair of gold;
But this is ugly and wrinkled,
    Cross, and cunning, and old.

"I hate the touch of her fingers,
    I hate the feel of her skin;
It's not the milk from my bosom,
    But my blood, that she sucks in.

"My face grows sharp with the torment;
    Look! my arms are skin and bone!—
Rake open the red coals, goodman,
    And the witch shall have her own.

"She'll come when she hears it crying,
    In the shape of an owl or bat,
And she'll bring us our darling Anna
    In place of her screeching brat."

Then the goodman, Ezra Dalton,
    Laid his hand upon her head:
"Thy sorrow is great, O woman!
    I sorrow with thee," he said.

"The paths to trouble are many,
    And never but one sure way
Leads out to the light beyond it:
    My poor wife, let us pray."

Then he said to the great All-Father,
    "Thy daughter is weak and blind;

Let her sight come back, and clothe her
    Once more in her right mind.

"Lead her out of this evil shadow,
    Out of these fancies wild;
Let the holy love of the mother
    Turn again to her child.

"Make her lips like the lips of Mary
    Kissing her blessed Son;
Let her hands, like the hands of Jesus,
    Rest on her little one.

"Comfort the soul of thy handmaid,
    Open her prison-door,
And thine shall be all the glory
    And praise forevermore."

Then into the face of its mother
    The baby looked up and smiled;
And the cloud of her soul was lifted,
    And she knew her little child.

A beam of the slant west sunshine
    Made the wan face almost fair,
Lit the blue eyes' patient wonder
    And the rings of pale gold hair.

She kissed it on lip and forehead,
    She kissed it on cheek and chin,
And she bared her snow-white bosom
    To the lips so pale and thin.

Oh, fair on her bridal morning
    Was the maid who blushed and smiled,
But fairer to Ezra Dalton
    Looked the mother of his child.

With more than a lover's fondness
    He stooped to her worn young face,
And the nursing child and the mother
    He folded in one embrace.

"Blessed be God!" he murmured.
    "Blessed be God!" she said;
"For I see, who once was blinded,—
    I live, who once was dead.

"Now mount and ride, my goodman,
    As thou lovest thy own soul!
Woe's me, if my wicked fancies
    Be the death of Goody Cole!"

His horse he saddled and bridled,
    And into the night rode he,—
Now through the great black woodland,
    Now by the white-beached sea.

He rode through the silent clearings,
    He came to the ferry wide,
And thrice he called to the boatman
    Asleep on the other side.

He set his horse to the river,
    He swam to Newbury town,
And he called up Justice Sewall
    In his nightcap and his gown.

And the grave and worshipful justice
    (Upon whose soul be peace!)
Set his name to the jailer's warrant
    For Goodwife Cole's release.

Then through the night the hoof-beats
    Went sounding like a flail;
And Goody Cole at cockcrow
    Came forth from Ipswich jail.

OSCAR WILDE

from *The Ballad of Reading Gaol*
II

For oak and elm have pleasant leaves
That in the spring-time shoot:

But grim to see is the gallows-tree,
With its adder-bitten root,
And, green or dry, a man must die
Before it bears its fruit!

The loftiest place is that seat of grace
For which all worldlings try:
But who would stand in hempen band
Upon a scaffold high,
And through a murderer's collar take
His last look at the sky?

It is sweet to dance to violins
When Love and Life are fair:
To dance to flutes, to dance to lutes
Is delicate and rare:
But it is not sweet with nimble feet
To dance upon the air!

So with curious eyes and sick surmise
We watched him day by day,
And wondered if each one of us
Would end the self-same way,
For none can tell to what red Hell
His sightless soul may stray.

At last the dead man walked no more
Amongst the Trial Men,
And I knew that he was standing up
In the black dock's dreadful pen,
And that never would I see his face
In God's sweet world again.

Like two doomed ships that pass in storm
We had crossed each other's way:
But we made no sign, we said no word,
We had no word to say;
For we did not meet in the holy night,
But in the shameful day.

ELINOR WYLIE

Peter and John

Twelve good friends
Walked under the leaves,
Binding the ends
Of the barley sheaves.

Peter and John
Lay down to sleep
Pillowed upon
A haymaker's heap.

John and Peter
Lay down to dream.
The air was sweeter
Than honey and cream.

Peter was bred
In the salty cold:
His hair was red
And his eyes were gold.

John had a mouth
Like a wing bent down:
His brow was smooth
And his eyes were brown.

Peter to slumber
Sank like a stone,
Of all their number
The bravest one.

John more slowly
Composed himself,
Young and holy
Among the Twelve.

John as he slept
Cried out in grief,
Turned and wept
On the golden leaf:

"Peter, Peter,
Stretch me your hand
Across the glitter
Of the harvest land!

"Peter, Peter,
Give me a sign!
This was a bitter
Dream of mine—

"Bitter as aloes
It parched my tongue.
Upon the gallows
My life was hung.

"Sharp it seemed
As a bloody sword.
Peter, I dreamed
I was Christ the Lord!"

Peter turned
To holy Saint John:
His body burned
In the falling sun.

In the falling sun
He burned like flame:
"John, Saint John,
I have dreamed the same!

"My bones were hung
On an elder tree;
Bells were rung
Over Galilee.

"A silver penny
Sealed each of my eyes.
Many and many
A cock crew thrice."

When Peter's word
Was spoken and done,

"Were you Christ the Lord
In your dream?" said John.

"No," said the other,
"That I was not.
I was our brother
Iscariot."

Bagpipe Music

It's no go the merrygoround, it's no go the rickshaw,
All we want is a limousine and a ticket for the peepshow.
Their knickers are made of crêpe-de-chine, their shoes are made of
    python,
Their halls are lined with tiger rugs and their walls with heads of
    bison.

John MacDonald found a corpse, put it under the sofa,
Waited till it came to life and hit it with a poker,
Sold its eyes for souvenirs, sold its blood for whiskey,
Kept its bones for dumbbells to use when he was fifty.

It's no go the Yogi-Man, it's no go Blavatsky,
All we want is a bank balance and a bit of skirt in a taxi.

Annie MacDougall went to milk, caught her foot in the heather,
Woke to hear a dance record playing of Old Vienna.
It's no go your maidenheads, it's no go your culture,
All we want is a Dunlop tire and the devil mend the puncture.

The Laird o' Phelps spent Hogmanay declaring he was sober,
Counted his feet to prove the fact and found he had one foot over.
Mrs. Carmichael had her fifth, looked at the job with repulsion,
Said to the midwife "Take it away; I'm through with over-
    production."

It's no go the gossip column, it's no go the Ceilidh,
All we want is a mother's help and a sugar-stick for the baby.

Willie Murray cut his thumb, couldn't count the damage,
Took the hide of an Ayrshire cow and used it for a bandage.

His brother caught three hundred cran when the seas were lavish,
Threw the bleeders back in the sea and went upon the parish.

It's no go the Herring Board, it's no go the Bible,
All we want is a packet of fags when our hands are idle.

It's no go the picture palace, it's no go the stadium,
It's no go the country cot with a pot of pink geraniums,
It's no go the Government grants, it's no go the elections,
Sit on your arse for fifty years and hang your hat on a pension.

It's no go my honey love, it's no go my poppet;
Work your hands from day to day, the winds will blow the profit.
The glass is falling hour by hour, the glass will fall forever,
But if you break the bloody glass you won't hold up the weather.

JOHN BETJEMAN

Death in Leamington

She died in the upstairs bedroom
   By the light of the evening star
That shone through the plate glass window
   From over Leamington Spa.

Beside her the lonely crochet
   Lay patiently and unstirred,
But the fingers that would have worked it
   Were dead as the spoken word.

And Nurse came in with the tea-things
   Breast high 'mid the stands and chairs—
But Nurse was alone with her own little soul,
   And the things were alone with theirs.

She bolted the big round window,
   She let the blinds unroll,
She set a match to the mantle,
   She covered the fire with coal.

And "Tea!" she said in a tiny voice
   "Wake up! It's nearly *five*."

Oh! Chintzy, chintzy cheeriness,
   Half dead and half alive!

Do you know that the stucco is peeling?
   Do you know that the heart will stop?
From those yellow Italianate arches
   Do you hear the plaster drop?

Nurse looked at the silent bedstead,
   At the gray, decaying face,
As the calm of a Leamington evening
   Drifted into the place.

She moved the table of bottles
   Away from the bed to the wall;
And tiptoeing gently over the stairs
   Turned down the gas in the hall.

OGDEN NASH

The Tale of Custard the Dragon

Belinda lived in a little white house,
With a little black kitten and a little gray mouse,
And a little yellow dog and a little red wagon,
And a realio, trulio, little pet dragon.

Now the name of the little black kitten was Ink,
And the little gray mouse, she called her Blink,
And the little yellow dog was sharp as Mustard,
But the dragon was a coward, and she called him Custard.

Custard the dragon had big sharp teeth,
And spikes on top of him and scales underneath,
Mouth like a fireplace, chimney for a nose,
And realio, trulio daggers on his toes.

Belinda was as brave as a barrel full of bears,
And Ink and Blink chased lions down the stairs,
Mustard was as brave as a tiger in a rage,
But Custard cried for a nice safe cage.

Belinda tickled him, she tickled him unmerciful,
Ink, Blink and Mustard, they rudely called him Percival,
They all sat laughing in the little red wagon
At the realio, trulio, cowardly dragon.

Belinda giggled till she shook the house,
And Blink said Weeck! which is giggling for a mouse,
Ink and Mustard rudely asked his age,
When Custard cried for a nice safe cage.

Suddenly, suddenly they heard a nasty sound,
And Mustard growled, and they all looked around.
Meowch! cried Ink, and Ooh! cried Belinda,
For there was a pirate, climbing in the winda.

Pistol in his left hand, pistol in his right,
And he held in his teeth a cutlass bright,
His beard was black, one leg was wood;
It was clear that the pirate meant no good.

Belinda paled, and she cried Help! Help!
But Mustard fled with a terrified yelp,
Ink trickled down to the bottom of the household,
And little mouse Blink strategically mouseholed.

But up jumped Custard, snorting like an engine,
Clashed his tail like irons in a dungeon,
With a clatter and a clank and a jangling squirm
He went at the pirate like a robin at a worm.

The pirate gaped at Belindas dragon,
And gulped some grog from his pocket flagon,
He fired two bullets, but they didn't hit,
And Custard gobbled him, every bit.

Belinda embraced him, Mustard licked him,
No one mourned for his pirate victim.
Ink and Blink in glee did gyrate
Around the dragon that ate the pyrate.

Belinda still lives in her little white house,
With her little black kitten and her little gray mouse,

And her little yellow dog and her little red wagon,
And her realio, trulio, little pet dragon.

Belinda is as brave as a barrel full of bears,
And Ink and Blink chase lions down the stairs,
Mustard is as brave as a tiger in a rage,
But Custard keeps crying for a nice safe cage.

GWENDOLYN BROOKS

We Real Cool
The Pool Players.
Seven at the Golden Shovel.

We real cool. We
Left school. We

Lurk Late. We
Strike straight. We

Sing sin. We
Thin gin. We

Jazz June. We
Die soon.

STERLING A. BROWN

Riverbank Blues

A man git his feet set in a sticky mudbank,
A man git dis yellow water in his blood,
No need for hopin', no need for doin',
Muddy streams keep him fixed for good.

Little Muddy, Big Muddy, Moreau and Osage,
Little Mary's, Big Mary's, Cedar Creek,
Flood deir muddy water roundabout a man's roots,
Keep him soaked and stranded and git him weak.

Lazy sun shinin' on a little cabin,
Lazy moon glistenin' over river trees;
Ole river whisperin', lappin' 'gainst de long roots:
"Plenty of rest and peace in these. . . ."

Big mules, black loam, apple and peach trees,
But seems lak de river washes us down
Past de rich farms, away from de fat lands,
Dumps us in some ornery riverbank town.

Went down to the river, sot me down an' listened,
Heard de water talkin' quiet, quiet lak an' slow:
"Ain' no need fo' hurry, take yo' time, take yo' time. . . ."
Heard it sayin'—*"Baby, hyeahs de way life go. . . ."*

Dat is what it tole me as I watched it slowly rollin',
But somp'n way inside me rared up an' say,
"Better be movin' . . . better be travelin' . . .
Riverbank'll git you ef you stay. . . ."

Towns are sinkin' deeper, deeper in de riverbank,
Takin' on de ways of deir sulky Ole Man—
Takin' on his creepy ways, takin' on his evil ways,
"Bes' git way, a long way . . . whiles you can.

"Man got his sea too lak de Mississippi
Ain't got so long for a whole lot longer way,
Man better move some, better not git rooted
Muddy water fool you, ef you stay. . . .

W. S. MERWIN

Ballad of John Cable and Three Gentlemen

He that had come that morning,
One after the other,
Over seven hills,
Each of a new color,

Came now by the last tree,
By the red-colored valley,
To a gray river
Wide as the sea.

There at the shingle
A listing wherry
Awash with dark water;
What should it carry?

There on the shelving,
Three dark gentlemen.
Might they direct him?
Three gentlemen.

"Cable, friend John, John Cable,"
When they saw him they said,
"Come and be company
As far as the far side."

"Come follow the feet," they said,
"Of your family,
Of your old father
That came already this way."

But Cable said, "First I must go
Once to my sister again;
What will she do come spring
And no man on her garden?

She will say "Weeds are alive
From here to the Stream of Friday;
I grieve for my brother's plowing,'
Then break and cry."

"Lose no sleep," they said, "for that fallow:
She will say before summer
'I can get me a daylong man,
Do better than a brother.' "

Cable said, "I think of my wife:
Dearly she needs consoling;
I must go back for a little
For fear she dies of grieving."

"Cable," they said, "John Cable,
Ask no such wild favor;
Still, if you fear she die soon,
The boat might wait for her."

But Cable said, "I remember:
Out of charity let me
Go shore up my poorly mother,
Cries all afternoon."

They said, "She is old and far,
Far and rheumy with years,
And, if you like, we shall take
No note of her tears."

But Cable said, "I am neither
Your hired man nor maid,
Your dog nor shadow
Nor your ape to be led."

He said, "I must go back:
Once I heard someone say
That the hollow Stream of Friday
Is a rank place to lie;

And this word, now I remember,
Makes me sorry: have you
Thought of my own body
I was always good to?

The frame that was my devotion
And my blessing was,
The straight bole whose limbs
Were long as stories—

Now, poor thing, left in the dirt
By the Stream of Friday
Might not remember me
Half tenderly."

They let him nurse no worry;
They said, "We give you our word:
Poor thing is made of patience;
Will not say a word."

"Cable, friend John, John Cable,"
After this they said,
"Come with no company
To the far side.

To a populous place,
A dense city
That shall not be changed
Before much sorrow dry."

Over shaking water
Toward the feet of his father,
Leaving the hills' color
And his poorly mother

And his wife at grieving
And his sister's fallow
And his body lying
In the rank hollow,

Now Cable is carried
On the dark river;
Not even a shadow
Followed him over.

On the wide river
Gray as the sea
Flags of white water
Are his company.

Close-Up of a Ballad

"WE REAL COOL"

by Gwendolyn Brooks

G wendolyn Brooks was born in 1917. She was a child when the Harlem Renaissance was testing and establishing new poetic styles for American poetry. In her book *A Street in Bronzeville* (1945), with its path-breaking insistence on the local and ordinary, she continued the adventure.

As an African-American poet, Gwendolyn Brooks innovated styles and melodies to convey the edge and power of a poetry that was often political, often a vehicle of resistance. Her celebrated poem "We Real Cool" is an example. It has a striking number of characteristics in common with the ballad of tradition. With its suppressed narrative, concealed drama, and communal theme, it conveys the power of the ballad in a contemporary context, disguising a sharp and public tone with deceptively musical cadences.

"We Real Cool" is witty and entertaining, despite its darkness.

No one, however, reading the poem again could doubt the irony and passionate engagement of the poet. The short lines become daggers of irony. The music of courage and the bleakness of reality are played off against each other in these brief, jumpy stanzas, like figures in fairytale. And the moral, as so often in the fable or the nursery rhyme, is clear: Personal risk is endangered. Society is about to punish the individual. The poem reminds us that the role of the ballad in our times can also be moral and satirical; that beneath the entertainment, the balladeer can make a secret and powerful claim on the reader.

Blank Verse

Blank Verse at a Glance

1) It is an iambic line with ten stresses and five beats.

2) It is unrhymed.

3) It is traditionally associated with dramatic speech and epic poetry.

4) The lack of rhyme makes enjambment more possible and often more effective.

5) It is often identified as the poetic form closest to human speech.

The History of the Form

lank verse came into English poetry from Italian literature.
The Italians called blank verse *verse sciolti da rima*—verse
free from rhyme. There was intense interest at the time in
finding an unrhymed line that would match the heft and weight of
the classical epic. This was, after all the Renaissance when imitation
of the classical epic, its scope and purpose, was still a priority for
poets. Italian poets such as Luigi Alamanni and Trissino were al-
ready using blank verse for plays in the early part of the sixteenth
century. But their blank verse was composed with eleven or ten or
nine syllables. There was still a need to naturalize the whole project
of blank verse in the English language.

The inventor of blank verse in England was Henry Howard, Earl
of Surrey—one of those raffish and unfortunate minor figures in
history who end up having a powerful influence on the poetry they
do not completely master. He was born in 1517, the son of a man who
would become the Duke of Norfolk. He would die at the age of
thirty, executed for no real reason by Henry VIII, except that he ad-
vised his sister to become the king's mistress and for some other
minor offenses.

In a short life he accomplished two major innovations in English
poetry. He helped Thomas Wyatt bring the sonnet to England. And
he translated *The Aeneid* into "this straunge meter" of blank verse.

His intention was to produce a strict ten-syllable line and this is what he endeavored to do.

The establishment of blank verse as a convention that could be used in English poetry had an immediate effect. Without rhyme, there was suddenly far more chance of natural and unforced speech. And it was another glamorous and doomed poet with whom blank verse came into its own.

Christopher Marlowe, born in 1564, electrified the London theater with his production of *Tamburlaine the Great,* which was published and performed in 1590. Here for the first time, blank verse was revealed to be a natural vehicle for rhythmic and sustained speech, where complex argument and emotion could be sustained without being drowned out by rhyme.

Shakespeare chose blank verse for most of his plays, although usually made it a near neighbor of rhyme and song. But it was John Milton who took blank verse further again, arguing in his prose statement at the beginning of *Paradise Lost* that this measure was preferable to "the jingling sound of like endings" and that it provided the music and example of "the sense variously drawn out from one verse into another."

The Contemporary Context

I n America blank verse has become something of a rarity toward the end of the twentieth century. The reason may have to do with the favor that plain speech enjoys. The poetic line has become shorter, so short that even a tetrameter line at times seems long. Today's poetry has taken on the directness of journalism and the simplicity of speech. Elaborate sentences are considered part of mandarin speech—inauthentic, self-involved, not committed to communication or at the very least not committed to delivering what might be easily, quickly acknowledged as the truth of a mood, say, or scene, or action. Our present-day preference for directness means fewer adjectives or adverbs, fewer subordinate or qualifying clauses (except in academic writing) that might lengthen the sentence. In much of today's poetry there are many sentences that could not contain a blank verse line, let alone two or three. Our mistrust of verbal play has made it hard for us to accept sentences that extend beyond a three or four stress line. Our rejection of elaboration is a Puritan inheritance to be sure, but never has it made such deep claims on a contemporary literary style as it has in the twentieth century. Short declarative sentences, usually in the past or present tense suggest a resistance to what blank verse offers—greater suspension of the sentence, an acceptance of duration, and, finally, an imitation or a description of thought.

It is also true that many of today's poets do not hear blank verse because they have not read it and if they had there is no certainty they would recognize it.

There is a misconception that blank verse must be as stressed as Marlowe's, and as obviously rhetorical. The complexity of Milton's blank verse or the subtlety and suppleness of Wordsworth's are largely unacknowledged by today's poets whose timing is more attuned to audience response (at readings) than to metrical considerations.

HENRY HOWARD, EARL OF SURREY

from his translation of *The Aeneid*

It was then night: the sound and quiet sleep
Had through the earth the wearied bodies caught;
The woods, the raging seas were fallen to rest;
When that the stars had half their course declined
The fields whist; beasts and fowls of divers hue,
And what so that in the broad lakes remained,
Or yet among the bushy thicks of briar
Laid down to sleep by silence of the night,
Gan 'suage their cares, mindless of travels past.
Not so the sprite of this Phoenician:
Unhappy she, that on no sleep could chance,
Nor yet night's rest enter in eye or breast.
Her cares redouble; love doth rise and rage again,
And overflows with swelling storms of wrath.

CHRISTOPHER MARLOWE

from *Tamburlaine the Great* (Part I, Act V, 160–173)

What is beauty, saith my sufferings, then?
If all the pens that ever poets held
Had fed the feeling of their masters' thoughts
And every sweetness that inspired their hearts,
Their minds and muses on admirèd themes;
If all the heavenly quintessence they still
From their immortal flowers of poesy,

Wherein as in a mirror we perceive
The highest reaches of a human wit—
If these had made one poem's period
And all combined in beauty's worthiness,
Yet should there hover in their restless heads
One thought, one grace, one wonder at the least,
Which into words no virtue can digest.

WILLIAM SHAKESPEARE

from *Julius Caesar* (III.ii. 70–104)

Friends, Romans, countrymen, lend me your ears.
I come to bury Caesar, not to praise him.
The evil that men do lives after them;
The good is oft interred with their bones.
So let it be with Caesar. The noble Brutus
Hath told you Caesar was ambitious.
If it were so, it was a grievous fault,
And grievously hath Caesar answered it.
Here, under leave of Brutus and the rest—
For Brutus is an honourable man,
So are they all, all honourable men—
Come I to speak in Caesar's funeral.
He was my friend, faithful and just to me.
But Brutus says he was ambitious,
And Brutus is an honourable man.
He hath brought many captives home to Rome,
Whose ransoms did the general coffers fill.
Did this in Caesar seem ambitious?
When that the poor have cried, Caesar hath wept.
Ambition should be made of sterner stuff.
Yet Brutus says he was ambitious.
And Brutus is an honourable man.
You all did see that on the Lupercal
I thrice presented him a kingly crown,
Which he did thrice refuse. Was this ambition?
Yet Brutus says he was ambitious.
And sure he is an honourable man.

I speak not to disprove what Brutus spoke,
But here I am to speak what I do know.
You all did love him once, not without cause.
What cause withholds you then to mourn for him?
O judgement, thou art fled to brutish beasts,
And men have lost their reason! Bear with me.
My heart is in the coffin there with Caesar,
And I must pause till it come back to me.

JOHN MILTON

from *Paradise Lost* (Book I, lines 710–746)

Anon out of the earth a fabric huge
Rose like an exhalation, with the sound
Of dulcet symphonies and voices sweet,
Built like a temple, where pilasters round
Were set, and Doric pillars overlaid
With golden architrave; nor did there want
Cornice or frieze, with bossy sculptures grav'n;
The roof was fretted gold. Not Babylon,
Nor great Alcairo such magnificence
Equaled in all their glories, to enshrine
Belus or Serapis their gods, or seat
Their kings, when Egypt with Assyria strove
In wealth and luxury. Th' ascending pile
Stood fixed her stately height, and straight the doors
Opening their brazen folds discover wide
Within, her ample spaces, o'er the smooth
And level pavement: from the archèd roof
Pendent by subtle magic many a row
Of starry lamps and blazing cressets fed
With naphtha and asphaltus yielded light
As from a sky. The hasty multitude
Admiring entered, and the work some praise
And some the architect: his hand was known
In Heav'n by many a towered structure high,
Where sceptred angels held their residence,
And sat as princes, whom the Súpreme King

Exalted to such power, and gave to rule,
Each in his hierarchy, the orders bright.
Nor was his name unheard or unadored
In ancient Greece and in Ausonian land
Men called him Mulciber and how he fell
From Heav'n, they fabled, thrown by angry Jove
Sheer o'er the crystal battlements: from morn
To noon he fell, from noon to dewy eve,
A summer's day; and with the setting sun
Dropped from the zenith like a falling star,
On Lemnos th' Aégean isle . . .

CHARLOTTE SMITH

from *Beachy Head*

An early worshipper at Nature's shrine,
I loved her rudest scenes—warrens, and heaths,
And yellow commons, and birch-shaded hollows,
And hedge rows, bordering unfrequented lanes
Bowered with wild roses, and the clasping woodbine
Where purple tassels of the tangling vetch
With bittersweet, and bryony inweave,
And the dew fills the silver bindweed's cups—
I loved to trace the brooks whose humid banks
Nourish the harebell, and the freckled pagil;
And stroll among o'ershadowing woods of beech,
Lending in Summer, from the heats of noon
A whispering shade; while haply there reclines
Some pensive lover of uncultured flowers,
Who, from the tumps with bright green mosses clad,
Plucks the wood sorrel, with its light thin leaves,
Heart-shaped, and triply folded; and its root
Creeping like beaded coral; or who there
Gathers, the copse's pride, anemones,
With rays like golden studs on ivory laid
Most delicate: but touched with purple clouds,
Fit crown for April's fair but changeful brow.

WILLIAM WORDSWORTH
from *The Prelude* (Book Thirteenth, 1805, 10–65)

It was a summer's night, a close warm night,
Wan, dull, and glaring, with a dripping mist
Low-hung and thick that covered all the sky,
Half threatening storm and rain; but on we went
Unchecked, being full of heart and having faith
In our tried pilot. Little could we see,
Hemmed round on every side with fog and damp,
And, after ordinary travellers' chat
With our conductor, silently we sunk
Each into commerce with his private thoughts.
Thus did we breast the ascent, and by myself
Was nothing either seen or heard the while
Which took me from my musings, save that once
The shepherd's cur did to his own great joy
Unearth a hedgehog in the mountain-crags,
Round which he made a barking turbulent.
This small adventure—for even such it seemed
In that wild place and at the dead of night—
Being over and forgotten, on we wound
In silence as before. With forehead bent
Earthward, as if in opposition set
Against an enemy, I panted up
With eager pace, and no less eager thoughts,
Thus might we wear perhaps an hour away,
Ascending at loose distance each from each,
And I, as chanced, the foremost of the band—
When at my feet the ground appeared to brighten,
And with a step or two seemed brighter still;
Nor had I time to ask the cause of this,
For instantly a light upon the turf
Fell like a flash. I looked about, and lo,
The moon stood naked in the heavens, at height
Immense above my head, and on the shore
I found myself of a huge sea of mist,
Which meek and silent rested at my feet.

A hundred hills their dusky backs upheaved
All over this still ocean, and beyond,
Far, far beyond, the vapours shot themselves
In headlands, tongues, and promontory shapes,
Into the sea, the real sea, that seemed
To dwindle and give up its majesty,
Usurped upon as far as sight could reach.
Meanwhile, the moon looked down upon this shew
In single glory, and we stood, the mist
Touching our very feet; and from the shore
At distance not the third part of a mile
Was a blue chasm; a fracture in the vapour,
A deep and gloomy breathing-place, through which
Mounted the roar of waters, torrents, streams
Innumerable, roaring with one voice.
The universal spectacle throughout
Was shaped for admiration and delight,
Grand in itself alone, but in that breach
Through which the homeless voice of waters rose,
That dark deep thoroughfare, had Nature lodged
The soul, the imagination of the whole.

ALFRED, LORD TENNYSON

Ulysses

It little profits that an idle king,
By this still hearth, among these barren crags,
Matched with an aged wife, I mete and dole
Unequal laws unto a savage race,
That hoard, and sleep, and feed, and know not me.

I cannot rest from travel: I will drink
Life to the lees: all times I have enjoyed
Greatly, have suffered greatly, both with those
That loved me, and alone; on shore, and when
Through scudding drifts the rainy Hyades
Vext the dim sea I am become a name;
For always roaming with a hungry heart
Much have I seen and known; cities of men

And manners, climates, councils, governments,
Myself not least, but honored of them all;
And drunk delight of battle with my peers,
Far on the ringing plains of windy Troy.
I am a part of all that I have met;
Yet all experience is an arch wherethrough
Gleams that untravelled world whose margin fades
For ever and for ever when I move.
How dull it is to pause, to make an end,
To rust unburnished, not to shine in use!
As though to breathe were life! Life piled on life
Were all too little, and of one to me
Little remains; but every hour is saved
From that eternal silence, something more,
A bringer of new things; and vile it were
For some three suns to store and hoard myself,
And this gray spirit yearning in desire
To follow knowledge like a sinking star,
Beyond the utmost bound of human thought.

This is my son, mine own Telemachus,
To whom I leave the scepter and the isle—
Well-loved of me, discerning to fulfill
This labor, by slow prudence to make mild
A rugged people, and through soft degrees
Subdue them to the useful and the good.
Most blameless is he, centered in the sphere
Of common duties, decent not to fail
In offices of tenderness, and pay
Meet adoration to my household gods,
When I am gone. He works his work, I mine.

There lies the port; the vessel puffs her sail:
There gloom the dark, broad seas. My mariners,
Souls that have toiled, and wrought, and thought with me—
That ever with a frolic welcome took
The thunder and the sunshine, and opposed
Free hearts, free foreheads—you and I are old;
Old age hath yet his honor and his toil.

Death closes all; but something ere the end,
Some work of noble note, may yet be done,
Not unbecoming men that strove with Gods.
The lights begin to twinkle from the rocks:
The long day wanes: the slow moon climbs: the deep
Moans round with many voices. Come, my friends,
'Tis not too late to seek a newer world.
Push off, and sitting well in order smite
The sounding furrows; for my purpose holds
To sail beyond the sunset, and the baths
Of all the western stars, until I die.
It may be that the gulfs will wash us down;
It may be we shall touch the Happy Isles,
And see the great Achilles, whom we knew.
Though much is taken, much abides; and though
We are not now that strength which in old days
Moved earth and heaven; that which we are, we are,
One equal temper of heroic hearts,
Made weak by time and fate, but strong in will
To strive, to seek, to find, and not to yield.

EDWARD THOMAS

Rain

Rain, midnight rain, nothing but the wild rain
On this bleak hut, and solitude, and me
Remembering again that I shall die
And neither hear the rain nor give it thanks
For washing me cleaner than I have been
Since I was born into this solitude.
Blessed are the dead that the rain rains upon:
But here I pray that none whom once I loved
Is dying tonight or lying still awake
Solitary, listening to the rain,
Either in pain or thus in sympathy
Helpless among the living and the dead,
Like a cold water among broken reeds,
Myriads of broken reeds all still and stiff,

Like me who have no love which this wild rain
Has not dissolved except the love of death,
If love it be towards what is perfect and
Cannot, the tempest tells me, disappoint.

ROBERT FROST

Directive

Back out of all this now too much for us,
Back in a time made simple by the loss
Of detail, burned, dissolved, and broken off
Like graveyard marble sculpture in the weather,
There is a house that is no more a house
Upon a farm that is no more a farm
And in a town that is no more a town.
The road there, if you'll let a guide direct you
Who only has at heart your getting lost,
May seem as if it should have been a quarry—
Great monolithic knees the former town
Long since gave up pretense of keeping covered.
And there's a story in a book about it:
Besides the wear of iron wagon wheels
The ledges show lines ruled southeast-northwest,
The chisel work of an enormous Glacier
That braced his feet against the Arctic Pole.
You must not mind a certain coolness from him
Still said to haunt this side of Panther Mountain.
Nor need you mind the serial ordeal
Of being watched from forty cellar holes
As if by eye pairs out of forty firkins.
As for the woods' excitement over you
That sends light rustle rushes to their leaves,
Charge that to upstart inexperience.
Where were they all not twenty years ago?
They think too much of having shaded out
A few old pecker-fretted apple trees.
Make yourself up a cheering song of how
Someone's road home from work this once was,

Who may be just ahead of you on foot
Or creaking with a buggy load of grain.
The height of the adventure is the height
Of country where two village cultures faded
Into each other. Both of them are lost.
And if you're lost enough to find yourself
By now, pull in your ladder road behind you
And put a sign up CLOSED to all but me.
Then make yourself at home. The only field
Now left's no bigger than a harness gall.
First there's the children's house of make-believe,
Some shattered dishes underneath a pine,
The playthings in the playhouse of the children.
Weep for what little things could make them glad.
Then for the house that is no more a house,
But only a belilaced cellar hole,
Now slowly closing like a dent in dough.
This was no playhouse but a house in earnest.
Your destination and your destiny's
A brook that was the water of the house,
Cold as a spring as yet so near its source,
Too lofty and original to rage.
(We know the valley streams that when aroused
Will leave their tatters hung on barb and thorn.)
I have kept hidden in the instep arch
Of an old cedar at the waterside
A broken drinking goblet like the Grail
Under a spell so the wrong ones can't find it,
So can't get saved, as Saint Mark says they mustn't.
(I stole the goblet from the children's playhouse.)
Here are your waters and your watering place.
Drink and be whole again beyond confusion.

RICHARD WILBUR

Lying

To claim, at a dead party, to have spotted a grackle,
When in fact you haven't of late, can do no harm.

Your reputation for saying things of interest
Will not be marred, if you hasten to other topics,
Nor will the delicate web of human trust
Be ruptured by that airy fabrication.
Later, however, talking with toxic zest
Of golf, or taxes, or the rest of it
Where the beaked ladle plies the chuckling ice,
You may enjoy a chill of severance, hearing
Above your head the shrug of unreal wings.
Not that the world is tiresome in itself:
We know what boredom is: it is a dull
Impatience or a fierce velleity,
A champing wish, stalled by our lassitude,
To make or do. In the strict sense, of course,
We invent nothing, merely bearing witness
To what each morning brings again to light:
Gold crosses, cornices, astonishment
Of panes, the turbine-vent which natural law
Spins on the grill-end of the diner's roof,
Then grass and grackles or, at the end of town
In sheen-swept pastureland, the horse's neck
Clothed with its usual thunder, and the stones
Beginning now to tug their shadows in
And track the air with glitter. All these things
Are there before us; there before we look
Or fail to look; there to be seen or not
By us, as by the bee's twelve thousand eyes,
According to our means and purposes.
So too with strangeness not to be ignored,
Total eclipse or snow upon the rose,
And so with that most rare conception, nothing.
What is it, after all, but something missed?
It is the water of a dried-up well
Gone to assail the cliffs of Labrador.
There is what galled the arch-negator, sprung
From Hell to probe with intellectual sight
The cells and heavens of a given world
Which he could take but as another prison:

Small wonder that, pretending not to be,
He drifted through the bar-like boles of Eden
In a *black mist low creeping,* dragging down
And darkening with moody self-absorption
What, when he left it, lifted and, if seen
From the sun's vantage, seethed with vaulting hues.
Closer to making than the deftest fraud
Is seeing how the catbird's tail was made
To counterpoise, on the mock-orange spray,
Its light, up-tilted spine; or, lighter still,
How the shucked tunic of an onion, brushed
To one side on a backlit chopping-board
And rocked by trifling currents, prints and prints
Its bright, ribbed shadow like a flapping sail.
Odd that a thing is most itself when likened:
The eye mists over, basil hints of clove,
The river glazes toward the dam and spills
To the drubbed rocks below its crashing cullet,
And in the barnyard near the sawdust-pile
Some great thing is tormented. Either it is
A tarp torn loose and in the groaning wind
Now puffed, now flattened, or a hip-shot beast
Which tries again, and once again, to rise.
What, though for pain there is no other word,
Finds pleasure in the cruellest simile?
It is something in us like the catbird's song
From neighbor bushes in the grey of morning
That, harsh or sweet, and of its own accord,
Proclaims its many kin. It is a chant
Of the first springs, and it is tributary
To the great lies told with the eyes half-shut
That have the truth in view: the tale of Chiron
Who, with sage head, wild heart, and planted hoof
Instructed brute Achilles in the lyre,
Or of the garden where we first mislaid
Simplicity of wish and will, forgetting
Out of what cognate splendor all things came

To take their scattering names; and nonetheless
That matter of a baggage-train surprised
By a few Gascons in the Pyrenees
Which, having worked three centuries and more
In the dark caves of France, poured out at last
The blood of Roland, who to Charles his king
And to the dove that hatched the dove-tailed world
Was faithful unto death, and shamed the Devil.

RICHARD HOWARD

Stanzas in Bloomsbury

(Mrs Woolf entertains the notion of a novel about Lord Byron)

> *. . . wanting to build up my imaginary figure with every scrap I could find, when suddenly the figure turns to merely one of the usual dead . . .*

In search of treasure near the Pyramids
they all become unconscionably coy
having unearthed a vessel tightly sealed
secluded special and being set upon
opening it they found that it contained
one object which they all agreed to be
honey by taste till hairs clinging to
just what was wanted—though it seemed to me
the private parts of an intrepid man
merely silly and tinkling as if once
drawn forth what met their eyes was a boy
—I had ventured into the men's urinal!
his limbs entire the flesh smooth what else
but lust and tenderness afford relief?

Each man is under his thumb—just conceive
living your life in fear of drying up
and on command plunging from the walls
though haven't envisaged that fate for myself
enticed with hope of inevitable paradise—
on the contrary shall I ever have time enough
and promise of pleasure—eternal ecstasy
to write out everything that's in my head

ordering this one or that to leap to his doom
—though suppose what's in my head becomes absurd
for the entertainment of others, after which
—but would I even know it afterwards?
still others were pledged that night for their desires
besides I cannot believe I shall ever die . . .
I thank you for the bishop's work on God
which I am reading though he prove no more
than what I have always thought: so I am
not impotent but I have had enough
where I was—verging toward Spinoza not
of a mind to write books but to become
alien to his gloomy creed—I would be
nice to other people (only now? this once?)
better than that? there is a power in me
obsessed beyond all reading to withstand:
I cannot shake it off. I deny nothing
of all the accumulation of the past
but doubt everything. Incessant guests
are quite as bad as solitary jail.

Close-Up of Blank Verse
"DIRECTIVE"

by Robert Frost

CORBIS/BETTMANN

R obert Lee Frost was born in 1874, not in the New England that haunts and enhances his best work, but in San Francisco. He had a restless, disaffected early manhood—staying only a semester at Harvard and finally, in 1912, when he was thirty-eight selling the farm in New Hampshire his grandfather had bought him, and moving with his family to England.

The English experience was crucial to the way Frost developed the cadences and style of his blank verse. He stayed for two years in an England where the influence of Tennyson's "Ulysses" and Browning's "My Last Duchess" were still in the vocabulary of the Georgian poets he associated with, like Edward Thomas, as well as an intellectual pastoral stance. Frost's blank verse line is slow, distinctive, and deceptively driven by a vernacular narrative tone. In fact, as "Directive" shows, it is intensely stylized.

The contemporary poet who may have gained most from the rich tradition of blank verse was Robert Frost. Returning to America from England in 1918, he set out to find an idiom that allowed a stylized, dark voice to be heard, but which would also be capable of fast and surprising narrative drama.

Blank verse also allowed Frost one of the most striking first lines in the century's poetry—a rare iambic rush of monosyllables "Back out of all this now too much for us" that forms the first line of "Directive."

The Heroic Couplet at a Glance

1) It is a rhyming pair of lines.

2) The meter is usually iambic pentameter but may also be tetrameter.

3) A pentameter couplet has ten syllables with alternating stresses.

4) The rhyme scheme progresses as *aabbcc,* etc.

5) The heroic couplet, so-called, denoted that it was a form in which a high subject matter could be written. This was the form often used for translation of epic poetry from the classical Latin and Greek.

6) It works by adapting the old Chaucerian line and allowing a strong pause or caesura in the middle of the line.

7) The caesura usually comes after the fifth or sixth syllable. Its sharp rhymes and regular beat made it widely used in the sixteenth, seventeenth, and eighteenth centuries for epigrammatic and satirical poetry.

The History of the Form

At first glance, the couplet seems to be an element of form rather than a form in itself. It evolved out of parts of a poem, and one model of a line in particular—Chaucer's spacious rhyming couplet. This is one of the few forms that we have not annotated with a contemporary context. We mean this section to be almost a small laboratory to show how a single, unassuming form could suddenly rise to express the grander hopes of a time.

Even as a useful, witty, and musical unit, no one could have predicted the extraordinary development in the couplet that happened in the sixteenth century. Suddenly poets began to think, to argue, and to explain in the couplet. This then took the name "the heroic couplet," denoting a high subject matter.

By the eighteenth century the heroic couplet reigned supreme. The sharp, end-stop rhymes, the regular stresses, and the pause that happened in the middle of the line all made it perfect for moralizing, warning, satirizing, and poking fun at another's expense.

In many cases, for the poets who adopted it so enthusiastically in the eighteenth century, the heroic couplet became a self-conscious reconnection to a golden age of wit and closure. Samuel Johnson's *The Vanity of Human Wishes* for example is subtitled *The Tenth Satire of Juvenal Imitated by Samuel Johnson.*

In the Augustan Age when order was the dream, and decorum a necessity, the couplet seemed a micro-model of the age's intentions:

closed-in, certain, attractive to the reason, and finally, reassuring to the limits of that elegant world.

The couplet allows us to observe an element of form becoming a form: by the eighteenth century the heroic couplet—for good and ill—was a form. It began to shape the concept of the poem, as well as being shaped by the poets. Its fashionable, tight enclosure of sense and sensibility became an emblem for the times.

AEMILIA LANYER

from *The Description of Cooke-ham*

Now let me come unto that stately tree,
Wherein such goodly prospects you did see;
That oak that did in height his fellows pass,
As much as lofty trees, low growing grass,
Much like a comely cedar straight and tall,
Whose beauteous stature far exceeded all.
How often did you visit this fair tree,
Which seeming joyful in receiving thee,
Would like a palm tree spread his arms abroad,
Desirous that you there should make abode;
Whose fair green leaves much like a comely veil,
Defended *Phoebus* when he would assail;
Whose pleasing boughs did yield a cool fresh air
Joying his happiness when you were there.
Where being seated, you might plainly see
Hills, vales, and woods, as if on bended knee
They had appeared, your honor to salute,
Or to prefer some strange unlooked-for suit;
All interlaced with brooks and crystal springs,
A prospect fit to please the eyes of kings.
And thirteen shires appeared all in your sight,
Europe could not afford much more delight.

ANNE BRADSTREET

The Author to Her Book

Thou ill-formed offspring of my feeble brain,
Who after birth didst by my side remain,

Till snatched from thence by friends, less wise than true,
Who thee abroad, exposed to public view,
Made thee in rags, halting to th' press to trudge,
Where errors were not lessened (all may judge).
At thy return my blushing was not small,
My rambling brat (in print) should mother call,
I cast thee by as one unfit for light,
Thy visage was so irksome in my sight;
Yet being mine own, at length affection would
Thy blemishes amend, if so I could:
I washed thy face, but more defects I saw,
And rubbing off a spot still made a flaw.
I stretched thy joints to make thee even feet,
Yet still thou run'st more hobbling than is meet;
In better dress to trim thee was my mind,
But nought save homespun cloth i' th' house I find.
In this array 'mongst vulgars may'st thou roam.
In critic's hands beware thou dost not come,
And take thy way where yet thou art not known
If for thy father asked, say thou hadst none;
And for thy mother, she alas is poor,
Which caused her thus to send thee out of door.

ANNE FINCH

A Letter to Daphnis, April 2, 1685

This to the crown and blessing of my life,
The much loved husband of a happy wife,
To him whose constant passion found the art
To win a stubborn and ungrateful heart;
And to the world by tenderest proof discovers
They err, who say that husbands can't be lovers.
With such return of passion, as is due,
Daphnis I love, Daphnis my thoughts pursue,
Daphnis, my hopes, my joys, are bounded all in you:
Even I, for Daphnis, and my promise sake,
What I in women censure, undertake.
But this from love, not vanity, proceeds;
You know who writes; and I who 'tis that reads.

Judge not my passion by my want of skill,
Many love well, though they express it ill;
And I your censure could with pleasure bear,
Would you but soon return, and speak it here.

JOHN DRYDEN

from *Absalom and Achitophel* (lines 1–30)

In pious times, e're priestcraft did begin,
Before polygamy was made a sin;
When man on many multiplied his kind,
Ere one to one was cursedly confined;
When nature prompted and no law denied
Promiscuous use of concubine and bride;
Then Israel's monarch after Heaven's own heart,
His vigorous warmth did variously impart
To wives and slaves; and, wide as his command,
Scattered his Maker's image through the land.
Michal, of royal blood, the crown did wear,
A soil ungrateful to the tiller's care:
Not so the rest; for several mothers bore
To godlike David several sons before.
But since like slaves his bed they did ascend,
No true succession could their seed attend.
Of all this numerous progeny was none
So beautiful, so brave, as Absalom:
Whether, inspired by some diviner lust,
His father got him with a greater gust,
Or that his conscious destiny made way,
By manly beauty, to imperial sway.
Early in foreign fields he won renown,
With kings and states allied to Israel's crown:
In peace the thoughts of war he could remove,
And seemed as he were onely born for love.
Whate'er he did, was done with so much ease,
In him alone 'twas natural to please;
His motions all accompanied with grace;
And paradise was opened in his face.

SAMUEL JOHNSON

from *The Vanity of Human Wishes*

In Imitation of the Tenth Satire of Juvenal (lines 1–36)

Let Observation, with extensive view,
Survey mankind, from China to Peru;
Remark each anxious toil, each eager strife,
And watch the busy scenes of crowded life;
Then say how hope and fear, desire and hate
O'erspread with snares the clouded maze of fate,
Where wavering man, betrayed by venturous pride
To tread the dreary paths without a guide,
As treacherous phantoms in the mist delude,
Shuns fancied ills, or chases airy good;
How rarely Reason guides the stubborn choice,
Rules the bold hand, or prompts the suppliant voice;
How nations sink, by darling schemes oppressed,
When Vengeance listens to the fool's request.
Fate wings with every wish the afflictive dart,
Each gift of nature, and each grace of art,
With fatal heat impetuous courage glows,
With fatal sweetness elocution flows,
Impeachment stops the speaker's powerful breath,
And restless fire precipitates on death.

But scarce observed, the knowing and the bold
Fall in the general massacre of gold;
Wide-wasting pest! that rages unconfined,
And crowds with crimes the records of mankind;
For gold his sword the hireling ruffian draws,
For gold the hireling judge distorts the laws;
Wealth heaped on wealth, nor truth nor safety buys,
The dangers gather as the treasures rise.

Let History tell where rival kings command,
And dubious title shakes the madded land,
When statutes glean the refuse of the sword,
How much more safe the vassal than the lord,
low skulks the hind beneath the rage of power,
And leaves the wealthy traitor in the Tower,

Untouched his cottage, and his slumbers sound,
Though Confiscation's vultures hover around.

PHILLIS WHEATLEY

To S. M., a Young African Painter, on Seeing His Works

To show the lab'ring bosom's deep intent,
And thought in living characters to paint,
When first thy pencil did those beauties give,
And breathing figures learnt from thee to live,
How did those prospects give my soul delight,
A new creation rushing on my sight?
Still, wond'rous youth! each noble path pursue,
On deathless glories fix thine ardent view:
Still may the painter's and the poet's fire
To aid thy pencil, and thy verse conspire!
And may the charms of each seraphic theme
Conduct thy footsteps to immortal fame!
High to the blissful wonders of the skies
Elate thy soul, and raise thy wishful eyes.
Thrice happy, when exalted to survey
That splendid city, crowned with endless day,
Whose twice six gates on radiant hinges ring:
Celestial Salem blooms in endless spring.

Calm and serene thy moments glide along,
And may the muse inspire each future song!
Still, with the sweets of contemplation blessed,
May peace with balmy wings your soul invest!
But when these shades of time are chased away,
And darkness ends in everlasting day,
On what seraphic pinions shall we move,
And view the landscapes in the realms above?
There shall thy tongue in heav'nly murmurs flow,
And there my muse with heav'nly transport glow:
No more to tell of Damon's tender sighs,
Or rising radiance of Aurora's eyes,
For nobler themes demand a nobler strain,
And purer language on th' ethereal plain.

Cease, gentle muse! the solemn gloom of night
Now seals the fair creation from my sight.

OLIVER GOLDSMITH

from *The Deserted Village* (lines 1–34)

Sweet Auburn! loveliest village of the plain,
Where health and plenty cheered the laboring swain,
Where smiling spring its earliest visit paid,
And parting summer's lingering blooms delayed:
Dear lovely bowers of innocence and ease,
Seats of my youth, when every sport could please,
How often have I loitered o'er thy green,
Where humble happiness endeared each scene;
How often have I paused on every charm,
The sheltered cot, the cultivated farm,
The never-failing brook, the busy mill,
The decent church that topped the neighboring hill,
The hawthorn bush, with seats beneath the shade,
For talking age and whispering lovers made;
How often have I blessed the coming day,
When toil remitting lent its turn to play,
And all the village train, from labor free,
Led up their sports beneath the spreading tree,
While many a pastime circled in the shade,
The young contending as the old surveyed;
And many a gambol frolicked o'er the ground,
And sleights of art and feats of strength went round;
And still as each repeated pleasure tired,
Succeeding sports the mirthful band inspired;
The dancing pair that simply sought renown,
By holding out to tire each other down;
The swain, mistrustless of his smutted face,
While secret laughter tittered round the place;
The bashful virgin's sidelong looks of love,
The matron's glance that would those looks reprove:
These were thy charms, sweet village! sports like these,
With sweet succession, taught even toil to please;

These round thy bowers their cheerful influence shed,
These were thy charms—But all these charms are fled.

ALEXANDER POPE
from *An Essay on Criticism* (lines 201–252)
Part II

Of all the causes which conspire to blind
Man's erring judgment, and misguide the mind,
What the weak head with strongest bias rules,
Is pride, the never-failing vice of fools.
Whatever Nature has in worth denied,
She gives in large recruits of needful pride;
For as in bodies, thus in souls, we find
What wants in blood and spirits swelled with wind:
Pride, where wit fails, steps in to our defense,
And fills up all the mighty void of sense.
If once right reason drives that cloud away,
Truth breaks upon us with resistless day.
Trust not yourself: but your defects to know,
Make use of every friend—and every foe.
A little learning is a dangerous thing;
Drink deep, or taste not the Pierian spring.
There shallow draughts intoxicate the brain,
And drinking largely sobers us again.
Fired at first sight with what the Muse imparts,
In fearless youth we tempt the heights of arts,
While from the bounded level of our mind
Short views we take, nor see the lengths behind;
Bur more advanced, behold with strange surprise
New distant scenes of endless science rise!
So pleased at first the towering Alps we try,
Mount o'er the vales, and seem to tread the sky,
The eternal snows appear already past,
And the first clouds and mountains seem the last;
But, those attained, we tremble to survey
The growing labors of the lengthened way,
The increasing prospect tires our wandering eyes,

Hills peep o'er hills, and Alps on Alps arise!
    A perfect judge will read each work of wit
With the same spirit that its author writ:
Survey the whole, not seek slight faults to find
Where Nature moves, and rapture warms the mind;
Nor lose, for that malignant dull delight,
The generous pleasure to be charmed with wit.
But in such lays as neither ebb nor flow,
Correctly cold, and regularly low,
That, shunning faults, one quiet tenor keep,
We cannot blame indeed—but we may sleep.
In wit, as nature, what affects our hearts
Is not the exactness of peculiar parts;
'Tis not a lip, or eye, we beauty call,
But the joint force and full result of all.
Thus when we view some well-proportioned dome
(The world's just wonder, and even thine, O Rome!),
No single parts unequally surprise,
All comes united to the admiring eyes:
No monstrous height, or breadth, or length appear;
The whole at once is bold and regular.

ROBERT BROWNING

My Last Duchess
Ferrara

That's my last duchess painted on the wall,
Looking as if she were alive. I call
That piece a wonder, now: Frà Pandolf's hands
Worked busily a day, and there she stands.
Will't please you sit and look at her? I said
"Frà Pandolf" by design, for never read
Strangers like you that pictured countenance,
The depth and passion of its earnest glance,
But to myself they turned (since none puts by
The curtain I have drawn for you, but I)
And seemed as they would ask me, if they durst,
How such a glance came there; so, not the first

Are you to turn and ask thus. Sir, 'twas not
Her husband's presence only, called that spot
Of joy into the Duchess' cheek: perhaps
Frà Pandolf chanced to say "Her mantle laps
Over my lady's wrist too much," or "Paint
Must never hope to reproduce the faint
Half-flush that dies along her throat": such stuff
Was courtesy, she thought, and cause enough
For calling up that spot of joy. She had
A heart—how shall I say?—too soon made glad,
Too easily impressed; she liked whate'er
She looked on, and her looks went everywhere.
Sir, 'twas all one! My favor at her breast,
The dropping of the daylight in the West,
The bough of cherries some officious fool
Broke in the orchard for her, the white mule
She rode with round the terrace—all and each
Would draw from her alike the approving speech,
Or blush, at least. She thanked men—good! but thanked
Somehow—I know not how—as if she ranked
My gift of a nine-hundred-years-old name
With anybody's gift. Who'd stoop to blame
This sort of trifling? Even had you skill
In speech—which I have not—to make your will
Quite clear to such an one, and say, "Just this
Or that in you disgusts me; here you miss,
Or there exceed the mark"—and if she let
Herself be lessoned so, nor plainly set
Her wits to yours, forsooth, and made excuse
—E'en then would be some stooping; and I choose
Never to stoop. Oh sir, she smiled, no doubt,
Whene'er I passed her; but who passed without
Much the same smile? This grew; I gave commands;
Then all smiles stopped together. There she stands
As if alive. Will 't please you rise? We'll meet
The company below, then. I repeat,
The Count your master's known munificence
Is ample warrant that no just pretense

Of mine for dowry will be disallowed;
Though his fair daughter's self, as I avowed
At starting, is my object. Nay, we'll go
Together down, sir. Notice Neptune, though,
Taming a sea-horse, thought a rarity,
Which Clause of Innsbruck cast in bronze for me!

WILFRED OWEN

Strange Meeting

It seemed that out of battle I escaped
Down some profound dull tunnel, long since scooped
Through granites which titanic wars had groined.

Yet also there encumbered sleepers groaned,
Too fast in thought or death to be bestirred.
Then, as I probed them, one sprang up, and stared
With piteous recognition in fixed eyes,
Lifting distressful hands, as if to bless.
And by his smile, I knew that sullen hall,—
By his dead smile I knew we stood in Hell.

With a thousand pains that vision's face was grained;
Yet no blood reached there from the upper ground,
And no guns thumped, or down the flues made moan.
"Strange friend," I said, "here is no cause to mourn."
"None," said the other, "save the undone years,
The hopelessness. Whatever hope is yours,
Was my life also; I went hunting wild
After the wildest beauty in the world,
Which lies not calm in eyes, or braided hair,
But mocks the steady running of the hour,
And if it grieves, grieves richlier than here.
For by my glee might many men have laughed.
And of my weeping something had been left,
Which must die now. I mean the truth untold,
The pity of war, the pity war distilled.
Now men will go content with what we spoiled,
Or, discontent, boil bloody, and be spilled.

They will be swift with swiftness of the tigress.
None will break ranks, though nations trek from progress.
Courage was mine, and I had mystery,
Wisdom was mine, and I had mastery:
To miss the march of this retreating world
Into vain citadels that are not walled.
Then, when much blood had clogged their chariot-wheels,
I would go up and wash them from sweet wells,
Even with truths that lie too deep for taint.
I would have poured my spirit without stint
But not through wounds; not on the cess of war.
Foreheads of men have bled where no wounds were.

"I am the enemy you killed, my friend.
I knew you in this dark: for so you frowned
Yesterday through me as you jabbed and killed.
I parried; but my hands were loath and cold.
"Let us sleep now . . ."

THOM GUNN

The J Car

Last year I used to ride the J CHURCH Line,
Climbing between small yards recessed with vine
—Their ordered privacy, their plots of flowers
Like blameless lives we might imagine ours.
Most trees were cut back, but some brushed the car
Before it swung round to the street once more
On which I rolled out almost to the end,
To 29th Street, calling for my friend.
      He'd be there at the door, smiling but gaunt,
To set out for the German restaurant.
There, since his sight was tattered now, I would
First read the menu out. He liked the food
In which a sourness and dark richness meet
For conflict without taste of a defeat,
As in the Sauerbraten. What he ate
I hoped would help him to put on some weight,
But though the crusted pancakes might attract

They did so more as concept than in fact,
And I'd eat his dessert before we both
Rose from the neat arrangement of the cloth,
Where the connection between life and food
Had briefly seemed so obvious if so crude.
Our conversation circumspectly cheerful,
We had sat here like children good but fearful
Who think if they behave everything might
Still against likelihood come out all right.
　　But it would not, and we could not stay here:
Finishing up the Optimator beer
I walked him home through the suburban cool
By dimming shape of church and Catholic school,
Only a few, white, teenagers about.
After the four blocks he would be tired out.
I'd leave him to the feverish sleep ahead,
Myself to ride through darkened yards instead
Back to my health. Of course I simplify.
Of course. It tears me still that he should die
As only an apprentice to his trade,
The ultimate engagements not yet made.
His gifts had been withdrawing one by one
Even before their usefulness was done:
This optic nerve would never be relit;
The other flickered, soon to be with it.
Unready, disappointed, unachieved,
He knew he would not write the much-conceived
Much-hoped-for work now, nor yet help create
A love he might in full reciprocate.

Close-Up of the Heroic Couplet
"MY LAST DUCHESS"
by Robert Browning

CORBIS/BETTMANN

obert Browning was born in London in 1812. In an age
when Romanticism was still the dominant poetic influence,
he soon struck out on his own and began exploring the dis-
tinctive tones of estrangement and rebellion that evolved into the
powerful dramatic monologues of his later work.

"My Last Duchess" is this sort of monologue. It canvasses the odd
tone and misfit emotional address of a nobleman, thinking aloud
about possession, art, power, and marriage—and plainly unable to
distinguish one from the other.

Browning took the eighteenth-century couplet and made it pecu-
liarly his own. In one sense here it remains the heroic couplet—set
aside for another life, a higher life, as the couplet was in that age. The
difference is that Browning has ironized it in a completely new way.
His couplet is darker, faster, and more disturbing than the ones of the
eighteenth century.

The Stanza

The Stanza at a Glance

1) Any unit of recurring meter and rhyme—or variants of them—used in an established pattern of repetition and separation in a single poem.

2) The stanza can be made up of lines of the same length. This is called an isometric stanza.

3) The stanza can also be made up of lines of different lengths. This is called heterometric.

4) There can also be a loose grouping of lines and paragraphs of verse. This is called quasi-stanzaic.

5) The effect of the stanza is gained by the combination of accumulating sense, from stanza to stanza, combined with repeated sound through the repetition of lineation and rhyming.

The History of the Form

There is almost no precise formal history for the stanza. Or to put it differently, it has always been there as an almost invisible and yet dynamic element of poetic form. The earliest poems, ballads and songs usually consisted of groups and patterns of sounds and rhymes. These patterns allowed the poem to build into an architecture of musical effects and the first stanzas often had refrains in them.

The word "stanza" in Italian means room. In a simple practical way, the stanza in poetry has that figurative purpose. It is as self-contained as any chamber or room. And yet to be in it is to have the consciousness at all times that it also leads somewhere.

These were, by and large, isometric stanzas—built on the one meter. They covered the speaking voice with music and created elements of tension and expectation that can be seen in ballad narrative. These elements have their source in some of the origins of poetry: They are communal and melodic. The very opposite of blank verse, which subordinates the speaking voice to verse structure. The stanza, on the other hand comes out of an oral culture.

By the end of the middle ages, poets were beginning to show considerable interest in making elaborate patterns with their stanzas. At this point the stanza shifted from isometric to heterometric structures.

The stanza with several meters opened the way for poets to achieve shifting patterns of sound and subtle arrangements of music and dissonance all within the one unit of relatively few lines. One of the most striking examples is Edmund Spenser, who devised what is called the *Spenserian stanza.* This consists of eight lines followed by a long final line. It became an influential unit, and was used by Keats in the "The Eve of St. Agnes."

The Contemporary Context

It might be wrong as well as irreverent to describe poetic forms as having long necks and being only fit to crop trees, or else having the clever thumbs and arms needed to evolve. Nevertheless there are, inevitably, Darwinian aspects to form. Just as blank verse has not always relished its new surroundings in this century, the stanza has proved itself to be one of the forms most adept at evolution.

At first it was hardly a form at all, merely an element of it. But as time has gone on, the stanza's superb capacity to maintain a tension between narrative and lyric elements, to close off a story and open up a drama, all on the same page—these have made it particularly suitable to both the musicians and the narrators within the poetic discipline.

The evolutionary capacity is shown in several ways. In Renaissance and metaphysical poetry the stanza was an instrument of wit: a place where sharp turns could be taken and epigrams were shown to advantage. In the Romantic movement it became an instrument of drama, for following the narrative of the lovers in the "The Eve of St. Agnes" and later for arranging the emotional colors of loss in "In Memoriam."

And yet in this century the stanza has been one of the building blocks of change. Poets from Eliot to Adrienne Rich have been able to take its open architecture and apply it to radical projects, while keeping its powerful traditional character as a resonance within the poem.

But the stanza is also often the place where poetry reconnects to song: where the sharp music of short lines reminded the reader of the troubadour at the window or the court poet. Some of the most beautiful stanzas in this section are also those where the poet—whether de la Mare or Stevie Smith—renews an old connection with both music and dissonance.

GEOFFREY CHAUCER

from *Troilus and Criseyde* (Book One, lines 1–42)

The double sorwe of Troilus to tellen,
That was the kyng Priamus sone of Troye,
In lovynge, how his aventures fellen
Fro wo to wele, and after out of joie,
My purpos is, er that I parte fro ye.
Thesiphone, thou help me for 'tendite
Thise woful vers, that wepen as I write.

To thee clepe I, thou goddesse of torment,
Thou cruwel Furie, sorwynge evere in peyne;
Help me, that am the sorwful instrument
That helpeth loveres, as I kan, to pleyne.
For wel sit it, the sothe for to seyne,
A woful wight to han a drery feere,
And, to a sorwful tale, a sory chere.

For I, that God of Loves servantz serve,
Ne dar to Love, for myn unliklynesse,
Preyen for speed, al sholde I therefore sterve,
So fer am I from his help in derknesse.
But natheles, if this may don gladnesse
To any lovere, and his cause availle,
Have he my thonk, and myn be this travaille!

But ye loveres, that bathen in gladnesse,
If any drope of pyte in yow be,
Remembreth yow on passed hevynesse

That ye han felt, and on the adversite
Of othere folk, and thynketh how that ye
Han felt that Love dorste yow displese,
Or ye han wonne hym with to gret an ese.

And preieth for hem that ben in the cas
Of Troilus, as ye may after here,
That Love hem brynge in hevene to solas,
And ek for me preieth to God so dere
That I have myght to shewe, in som manere,
Swich peyne and wo as Loves folk endure,
In Troilus unsely aventure.

And biddeth ek for hem that ben despeired
In love that nevere nyl recovered be,
And ek for hem that falsly been apeired
Thorugh wikked tonges, be it he or she;
Thus biddeth God, for his benignite,
So graunte hem sone owt of this world to pace,
That ben despeired out of Loves grace.

EDMUND SPENSER

From *The Faerie Queene*: Mutabilitie Cantas (Book VII, 504–530)

So having ended, silence long ensewed,
  Ne Nature to or fro spake for a space,
  But with firme eyes affixt, the ground still viewed.
  Meane while, all creatures, looking in her face,
  Expecting th' end of this so doubtfull case,
  Did hang in long suspence what would ensew,
  To whether side should fall the soveraigne place:
  At length, she looking up with chearefull view,
The silence brake, and gave her doome in speeches few.

"I well consider all that ye have sayd,
  And find that all things stedfastnes doe hate
  And changéd be: yet being rightly wayd
  They are not changed from their first estate;

But by their change their being doe dilate:
And turning to themselves at length againe,
Doe worke their owne perfection so by fate:
Then over them Change doth not rule and raigne;
But they raigne over change, and doe their states maintaine.

Cease therefore daughter further to aspire,
    And thee content thus to be ruled by me:
    For thy decay thou seekst by thy desire;
    But time shall come that all shall changéd bee,
    And from thenceforth, none no more change shall see."
So was the Titaness put downe and whist,
And Jove confirmed in his imperiall see.
Then was that whole assembly quite dismist,
And Natur's selfe did vanish, whither no man wist.

THOMAS WYATT

They Flee from Me

They flee from me that sometime did me seek
    With naked foot stalking in my chamber.
I have seen them gentle tame and meek
    That now are wild and do not remember
    That sometime they put themselves in danger
To take bread at my hand; and now they range
Busily seeking with a continual change.

Thanked be fortune, it hath been otherwise
    Twenty times better; but once in special,
In thin array after a pleasant guise,
    When her loose gown from her shoulders did fall,
    And she me caught in her arms long and small;
And therewithal sweetly did me kiss,
And softly said, *Dear heart, how like you this?*

It was no dream, I lay broad waking.
    But all is turned thorough my gentleness
Into a strange fashion of forsaking;

And I have leave to go of her goodness
And she also to use newfangleness.
But since that I kindely so am served,
I would fain know what she hath deserved.

GEORGE HERBERT

Easter Wings

Lord, who createdst man in wealth and store,
   Though foolishly he lost the same,
      Decaying more and more
         Till he became
            Most poor:
            With thee
         O let me rise
      As larks, harmoniously,
   And sing this day thy victories:
Then shall the fall further the flight in me.

My tender age in sorrow did begin;
   And still with sicknesses and shame
      Thou didst so punish sin,
         That I became
            Most thin.
            With thee
         Let me combine,
      And feel this day thy victory;
   For, if I imp my wing on thine,
Affliction shall advance the flight in me.

WILLIAM BLAKE

The Tyger

Tyger! Tyger! burning bright
In the forests of the night,
What immortal hand or eye
Could frame thy fearful symmetry?

In what distant deeps or skies
Burnt the fire of thine eyes?

On what wings dare he aspire?
What the hand, dare seize the fire?

And what shoulder, & what art,
Could twist the sinews of thy heart?
And when thy heart began to beat,
What dread hand? & what dread feet?

What the hammer? what the chain?
In what furnace was thy brain?
What the anvil? what dread grasp
Dare its deadly terrors clasp?

When the stars threw down their spears,
And water'd heaven with their tears,
Did he smile his work to see?
Did he who made the Lamb make thee?

Tyger! Tyger! burning bright
In the forests of the night,
What immortal hand or eye
Dare frame thy fearful symmetry?

GEORGE GORDON, LORD BYRON
So We'll Go No More A-Roving

So we'll go no more a-roving
    So late into the night,
Though the heart be still as loving,
    And the moon be still as bright.

For the sword outwears its sheath,
    And the soul wears out the breast,
And the heart must pause to breathe,
    And Love itself have rest.

Though the night was made for loving,
    And the day returns too soon,
Yet we'll go no more a-roving
    By the light of the moon.

EMILY DICKINSON

I died for Beauty—but was scarce

I died for Beauty—but was scarce
Adjusted in the Tomb
When One who died for Truth, was lain
In an adjoining Room—

He questioned softly "Why I failed"?
"For Beauty," I replied—
"And I—for Truth—Themself are One—
We Brethren, are," He said—

And so, as Kinsmen, met a Night—
We talked between the Rooms—
Until the Moss had reached our lips—
And covered up—our names—

THOMAS HARDY

The Convergence of the Twain
(Lines on the loss of the 'Titanic')

I

In a solitude of the sea
Deep from human vanity,
And the Pride of Life that planned her, stilly couches she.

II

Steel chambers, late the pyres
Of her salamandrine fires,
Cold currents third, and turn to rhythmic tidal lyres.

III

Over the mirrors meant
To glass the opulent
The sea-worm crawls—grotesque, slimed, dumb, indifferent.

IV

Jewels in joy designed
To ravish the sensuous mind
Lie lightless, all their sparkles bleared and black and blind.

V

      Dim moon-eyed fishes near
      Gaze at the gilded gear
And query: 'What does this vaingloriousness down here?' . . .

VI

      Well: while was fashioning
      This creature of cleaving wing,
The Immanent Will that stirs and urges everything

VII

      Prepared a sinister mate
      For her—so gaily great—
A Shape of Ice, for the time far and dissociate.

VIII

      And as the smart ship grew
      In stature, grace, and hue,
In shadowy silent distance grew the Iceberg too.

IX

      Alien they seemed to be:
      No mortal eye could see
The intimate welding of their later history,

X

      Or sign that they were bent
      By paths coincident
On being anon twin halves of one august event,

XI

      Till the Spinner of the Years
      Said 'Now!' And each one hears,
And consummation comes, and jars two hemispheres.

WALTER DE LA MARE

The Song of the Mad Prince

Who said, "Peacock Pie"?
    The old King to the sparrow:
Who said, "Crops are ripe"?
    Rust to the harrow:

Who said, "Where sleeps she now?
    Where rests she now her head,
Bathed in eve's loveliness"?—
    That's what I said.

Who said, "Ay, mum's the word"?
    Sexton to willow:
Who said, "Green dusk for dreams,
    Moss for a pillow"?
Who said, "All Time's delight
    Hath she for narrow bed;
Life's troubled bubble broken"?
    That's what I said.

CHARLOTTE MEW

À Quoi Bon Dire

Seventeen years ago you said
Something that sounded like Good-bye;
    And everybody thinks that you are dead,
            But I.

So I, as I grow stiff and cold
To this and that say Good-bye too;
    And everybody sees that I am old
            But you.

And one fine morning in a sunny lane
Some boy and girl will meet and kiss and swear
    That nobody can love their way again
            While over there
You will have smiled, I shall have tossed your hair.

JEAN TOOMER

Song of the Son

Pour O pour that parting soul in song,
    O pour it in the sawdust glow of night,
    Into the velvet pine-smoke air to-night,

And let the valley carry it along.
And let the valley carry it along.

O land and soil, red soil and sweet-gum tree,
So scant of grass, so profligate of pines,
Now just before an epoch's sun declines
Thy son, in time, I have returned to thee,
Thy son, I have in time returned to thee.

In time, for though the sun is setting on
A song-lit race of slaves, it has not set;
Though late, O soil, it is not too late yet
To catch thy plaintive soul, leaving, soon gone,
Leaving, to catch thy plaintive soul soon gone.

O Negro slaves, dark purple ripened plums,
Squeezed, and bursting in the pine-wood air,
Passing, before they stripped the old tree bare
One plum was saved for me, one seed becomes

An everlasting song, a singing tree,
Caroling softly souls of slavery,
What they were, and what they are to me,
Caroling softly souls of slavery.

CLAUDE McKAY

The Tropics in New York

Bananas ripe and green, and ginger root,
    Cocoa in pods and alligator pears,
And tangerines and mangoes and grape fruit,
    Fit for the highest prize at parish fairs,

Set in the window, bringing memories
    Of fruit-trees laden by low-singing rills,
And dewy dawns, and mystical skies
    In benediction over nun-like hills.

My eyes grow dim, and I could no more gaze;
    A wave of longing through my body swept,
And, hungry for the old, familiar ways,
    I turned aside and bowed my head and wept.

SARA TEASDALE

Night Song at Amalfi

I asked the heaven of stars
    What I should I give my love—
It answered me with silence,
    Silence above.

I asked the darkened sea
    Down where the fishes go—
It answered me with silence,
    Silence below.

Oh, I could give him weeping,
    Or I could give him song—
But how can I give silence
    My whole life long?

STEVIE SMITH

Not Waving but Drowning

Nobody heard him, the dead man,
But still he lay moaning:
I was much further out than you thought
And not waving but drowning.

Poor chap, he always loved larking
And now he's dead
It must have been too cold for him his heart gave way,
They said.

Oh, no no no, it was too cold always
(Still the dead one lay moaning)
I was much too far out all my life
And not waving but drowning.

YVOR WINTERS

On Teaching the Young

The young are quick of speech.
Grown middle-aged, I teach

Corrosion and distrust,
Exacting what I must.

A poem is what stands
When imperceptive hands,
Feeling, have gone astray.
It is what one should say.

Few minds will come to this.
The poet's only bliss
Is in cold certitude—
Laurel, archaic, rude.

ROBERT HAYDEN

Those Winter Sundays

Sundays too my father got up early
and put his clothes on in the blueblack cold,
then with cracked hands that ached
from labor in the weekday weather made
banked fires blaze. No one ever thanked him.

I'd wake and hear the cold splintering, breaking.
When the rooms were warm, he'd call,
and slowly I would rise and dress,
fearing the chronic angers of that house,

Speaking indifferently to him,
who had driven out the cold
and polished my good shoes as well.
What did I know, what did I know
of love's austere and lonely offices?

MURIEL RUKEYSER

Yes

It's like a tap-dance
Or a new pink dress,
A shit-naive feeling
Saying Yes.

Some say Good morning
Some say God bless—
Some say Possibly
Some say Yes.

Some say Never
Some say Unless
It's stupid and lovely
To rush into Yes.

What can it mean?
It's just like life,
One thing to you
One to your wife.

Some go local
Some go express
Some can't wait
To answer Yes.

Some complain
Of strain and stress
The answer may be
No for Yes.

Some like failure
Some like success
Some like Yes Yes
Yes Yes Yes.

Open your eyes,
Dream but don't guess.
Your biggest surprise
Comes after Yes.

CAROL ANN DUFFY

Warming Her Pearls

Next to my own skin, her pearls. My mistress
bids me wear them, warm them, until evening
when I'll brush her hair. At six, I place them
round her cool, white throat. All day I think of her,

resting in the Yellow Room, contemplating silk
or taffeta, which gown tonight? She fans herself
whilst I work willingly, my slow heat entering
each pearl. Slack on my neck, her rope.

She's beautiful. I dream about her
in my attic bed; picture her dancing
with tall men, puzzled by my faint, persistent scent
beneath her French perfume, her milky stones.

I dust her shoulders with a rabbit's foot,
watch the soft blush seep through her skin
like an indolent sigh. In her looking-glass
my red lips part as though I want to speak.

Full moon. Her carriage brings her home. I see
her every movement in my head. . . . Undressing,
taking off her jewels, her slim hand reaching
for the case, slipping naked into bed, the way

she always does. . . . And I lie here awake,
knowing the pearls are cooling even now
in the room where my mistress sleeps. All night
I feel their absence and I burn.

CAROL MUSKE

Epith

Here's the little dressmaker
on her knees at your feet,
mouth full of pins:
fixing you in the dummy's image.

Your belled satin shivers like
a goblet of fizzled brut—
You wanted it late in life,
happiness, wanted a little family

but after the kids grew up.
Like a saint on her death pallet,
you longed for an erotic God
but a refined deity—

not some oversexed Zeus
in a see-through raincoat,
spritzing gold coins,
rattling the canopy. No,

at last you've found a groom
born to forget the ring,
the bride's name—
a regular holy ghost.

You forget yourself
with each glittering pin,
each chip off the old rock,
each sip of the long toast

to your famous independence,
negotiated at such cost—
and still refusing to fit.

Close-Up of a Stanza
"I DIED FOR BEAUTY—
BUT WAS SCARCE"

by Emily Dickinson

Emily Dickinson was born in Amherst, Massachusetts, in 1830. She lived with her family and became something of a recluse in her last years. Despite an intense and powerful history of composition, her *Collected Poems* were not published until 1924, nearly forty years after her death.

Dickinson was a superb technician: original, volatile, and explosive in her arrangements of language and image. But perhaps her most distinguishing strength is the perfect timing of the quatrains she used. These four-line charges carried the force of her vision. They were perfectly and intuitively spaced, achieving maximum drama between stanza and stanza.

"I died for Beauty—but was scarce" is a case in point. The big, colorful argument she is making—a poignant update on Keats's claim for the relation between the two—is achieved in terms of three taut stanzas. The erotic drama unfolds as a suppressed narrative: Who are these two people, this man and woman who have lost their opportunities and become siblings and not lovers in death? This is a case in which the hidden story is superbly counterpointed by these powerful, heraldic stanzas. The questions are also maintained by the quick fire music and dramatic closure of each stanza.

II

Meter

Meter at a Glance

I: Types of Meter

1) Meter is the Greek word for "measure."

2) There are three meters most commonly used by poets in the English language.

3) These are accentual meter, syllabic meter, and accentual-syllabic meter.

4) In accentual meter the stresses are counted and the syllables are variable.

5) In syllabic meter the syllables are counted but the stresses are varied.

6) In accentual-syllabic meter both accents and syllables are measured and counted.

7) In English, one tradition established its dominance: the accentual-syllabic meter.

II: The Character of Different Types of Meter

1) Accentual meter is often called "stress meter" or "strong stress meter." Its origins lie far back in English poetry.

2) Accentual meter is common in the ballad and the nursery rhyme. It is heavily stressed and clearly heard when the poem is read.

3) Syllabic meters, on the other hand, are not easily heard. Because they count syllables, their force is most easily seen on the page: Syllabics are essentially a visual contract with the reader.

4) In accentual-syllabic meters—the combination of these—both syllables and accents are measured and counted and are often referred to as "feet."

5) These "feet" are patterns of stressed and unstressed syllables. The variations, pauses, musical effects, and dissonances within the accentual-syllabic line are where much of the force and power of meter occurs.

III: DEFINITIONS OF THE MOST COMMON "FEET" IN ACCENTUAL-SYLLABIC METER.

1) A poetic foot is a measured unit of meter, made up of stressed and unstressed syllables.

2) The iamb is the most common foot. It is a short stress followed by a long one. An example is *about.*

3) A trochee is a less commonly used foot, but it is clear and striking at the start of a line. It is a long stress followed by a short one. An example is *That is.* Or *dropsy.*

4) A dactyl is a long stress followed by two short ones. An example is *happily.*

5) An anapest is two short stresses followed by a long one. An example is *in a tree.*

6) A spondee is two long stresses. An example is *humdrum.*

A Brief Checklist of
Further Reading on Meter

Poetic Rhythm: An Introduction Derek Attridge, Cambridge
University Press (1996)

The Poem's Heartbeat: A Manual of Prosody Alfred Corn, Story Line
Press (1997)

Poetic Meter and Poetic Form Paul Fussell, McGraw Hill (1979)

Rhymes Reason: A Guide to English Verse John Hollander, Yale
University (1989)

A Poet's Guide to Poetry Mary Kinzie, University of Chicago Press
(1999)

The Sounds of Poetry: A Brief Guide Robert Pinsky, FSG (1999)

*All the Fun's in How You Say a Thing: An Explanation of Meter and
Versification* Timothy Steele, Ohio University Press (1999)

The New Book of Forms: A Handbook of Poetics Lewis Turco, New
England University Press (1986)

III

Shaping Forms

Overview

Poetic form has come to have a strong association—in class-
room and colloquium reference—with poetic meter and
rhyme. Although meter is a powerful constituent, form in
poetry is deeper, richer, and more complex than that. Its history
reaches back into an architecture of sense as well as sounds. This sec-
tion is intended as a fresh glance at this other dimension of form. This
is not a place where we provide the history or contemporary context
of a form. The shape and influence of these forms is too wide, too elu-
sive to be exactly regulated in this way. But rather a space where we
offer a wider view of the origins of form, rather than their outcome.

If metrical forms are the architecture of poetry, then the shaping
forms of ode, elegy, and pastoral are its environment. We have se-
lected these especially to address and illustrate because the need to re-
member the dead, to address the living and idealize a place of peace
and renewal—in all these it is possible to glimpse what poetry
achieved thousands of years ago and what that achievement contin-
ues to mean today.

More importantly, it is these forms—more than the closed metri-
cal ones—that allow us to reenter the public role of poetry in history
and society. The ode, elegy, and pastoral originate in the public role
of the poet—whether a funerary address or a poem for a court: They
bring us back to the charged corridor between a poem and its com-

munity. They remind us of times when a poem was at the heart of a society's self-definition.

These powerful modes of celebration and consolation, therefore, return the poem to some of its lost purposes. Although the guidelines for these shaping forms are not nearly as exact as those for a villanelle or a pantoum, the spirit of these forms remains profoundly influential on poetry up to the present moment.

This section is a time line. It follows these forms from their most public and rigorous expression in earlier centuries, to the shadow play they have become in the more private work of poets in our time. The twentieth-century versions are deliberately only approximate here. Sometimes the contemporary elegy—see Dylan Thomas's villanelle for instance—is no more than a passing reference, even a subversion, of the old decorums of these forms. Yet without that reference, outside that shadow, the poem would not have had such a forceful point of departure. And however free, informal, or contemporary these poems are, it is still possible to see in them the old watermarks of celebration and consolation toward which these forms have guided poets for thousands of years.

The Elegy

Overview

An elegy is a lament. It sets out the circumstances and character of a loss. It mourns for a dead person, lists his or her virtues, and seeks consolation beyond the momentary event. Despite this, an elegy, unlike a metrical form, is not associated with any required pattern or cadence or repetition.

For this reason, the structure of an elegy is less visible than a regulated form such as a sonnet or a villanelle. But the structure is there nonetheless—made of the slowly evolving customs and decorums, the coral reef of what each society expects a public poem of lament to contain and an elegiac poet to focus on.

Therefore—despite lacking a characteristic metrical structure—the elegy is a crucial formal link with the history and tradition of public poetry, serving notice that there was once a past where the corridor between the public utterance of poetry and cultural assumptions was both charged and narrow.

Because of its public role, the elegy is also one of the forms that can be said to have been coauthored by its community—so powerfully shared are the household gods it salutes. Interestingly, as the role of the public poet has altered, the elegy has altered also, and turned inward. Several of the formidable elegies of the last two centuries—Auden's for Yeats is included here—are for poets by poets.

In the traditional elegy, the grief the poet expresses is rarely a private one. More often it is a cultural grief: the lamented and lost subject of an elegy is shown to be possessed of social virtues, as in Milton's "Lycidas," or manifest pieties as in Tennyson's "In Memoriam." In all societies, death constitutes a cultural event—with all the superstitions and household gods of such an event—as well as an individual loss. That the elegy speaks to this: that it locates the cultural customs of death in whichever society it occurs, adds greatly to its power. The best elegies will always be sites of struggle between custom and decorum on the one hand, and private feeling on the other.

WILLIAM DUNBAR

Lament for the Makaris

I that in heill was and gladness,
Am troublit now with great seikness,
And feeblit with infirmity:
　　Timor Mortis conturbat me.

Our plesance here is all vain-glory
This false warld is bot transitory,
The fleshe is brukill, the Fiend is sle;
　　Timor Mortis conturbat me.

The state of man dois change and vary,
Now sound, now seik, now blyth, now sary,
Now dansand merry, now like to die;
　　Timor Mortis conturbat me.

No state in erd here standis siccar;
As with the wind wavis the wicker,
Wavis this warldis vanitie;
　　Timor Mortis conturbat me.

Unto the deid gois all Estatis,
Princes, Prelatis, and Potestatis,
Baith riche and puir of all degree;
　　Timor Mortis conturbat me.

He takis the knichtis into the field,
Enarmit under helm and shield;

Victor he is at all mêlée;
   Timor Mortis conturbat me.

That strang unmerciful tyrand
Takis on the moderis breist soukand
The babe, full of benignite;
   Timor Mortis conturbat me.

He takis the champion in the stour,
The capitane closit in the tour,
The lady in bour full of beautie;
   Timor Mortis conturbat me.

He sparis no lord for his puissance,
Na clerk for his intelligence;
His awful straik may no man flee;
   Timor Mortis conturbat me.

Art magicianis, and astrologis,
Rethoris, logicianis, and theologis,
Them helpis no conclusionis sle;
   Timor Mortis conturbat me.

In medicine the most practicianis,
Leechis, surigianis, and phisicianis,
Them-self fra deid may not supple;
   Timor Mortis conturbat me.

I see that makaris amang the lave
Playis here their pageant, syne gois to grave;
Sparit is nocht their facultie;
   Timor Mortis conturbat me.

He has done piteously devour
The noble Chaucer, of makaris flour,
The Monk of Bery, and Gower, all three;
   Timor Mortis conturbat me.

The gude Sir Hew of Eglintoun,
And eik Heriot, and Wintoun,
He has ta'en out of this countrie;
   Timor Mortis conturbat me.

That scorpion fell has done infec'
Maister John Clerk and James Affleck,
Fra ballad-making and tragedie;
    Timor Mortis conturbat me.

Holland and Barbour he has beravit;
Alas! that he nought with us leavit
Sir Mungo Lockhart of the Lea;
    Timor Mortis conturbat me.

Clerk of Tranent eke he has ta'en,
That made the Aunteris of Gawain;
Sir Gilbert Hay endit has he;
    Timor Mortis conturbat me.

He has Blind Harry, and Sandy Traill
Slain with his shour of mortal hail,
Whilk Patrick Johnstoun micht nocht flee;
    Timor Mortis conturbat me.

He has reft Merser endite,
That did in luve so lively write,
So short, so quick, of sentence hie;
    Timor Mortis conturbat me.

He has ta'en Roull of Aberdeen,
And gentle Roull of Corstorphin;
Two better fellowis did no man see;
    Timor Mortis conturbat me.

In Dunfermline he has done roune
With Maister Robert Henryson;
Sir John the Ross embraced has he;
    Timor Mortis conturbat me.

And he has now ta'en, last of a',
Gude gentle Stobo and Quintin Shaw,
Of wham all wichtis has pitie:
    Timor Mortis conturbat me.

Gude Maister Walter Kennedy
In point of deid lies verily,

Great ruth it were that so suld be;
    Timor Mortis conturbat me.

Sen he has all my brether ta'en,
He will nocht lat me live alane,
On force I maun his next prey be;
    Timor Mortis conturbat me.

Sen for the deid remead is none,
Best is that we for deid dispone,
Eftir our deid that live may we;
    Timor Mortis conturbat me.

MARY SIDNEY HERBERT, COUNTESS OF PEMBROKE

If Ever Hapless Woman Had a Cause

If ever hapless woman had a cause
    To breathe her plaints into the open air,
And never suffer inward grief to pause.
    Or seek her sorrow-shaken soul's repair;
Then I, for I have lost my only brother,
Whose like this age can scarcely yield another.

Come therefore, mournful Muses, and lament;
    Forsake all wanton pleasing motions;
Bedew your cheeks. Still shall my tears be spent,
    Yet still increased with inundations.
For I must weep, since I have lost my brother,
Whose like this age can scarcely yield another.

The cruel hand of murder cloyed with blood
    Lewdly deprived him of his mortal life.
Woe the death-attended blades that stood
    In opposition 'gainst him in the strife
Wherein he fell, and where I lost a brother,
Whose like this age can scarcely yield another.

Then unto Grief let me a temple make,
    And, mourning, daily enter Sorrow's ports,
Knock on my breast, sweet brother, for thy sake,

Nature and love will both be my consorts,
And help meaye to wail my only brother,
Whose like this age can scarcely yield another.

BEN JONSON

On My First Son

Farewell, thou child of my right hand, and joy;
My sin was too much hope of thee, loved boy:
Seven years thou' wert lent to me, and I thee pay,
Exacted by thy fate, on the just day.
O could I lose all father now! for why
Will man lament the state he should envỳ,
To have so soon 'scaped world's and flesh's rage,
And, if no other misery, yet age?
Rest in soft peace, and asked, say, "Here doth lie
Ben Jonson his best piece of poetry."
For whose sake henceforth all his vows be such
As what he loves may never like too much.

KATHERINE PHILIPS

Epitaph. On her Son H.P. at St. Syth's Church where her body also lies Interred

What on Earth deserves our Trust?
Youth and Beauty both are dust.
Long we gathering are with pain,
What one Moment calls again.
Seaven years Childless Marriage past,
A Son, A Son is born at last;
So exactly limmed and Fair,
Full of good Spirits, Meen, and Aier,
As a long life promised;
Yet, in less than six weeks, dead.
Too promising, too great a Mind
In so small room to be confin'd:
Therefore, fit in Heav'n to dwell,
He quickly broke the Prison shell.

So the Subtle Alchymist,
Can't with Hermes seal resist
The Powerfull Spirit's subtler flight,
But 'twill bid him long good night.
So the Sun, if it arise
Half so Glorious as his Eye's,
Like this Infant, takes a shroud,
Bury'd in a morning Cloud.

JOHN MILTON

Lycidas

**In this Monody the author bewails a learned friend,
unfortunately drowned in his passage from Chester
on the Irish Seas, 1637. And by occasion foretells
the ruin of our corrupted clergy,
then in their height.**

Yet once more, O ye laurels, and once more
Ye myrtles brown, with ivy never sere,
I come to pluck your berries harsh and crude,
And with forced fingers rude
Shatter your leaves before the mellowing year.
Bitter constraint, and sad occasion dear,
Compels me to disturb your season due;
For Lycidas is dead, dead ere his prime,
Young Lycidas, and hath not left his peer.
Who would not sing for Lycidas? He knew
Himself to sing, and build the lofty rhyme.
He must not float upon his watery bier
Unwept, and welter to the parching wind,
Without the meed of some melodious tear.
    Begin then, sisters of the sacred well
That from beneath the seat of Jove doth spring,
Begin, and somewhat loudly sweep the string.
Hence with denial vain, and coy excuse;
So may some gentle Muse
With lucky words favor my destined urn,
And as he passes turn,

And bid fair peace be to my sable shroud.
For we were nursed upon the selfsame hill,
Fed the same flock, by fountain, shade, and rill.

   Together both, ere the high lawns appeared
Under the opening eyelids of the morn,
We drove afield, and both together heard
What time the grayfly winds her sultry horn,
Battening our flocks with the fresh dews of night,
Oft till the star that rose at evening bright
Toward heaven's descent had sloped his westering wheel.
Meanwhile the rural ditties were not mute,
Tempered to th' oaten flute,
Rough satyrs danced, and fauns with cloven heel
From the glad sound would not be absent long,
And old Damoetas loved to hear our song.

   But O the heavy change, now thou art gone,
Now thou art gone, and never must return!
Thee, shepherd, thee the woods and desert caves,
With wild thyme and the gadding vine o'ergrown,
And all their echoes mourn.
The willows and the hazel copses green
Shall now no more be seen,
Fanning their joyous leaves to thy soft lays.
As killing as the canker to the rose,
Or taint-worm to the weanling herds that graze,
Or frost to flowers that their gay wardrobe wear
When first the white-thorn blows;
Such, Lycidas, thy loss to shepherd's ear.

   Where were ye, nymphs, when the remorseless deep
Clos'd o'er the head of your loved Lycidas?
For neither were ye playing on the steep
Where your old bards, the famous Druids, lie,
Nor on the shaggy top of Mona high,
Nor yet where Deva spreads her wizard stream:
Ay me! I fondly dream—
Had ye bin there—for what could that have done?
What could the Muse herself that Orpheus bore,
The Muse herself, for her inchanting son

Whom universal Nature did lament,
When by the rout that made the hideous roar
His gory visage down the stream was sent,
Down the swift Hebrus to the Lesbian shore?
   Alas! What boots it with incessant care
To tend the homely, slighted shepherd's trade,
And strictly meditate the thankless Muse?
Were it not better done as others use,
To sport with Amaryllis in the shade,
Or with the tangles of Neaera's hair?
Fame is the spur that the clear spirit doth raise
(That last infirmity of noble mind)
To scorn delights and live laborious days;
But the fair guerdon when we hope to find,
And think to burst out into sudden blaze,
Comes the blind Fury with th' abhorred shears,
And slits the thin-spun life. "But not the praise,"
Phoebus replied, and touched my trembling ears;
"Fame is no plant that grows on mortal soil,
Nor in the glistering foil
Set off to th' world, nor in broad rumor lies,
But lives and spreads aloft by those pure eyes,
And perfect witness of all-judging Jove;
As he pronounces lastly on each deed,
Of so much fame in heaven expect thy meed."
   O fountain Arethuse, and thou honored flood,
Smooth-sliding Minicius, crowned with vocal reeds,
That strain I heard was of a higher mood.
But now my oat proceeds,
And listens to the herald of the sea
That came in Neptune's plea.
He asked the waves, and asked the felon winds,
"What hard mishap hath doomed this gentle swain?"
And questioned every gust of rugged wings
That blows from off each beaked promontory;
They knew not of his story,
And sage Hippotades their answer brings,
That not a blast was from his dungeon strayed;

The air was calm, and on the level brine,
Sleek Panope with all her sisters played.
It was that fatal and perfidious bark,
Built in th' eclipse, and rigged with curses dark,
That sunk so low that sacred head of thine.
    Next Camus, reverend sire, went footing slow,
His mantle hairy, and his bonnet sedge,
Inwrought with figures dim, and on the edge
Like to that sanguine flower inscribed with woe.
"Ah! who hath reft," quoth he, "my dearest pledge?"
Last came and last did go,
The pilot of the Galilean lake;
Two massy keys he bore of metals twain
(The golden opes, the iron shuts amain).
He shook his mitered locks, and stern bespake:
"How well could I have spared for thee, young swain,
Enow of such as for their bellies' sake
Creep and intrude and climb into the fold?
Of other care they little reckoning make,
Than how to scramble at the shearers' feast,
And shove away the worthy bidden guest.
Blind mouths! that scarce themselves know how to hold
A sheep-hook, or have learned aught else the least
That to the faithful herdsman's art belongs!
What recks it them? What need they? They are sped;
And when they list, their lean and flashy songs
Grate on their scrannel pipes of wretched straw.
The hungry sheep look up, and are not fed,
But, swoln with wind, and the rank mist they draw,
Rot inwardly, and foul contagion spread,
Besides what the grim wolf with privy paw
Daily devours apace, and nothing said.
But that two-handed engine at the door
Stands ready to smite once, and smite no more."
    Return, Alpheus, the dread voice is past,
That shrunk thy streams; return, Sicilian muse,
And call the vales and bid them hither cast
Their bells and flowerets of a thousand hues.

Ye valleys low, where the mild whispers use,
Of shades and wanton winds, and gushing brooks,
On whose fresh lap the swart star sparely looks,
Throw hither all your quaint enameled eyes,
That on the green turf suck the honeyed showers,
And purple all the ground with vernal flowers.
Bring the rathe primrose that forsaken dies,
The tufted crow-toe, and pale jessamine,
The white pink, and the pansy freaked with jet,
The glowing violet,
The musk-rose, and the well attired woodbine,
With cowslips wan that hang the pensive head,
And every flower that sad embroidery wears:
Bid amaranthus all his beauty shed,
And daffadillies fill their cups with tears,
To strew the laureate hearse where Lycid lies.
For so to interpose a little ease,
Let our frail thoughts dally with false surmise.
Ay me! whilst thee the shores and sounding seas
Wash far away, where'er thy bones are hurled,
Whether beyond the stormy Hebrides,
Where thou perhaps under the whelming tide
Visit'st the bottom of the monstrous world;
Or whether thou, to our moist vows denied,
Sleep'st by the fable of Bellerus old,
Where the great vision of the guarded mount
Looks toward Namancos and Bayona's hold;
Look homeward angel now, and melt with ruth:
And, O ye dolphins, waft the hapless youth.
   Weep no more, woeful shepherds, weep no more,
For Lycidas your sorrow is not dead,
Sunk though he be beneath the wat'ry floor;
So sinks the day-star in the ocean bed,
And yet anon repairs his drooping head,
And tricks his beams, and with new-spangled ore
Flames in the forehead of the morning sky:
So Lycidas sunk low, but mounted high,
Through the dear might of him that walked the waves,

Where, other groves and other streams along,
With nectar pure his oozy locks he laves,
And hears the unexpressive nuptial song,
In the blest kingdoms meek of joy and love.
There entertain him all the saints above,
In solemn troops and sweet societies
That sing, and singing in their glory move,
And wipe the tears for ever from his eyes.
Now, Lycidas, the shepherds weep no more;
Henceforth thou art the genius of the shore,
In thy large recompense, and shalt be good
To all that wander in that perilous flood.

    Thus sang the uncouth swain to th' oaks and rills,
While the still morn went out with sandals gray;
He touched the tender stops of various quills,
With eager thought warbling his Doric lay:
And now the sun had stretched out all the hills,
And now was dropped into the western bay;
At last he rose, and twitched his mantle blue:
Tomorrow to fresh woods, and pastures new.

ANNE BRADSTREET

Here Follows Some Verses upon the Burning of Our House July 10th, 1666. Copied out of a Loose Paper

In silent night when rest I took
For sorrow near I did not look
I wakened was with thund'ring noise
And piteous shrieks of dreadful voice.
That fearful sound of "Fire!" and "Fire!"
Let no man know is my desire.
I, starting up, the light did spy,
And to my God my heart did cry
To strengthen me in my distress
And not to leave me succorless.
Then, coming out, beheld a space
The flame consume my dwelling place.
And when I could no longer look,

I blest His name that gave and took,
That laid my goods now in the dust.
Yea, so it was, and so 'twas just.
It was His own, it was not mine,
Far be it that I should repine;
He might of all justly bereft
But yet sufficient for us left.
When by the ruins oft I passed
My sorrowing eyes aside did cast,
And here and there the places spy
Where oft I sat and long did lie,
Here stood that trunk, and there that chest,
There lay that store I counted best.
My pleasant things in ashes lie,
And them behold no more shall I.
Under thy roof no guest shall sit,
Nor at thy table eat a bit.
No pleasant tale shall e'er be told,
Nor things recounted done of old.
No candle e'er shall shine in thee,
Nor bridegroom's voice e're heard shall be.
In silence ever shall thou lie,
Adieu, Adieu, all's vanity.
Then straight I' gin my heart to chide,
And did thy wealth on earth abide?
Didst fix thy hope on mold'ring dust?
The arm of flesh didst make thy trust?
Raise up thy thoughts above the sky
That dunghill mists away may fly.
Thou hast an house on high erect,
Framed by that mighty Architect,
With glory richly furnishéd,
Stands permanent though this be fled.
It's purchaséd and paid for too
By Him who hath enough to do.
A price so vast as is unknown
Yet by His gift is made thine own;
There's wealth enough, I need no more,

Farewell, my pelf, farewell my store.
The world no longer let me love,
My hope and treasure lies above.

THOMAS GRAY

Elegy Written in a Country Churchyard

The curfew tolls the knell of parting day,
   The lowing herd wind slowly o'er the lea,
The plowman homeward plods his weary way,
   And leaves the world to darkness and to me.

Now fades the glimmering landscape on the sight,
   And all the air a solemn stillness holds,
Save where the beetle wheels his droning flight,
   And drowsy tinklings lull the distant folds;

Save that from yonder ivy-mantled tower
   The moping owl does to the moon complain
Of such, as wandering near her secret bower,
   Molest her ancient solitary reign.

Beneath those rugged elms, that yew-tree's shade,
   Where heaves the turf in many a moldering heap,
Each in his narrow cell for ever laid,
   The rude forefathers of the hamlet sleep.

The breezy call of incense-breathing morn,
   The swallow twittering from the straw-built shed,
The cock's shrill clarion, or the echoing horn,
   No more shall rouse them from their lowly bed.

For them no more the blazing hearth shall burn,
   Or busy housewife ply her evening care;
No children run to lisp their sire's return,
   Or climb his knees the envied kiss to share.

Oft did the harvest to their sickle yield,
   Their furrow oft the stubborn glebe has broke;
How jocund did they drive their team afield!
   How bowed the woods beneath their sturdy stroke!

Let not Ambition mock their useful toil,
    Their homely joys, and destiny obscure;
Nor Grandeur hear with a disdainful smile
    The short and simple annals of the poor.

The boast of heraldry, the pomp of power,
    And all that beauty, all that wealth e'er gave,
Awaits alike the inevitable hour.
    The paths of glory lead but to the grave.

Nor you, ye proud, impute to these the fault,
    If Memory o'er their tomb no trophies raise,
Where through the long-drawn aisle and fretted vault
    The pealing anthem swells the note of praise.

Can storied urn or animated bust
    Back to its mansion call the fleeting breath?
Can Honor's voice provoke the silent dust,
    Or Flattery soothe the dull cold ear of Death?

Perhaps in this neglected spot is laid
    Some heart once pregnant with celestial fire;
Hands, that the rod of empire might have swayed,
    Or waked to ecstasy the living lyre.

But Knowledge to their eyes her ample page
    Rich with the spoils of time did ne'er unroll;
Chill Penury repressed their noble rage,
    And froze the genial current of the soul.

Full many a gem of purest ray serene,
    The dark unfathomed caves of ocean bear:
Full many a flower is born to blush unseen,
    And waste its sweetness on the desert air.

Some village Hampden, that with dauntless breast
    The little tyrant of his fields withstood;
Some mute inglorious Milton here may rest,
    Some Cromwell guiltless of his country's blood.

The applause of listening senates to command,
    The threats of pain and ruin to despise,

To scatter plenty o'er a smiling land,
  And read their history in a nation's eyes,

Their lot forbade: nor circumscribed alone
  Their glowing virtues, but their crimes confined;
Forbade to wade through slaughter to a throne,
  And shut the gates of mercy on mankind,

The struggling pangs of conscious truth to hide,
  To quench the blushes of ingenuous shame,
Or heap the shrine of Luxury and Pride
  With incense kindled at the Muse's flame.

Far from the madding crowd's ignoble strife,
  Their sober wishes never learned to stray;
Along the cool sequestered vale of life
  They kept the noiseless tenor of their way.

Yet even these bones from insult to protect
  Some frail memorial still erected nigh,
With uncouth rhymes and shapeless sculpture decked,
  Implores the passing tribute of a sigh.

Their name, their years, spelt by the unlettered Muse,
  The place of fame and elegy supply:
And many a holy text around she strews,
  That teach the rustic moralist to die.

For who to dumb Forgetfulness a prey,
  This pleasing anxious being e'er resign'd,
Left the warm precincts of the cheerful day,
  Nor cast one longing lingering look behind?

On some fond breast the parting soul relies,
  Some pious drops the closing eye requires;
Even from the tomb the voice of Nature cries,
  Even in our ashes live their wonted fires.

For thee, who mindful of the unhonored dead
  Dost in these lines their artless tale relate;
If chance, by lonely contemplation led,
  Some kindred spirit shall inquire thy fate,

Haply some hoary-headed swain may say,
   "Oft have we seen him at the peep of dawn
Brushing with hasty steps the dews away
   To meet the sun upon the upland lawn.

"There at the foot of yonder nodding beech
   That wreathes its old fantastic roots so high,
His listless length at noontide would he stretch,
   And pore upon the brook that babbles by.

"Hard by yon wood, now smiling as in scorn,
   Muttering his wayward fancies he would rove,
Now drooping, woeful wan, like one forlorn,
   Or crazed with care, or crossed in hopeless love.

"One morn I missed him on the customed hill,
   Along the heath and near his favorite tree;
Another came; nor yet beside the rill,
   Nor up the lawn, nor at the wood was he;

"The next with dirges due in sad array
   Slow through the churchway path we saw him borne.
Approach and read (for thou canst read) the lay,
   Graved on the stone beneath yon aged thorn."

THE EPITAPH

Here rests his head upon the lap of Earth
   A youth to Fortune and to Fame unknown.
Fair Science frowned not on his humble birth,
   And Melancholy marked him for her own.

Large was his bounty, and his soul sincere,
   Heaven did a recompense as largely send:
He gave to Misery all he had, a tear,
   He gained from Heaven ('twas all he wished) a friend.

No farther seek his merits to disclose,
   Or draw his frailties from their dread abode
(There they alike in trembling hope repose),
   The bosom of his Father and his God.

EMILY BRONTË
R. Alcona to J. Brenzaida

Cold in the earth, and the deep snow piled above thee!
Far, far removed, cold in the dreary grave!
Have I forgot, my Only Love, to love thee,
Severed at last by Time's all-wearing wave?

Now, when alone, do my thoughts no longer hover
Over the mountains on Angora's shore;
Resting their wings where heath and fern-leaves cover
Thy noble heart for ever, ever more?

Cold in the earth, and fifteen wild Decembers
From those brown hills have melted into spring—
Faithful indeed is the spirit that remembers
After such years of change and suffering!

Sweet Love of youth, forgive if I forget thee
While the World's tide is bearing me along:
Sterner desires and darker hopes beset me,
Hopes which obscure but cannot do thee wrong.

No other Sun has lightened up my heaven;
No other Star has ever shone for me:
All my life's bliss from thy dear life was given—
All my life's bliss is in the grave with thee.

But when the days of golden dreams had perished
And even Despair was powerless to destroy,
Then did I learn how existence could be cherished,
Strengthened and fed without the aid of joy;

Then did I check the tears of useless passion,
Weaned my young soul from yearning after thine;
Sternly denied its burning wish to hasten
Down to that tomb already more than mine!

And even yet, I dare not let it languish,
Dare not indulge in Memory's rapturous pain;
Once drinking deep of that divinest anguish,
How could I seek the empty world again?

WALT WHITMAN

O Captain! My Captain!

O Captain! my Captain! our fearful trip is done,
The ship has weather'd every rack, the prize we sought is won,
The port is near, the bells I hear, the people all exulting,
While follow eyes the steady keel, the vessel grim and daring;
  But O heart! heart! heart!
   O the bleeding drops of red!
    Where on the deck my Captain lies,
     Fallen cold and dead.

O Captain! my Captain! rise up and hear the bells;
Rise up—for you the flag is flung—for you the bugle trills,
For you bouquets and ribbon'd wreaths—for you the shores a-
  crowding,
For you they call, the swaying mass, their eager faces turning;
  Here Captain! dear father!
   This arm beneath your head!
    It is some dream that on the deck,
     You've fallen cold and dead.

My Captain does not answer, his lips are pale and still,
My father does not feel my arm, he has no pulse nor will,
The ship is anchor'd safe and sound, its voyage closed and done,
From fearful trip the victor ship comes in with object won;
  Exult, O shores, and ring, O bells!
   But I, with mournful tread,
    Walk the deck my Captain lies,
     Fallen cold and dead.

MATTHEW ARNOLD

Dover Beach

The sea is calm tonight.
The tide is full, the moon lies fair
Upon the straits; on the French coast the light
Gleams and is gone; the cliffs of England stand,
Glimmering and vast, out in the tranquil bay.

Come to the window, sweet is the night-air!
Only, from the long line of spray
Where the sea meets the moon-blanched land,
Listen! you hear the grating roar
Of pebbles which the waves draw back, and fling,
At their return, up the high strand,
Begin, and cease, and then again begin,
With tremulous cadence slow, and bring
The eternal note of sadness in.

Sophocles long ago
Heard it on the Aegean, and it brought
Into his mind the turbid ebb and flow
Of human misery; we
Find also in the sound a thought,
Hearing it by this distant northern sea.

The Sea of Faith
Was once, too, at the full, and round earth's shore
Lay like the folds of a bright girdle furled.
But now I only hear
Its melancholy, long withdrawing roar,
Retreating, to the breath
Of the night-wind, down the vast edges drear
And naked shingles of the world.

Ah, love, let us be true
To one another! for the world, which seems
To lie before us like a land of dreams,
So various, so beautiful, so new,
Hath really neither joy, nor love, nor light,
Nor certitude, nor peace, nor help for pain;
And we are here as on a darkling plain
Swept with confused alarms of struggle and flight,
Where ignorant armies clash by night.

IVOR GURNEY

To His Love

He's gone, and all our plans
    Are useless indeed.
We'll walk no more on Cotswold
    Where the sheep feed
    Quietly and take no heed.

His body that was so quick
    Is not as you
Knew it, on Severn river
    Under the blue
    Driving our small boat through.

You would not know him now . . .
    But still he died
Nobly, so cover him over
    With violets of pride
    Purple from Severn side.

Cover him, cover him soon!
    And with thick-set
Masses of memoried flowers—
    Hide that red wet
    Thing I must somehow forget.

JOHN CROWE RANSOM

Bells for John Whiteside's Daughter

There was such speed in her little body,
And such lightness in her footfall,
It is no wonder her brown study
Astonishes us all.

Her wars were bruited in our high window.
We looked among orchard trees and beyond
Where she took arms against her shadow,
Or harried unto the pond

The lazy geese, like a snow cloud
Dropping their snow on the green grass,
Tricking and stopping, sleepy and proud,
Who cried in goose, Alas,

For the tireless heart within the little
Lady with rod that made them rise
From their noon apple-dreams and scuttle
Goose-fashion under the skies!

But now go the bells, and we are ready,
In one house we are sternly stopped
To say we are vexed at her brown study,
Lying so primly propped.

LOUISE BOGAN

Tears in Sleep

All night the cocks crew, under a moon like day,
And I, in the cage of sleep, on a stranger's breast,
Shed tears, like a task not to be put away—
In the false light, false grief in my happy bed,
A labor of tears, set against joy's undoing.
I would not wake at your word, I had tears to say.
I clung to the bars of the dream and they were said,
And pain's derisive hand had given me rest
From the night giving off flames, and the dark renewing.

W. H. AUDEN

In Memory of W. B. Yeats

(d. Jan. 1939)

I

He disappeared in the dead of winter:
The brooks were frozen, the airports almost deserted,
And snow disfigured the public statues;
The mercury sank in the mouth of the dying day.
What instruments we have agree
The day of his death was a dark cold day.

Far from his illness
The wolves ran on through the evergreen forests,
The peasant river was untempted by the fashionable quays;
By mourning tongues
The death of the poet was kept from his poems.

But for him it was his last afternoon as himself,
An afternoon of nurses and rumours;
The provinces of his body revolted,
The squares of his mind were empty,
Silence invaded the suburbs,
The current of his feeling failed; he became his admirers.

Now he is scattered among a hundred cities
And wholly given over to unfamiliar affections,
To find his happiness in another kind of wood
And be punished under a foreign code of conscience.
The words of a dead man
Are modified in the guts of the living.

But in the importance and noise of to-morrow
When the brokers are roaring like beasts on the floor of the
Bourse,
And the poor have the sufferings to which they are fairly
accustomed,
And each in the cell of himself is almost convinced of his freedom,
A few thousand will think of this day
As one thinks of a day when one did something slightly unusual.

What instruments we have agree
The day of his death was a dark cold day.

II

You were silly like us; your gift survived it all:
The parish of rich women, physical decay,
Yourself. Mad Ireland hurt you into poetry.
Now Ireland has her madness and her weather still,
For poetry makes nothing happen: it survives
In the valley of its making where executives
Would never want to tamper, flows on south

From ranches of isolation and the busy griefs,
Raw towns that we believe and die in; it survives,
A way of happening, a mouth.

III

Earth, receive an honoured guest:
William Yeats is laid to rest.
Let the Irish vessel lie
Emptied of its poetry.

In the nightmare of the dark
All the dogs of Europe bark,
And the living nations wait,
Each sequestered in its hate;

Intellectual disgrace
Stares from every human face,
And the seas of pity lie
Locked and frozen in each eye.

Follow, poet, follow right
To the bottom of the night,
With your unconstraining voice
Still persuade us to rejoice;

With the farming of a verse
Make a vineyard of the curse,
Sing of human unsuccess
In a rapture of distress;

In the deserts of the heart
Let the healing fountain start,
In the prison of his days
Teach the free man how to praise.

ROBERT LOWELL

from *The Quaker Graveyard in Nantucket*

(For Warren Winslow, Dead at Sea)

Let man have dominion over the fishes of the sea and the fowls of the air and the beasts of the whole earth, and every creeping creature that moveth upon the earth.

I

A brackish reach of shoal off Madaket—
The sea was still breaking violently and night
Had steamed into our North Atlantic Fleet,
When the drowned sailor clutched the drag-net. Light
Flashed from his matted head and marble feet,
He grappled at the net
With the coiled, hurdling muscles of his thighs:
The corpse was bloodless, a botch of reds and whites,
Its open, staring eyes
Were lustreless dead-lights
Or cabin-windows on a stranded hulk
Heavy with sand. We weight the body, close
Its eyes and heave it seaward whence it came,
Where the heel-headed dogfish barks its nose
On Ahab's void and forehead; and the name
Is blocked in yellow chalk.
Sailors, who pitch this portent at the sea
Where dreadnaughts shall confess
Its heel-bent deity,
When you are powerless
To sand-bag this Atlantic bulwark, faced
By the earth-shaker, green, unwearied, chaste
In his steel scales: ask for no Orphean lute
To pluck life back. The guns of the steeled fleet
Recoil and then repeat
The hoarse salute.

II

Whenever winds are moving and their breath
Heaves at the roped-in bulwarks of this pier,

The terns and sea-gulls tremble at your death
In these home waters. Sailor, can you hear
The Pequod's sea wings, beating landward, fall
Headlong and break on our Atlantic wall
Off 'Sconset, where the yawing S-boats splash
The bellbuoy, with ballooning spinnakers,
As the entangled, screeching mainsheet clears
The blocks: off Madaket, where lubbers lash
The heavy surf and throw their long lead squids
For blue-fish? Sea-gulls blink their heavy lids
Seaward. The winds' wings beat upon the stones,
Cousin, and scream for you and the claws rush
At the sea's throat and wring it in the slush
Of this old Quaker graveyard where the bones
Cry out in the long night for the hurt beast
Bobbing by Ahab's whaleboats in the East.

III

All you recovered from Poseidon died
With you, my cousin, and the harrowed brine
Is fruitless on the blue beard of the god,
Stretching beyond us to the castles in Spain,
Nantucket's westward haven. To Cape Cod
Guns, cradled on the tide,
Blast the eelgrass about a waterclock
Of bilge and backwash, roil the salt and sand
Lashing earth's scaffold, rock
Our warships in the hand
Of the great God, where time's contrition blues
Whatever it was these Quaker sailors lost
In the mad scramble of their lives. They died
When time was open-eyed,
Wooden and childish; only bones abide
There, in the nowhere, where their boats were tossed
Sky-high, where mariners had fabled news
Of IS, the whited monster. What it cost
Them is their secret. In the sperm-whale's slick
I see the Quakers drown and hear their cry:

"If God himself had not been on our side,
If God himself had not been on our side,
When the Atlantic rose against us, why,
Then it had swallowed us up quick."

IV

This is the end of the whaleroad and the whale
Who spewed Nantucket bones on the thrashed swell
And stirred the troubled waters to whirlpools
To send the Pequod packing off to hell:
This is the end of them, three-quarters fools,
Snatching at straws to sail
Seaward and seaward on the turntail whale,
Spouting out blood and water as it rolls,
Sick as a dog to these Atlantic shoals:
Clamavimus, O depths. Let the sea-gulls wail

For water, for the deep where the high tide
Mutters to its hurt self, mutters and ebbs.
Waves wallow in their wash, go out and out,
Leave only the death-rattle of the crabs,
The beach increasing, its enormous snout
Sucking the ocean's side.
This is the end of running on the waves;
We are poured out like water. Who will dance
The mast-lashed master of Leviathans
Up from this field of Quakers in their unstoned graves?

V

When the whale's viscera go and the roll
Of its corruption overruns this world
Beyond tree-swept Nantucket and Woods Hole
And Martha's Vineyard, Sailor, will your sword
Whistle and fall and sink into the fat?
In the great ash-pit of Jehoshaphat
The bones cry for the blood of the white whale,
The fat flukes arch and whack about its ears,
The death-lance churns into the sanctuary, tears
The gun-blue swingle, heaving like a flail,

And hacks the coiling life out: it works and drags
And rips the sperm-whale's midriff into rags,
Gobbets of blubber spill to wind and weather,
Sailor, and gulls go round the stoven timbers
Where the morning stars sing out together
And thunder shakes the white surf and dismembers
The red flag hammered in the mast-head. Hide,
Our steel, Jonas Messias, in Thy side.

JOHN BERRYMAN

Dream Song 324

An Elegy for W.C.W., the lovely man

Henry in Ireland to Bill underground:
Rest well, who worked so hard, who made a good sound
constantly, for so many years:
your high-jinks delighted the continents & our ears:
you had so many girls your life was a triumph
and you loved your one wife.

At dawn you rose & wrote—the books poured forth—
you delivered infinite babies, in one great birth—
and your generosity
to juniors made you deeply loved, deeply:
if envy was a Henry trademark, he would envy you,
especially the being through.

Too many journeys lie for him ahead,
too many galleys & page-proofs to be read,
he would like to lie down
in your sweet silence, to whom was not denied
the mysterious late excellence which is the crown
of our trials & our last bride.

FRANK BIDART

To the Dead

What I hope (when I hope) is that we'll
see each other again,—

... and again reach the VEIN

in which we loved each other ...
It existed. *It existed.*

There is a NIGHT within the NIGHT,—

... for, like the detectives (the Ritz Brothers)
in *The Gorilla,*

once we'd been battered by the gorilla

we searched the walls, the intricately carved
impenetrable panelling

for a button, lever, latch

that unlocks a secret door that
reveals at last the secret chambers,

CORRIDORS within WALLS,

(the disenthralling, necessary, dreamed structure
beneath the structure we see,)

that is the HOUSE within the HOUSE ...

There is a NIGHT within the NIGHT,—

... there were (for example) months when I seemed only
to displease, frustrate,

disappoint you—; then, something triggered

a drunk lasting for days, and as you
slowly and shakily sobered up,

sick, throbbing with remorse and self-loathing,

insight like ashes: clung
to; useless; hated ...

This was the viewing of the power of the waters

while the waters were asleep:—
secrets, histories of loves, betrayals, double-binds

not fit (you thought) for the light of day . . .

There is a NIGHT within the NIGHT,—

. . . for, there at times at night, still we
inhabit the secret place together . . .

Is this wisdom, or self-pity?—

The love I've known is the love of
two people staring

not at each other, but in the same direction.

EDWARD HIRSCH

In Memoriam Paul Celan

Lay these words into the dead man's grave
next to the almonds and black cherries—
tiny skulls and flowering blood-drops, eyes,
and Thou, O bitterness that pillows his head.

Lay these words on the dead man's eyelids
like eyebrights, like medieval trumpet flowers
that will flourish, this time, in the shade.
Let the beheaded tulips glisten with rain.

Lay these words on his drowned eyelids
like coins or stars, ancillary eyes.
Canopy the swollen sky with sunspots
while thunder addresses the ground.

Syllable by syllable, clawed and handled,
the words have united in grief.
It is the ghostly hour of lamentation,
the void's turn, mournful and absolute.

Lay these words on the dead man's lips
like burning tongs, a tongue of flame.
A scouring eagle wheels and shrieks.
Let God pray to us for this man.

GARRETT HONGO

The Legend

In memory of Jay Kashiwamura

In Chicago, it is snowing softly
and a man has just done his wash for the week.
He steps into the twilight of early evening,
carrying a wrinkled shopping bag
full of neatly folded clothes,
and, for a moment, enjoys
the feel of warm laundry and crinkled paper,
flannellike against his gloveless hands.
There's a Rembrandt glow on his face,
a triangle of orange in the hollow of his cheek
as a last flash of sunset
blazes the storefronts and lit windows of the street.

He is Asian, Thai or Vietnamese,
and very skinny, dressed as one of the poor
in rumpled suit pants and a plaid mackinaw,
dingy and too large.
He negotiates the slick of ice
on the sidewalk by his car,
opens the Fairlane's back door,
leans to place the laundry in,
and turns, for an instant,
toward the flurry of footsteps
and cries of pedestrians
as a boy—that's all he was—
backs from the corner package store
shooting a pistol, firing it,
once, at the dumbfounded man
who falls forward,
grabbing at his chest.

A few sounds escape from his mouth,
a babbling no one understands
as people surround him
bewildered at his speech.

The noises he makes are nothing to them.
The boy has gone, lost
in the light array of foot traffic
dappling the snow with fresh prints.

Tonight, I read about Descartes'
grand courage to doubt everything
except his own miraculous existence
and I feel so distinct
from the wounded man lying on the concrete
I am ashamed.

Let the night sky cover him as he dies.
Let the weaver girl cross the bridge of heaven
and take up his cold hands.

DOUGLAS CRASE

The Elegy for New York

The buildings are at their stations, untimely
On the tick of property which can always assemble
To a bid. The air rights fidget about the vents,
Zoning and setback line up to be invested in. Today
The last holdout on the block was satisfied in brick,
Six derelict kittens moved blind to their rescue
Along *n*th Avenue, and the once individual rooms
Close rank in a take-it-or-leave-it portfolio:
Solid front. Steam rises from beneath the street
No higher than the metal cornices, applications
Were filed this afternoon, my days in the city
Made ready to appear (stretcher to header as dear
As Flemish bond and tiny among the derricks and drawn
Cranes). I arrived in the visible city to look for you
Where "time becomes visible with shape," as someone said.
With *shape?*
                    Each hour on the place will throw
Its sediment, the quarries are spent, the fortunes
Piece by bay in the scrapyard, numbered,
No questions asked. I've known travertine faces
Torn from a rich entablature and rushed out of town

To landfill the planned communities nearby.
Their kitchens gleam on a soil of terracotta winks
And smiles. In the Home and Garden Center
They have pressed-wood panelling on hand: old mill,
Old barn, and gothic oak. The Animal Hospital
Lengthens and opens its doors. From time to time
On their errands they see you (dripping with gravity
As if you were another world) hesitate over
The parkway's end, recoil, and burst outrageous
As before to riddle Connecticut, light-years off,
With the unkempt traffic of a star.

MARK DOTY

Tiara

Peter died in a paper tiara
cut from a book of princess paper dolls;
he loved royalty, sashes

and jewels. *I don't know,*
he said, when he woke in the hospice,
I was watching the Bette Davis film festival

on Channel 57 and then—
At the wake, the tension broke
when someone guessed

the casket closed because
he was *in there in a big wig
and heels,* and someone said,

*You know he's always late,
he probably isn't here yet—
he's still fixing his makeup.*

And someone said he asked for it.
Asked for it—
when all he did was go down

into the salt tide
of wanting as much as he wanted,
giving himself over so drunk

or stoned it almost didn't matter who,
though they were beautiful,
stampeding into him in the simple,

ravishing music of their hurry.
I think heaven is perfect stasis
poised over the realms of desire,

where dreaming and waking men lie
on the grass while wet horses
roam among them, huge fragments

of the music we die into
in the body's paradise.
Sometimes we wake not knowing

how we came to lie here,
or who has crowned us with these temporary,
precious stones. And given

the world's perfectly turned shoulders,
the deep hollows blued by longing,
given the irreplaceable silk

of horses rippling in orchards,
fruit thundering and chiming down,
given the ordinary marvels of form

and gravity, what could he do,
what could any of us ever do
but ask for it?

GJERTRUD SCHNACKENBERG

Supernatural Love

My father at the dictionary-stand
Touches the page to fully understand
The lamplit answer, tilting in his hand

His slowly scanning magnifying lens,
A blurry, glistening circle he suspends
Above the word "Carnation." Then he bends

So near his eyes are magnified and blurred,
One finger on the miniature word,
As if he touched a single key and heard

A distant, plucked, infinitesimal string,
"The obligation due to every thing
That's smaller than the universe." I bring

My sewing needle close enough that I
Can watch my father through the needle's eye,
As through a lens ground for a butterfly

Who peers down flower-hallways toward a room
Shadowed and fathomed as this study's gloom
Where, as a scholar bends above a tomb

To read what's buried there, he bends to pore
Over the Latin blossom. I am four,
I spill my pins and needles on the floor

Trying to stitch "Beloved" X by X.
My dangerous, bright needle's point connects
Myself illiterate to this perfect text

I cannot read. My father puzzles why
It is my habit to identify
Carnations as "Christ's flowers," knowing I

Can give no explanation but "Because."
Word-roots blossom in speechless messages
The way the thread behind my sampler does

Where following each X I awkward move
My needle through the word whose root is love.
He reads, "A pink variety of Clove,

Carnatio, the Latin, meaning flesh."
As if the bud's essential oils brush
Christ's fragrance through the room, the iron-fresh

Odor carnations have floats up to me,
A drifted, secret, bitter ecstasy,
The stems squeak in my scissors, *Child, it's me,*

He turns the page to "Clove" and reads aloud:
"The clove, a spice, dried from a flower-bud."
Then twice, as if he hasn't understood,

He reads, "From French, for *clou,* meaning a nail."
He gazes, motionless. "Meaning a nail."
The incarnation blossoms, flesh and nail,

I twist my threads like stems into a knot
And smooth "Beloved," but my needle caught
Within the threads, *Thy blood so dearly bought,*

The needle strikes my finger to the bone.
I lift my hand, it is myself I've sewn,
The flesh laid bare, the threads of blood my own,

I lift my hand in startled agony
And call upon his name, "Daddy daddy"—
My father's hand touches the injury

As lightly as he touched the page before,
Where incarnation bloomed from roots that bore
The flowers I called Christ's when I was four.

THOMAS KINSELLA

Mirror in February

The day dawns with scent of must and rain,
Of opened soil, dark trees, dry bedroom air.
Under the fading lamp, half dressed—my brain
Idling on some compulsive fantasy—
I towel my shaven jaw and stop, and stare,
Riveted by a dark exhausted eye,
A dry downturning mouth.

It seems again that it is time to learn,
In this untiring, crumbling place of growth
To which, for the time being, I return.
Now plainly in the mirror of my soul
I read that I have looked my last on youth
And little more; for they are not made whole
That reach the age of Christ.

Below my window the awakening trees,
Hacked clean for better bearing, stand defaced
Suffering their brute necessities,
And how should the flesh not quail that span for span
Is mutilated more? In slow distaste
I fold my towel with what grace I can,
Not young and not renewable, but man.

DAVID ST. JOHN

Iris

Vivian St. John (1891–1974)

There is a train inside this iris:

You think I'm crazy, & like to say boyish
& outrageous things. No, there is

A train inside this iris.

It's a child's finger bearded in black banners.
A single window like a child's nail,

A darkened porthole lit by the white, angular face

Of an old woman, or perhaps the boy beside her in the stuffy,
Hot compartment. Her hair is silver, & sweeps

Back off her forehead, onto her cold & bruised shoulders.

The prairies fail along Chicago. Past the five
Lakes. Into the black woods of her New York; & as I bend

Close above the iris, I see the train

Drive deep into the damp heart of its stem, & the gravel
Of the garden path

Cracks under my feet as I walk this long corridor

Of elms, arched
Like the ceiling of a French railway pier where a boy

With pale curls holding

A fresh iris is waving goodbye to a grandmother, gazing
A long time

Into the flower, as if he were looking some great

Distance, or down an empty garden path & he believes a man
Is walking toward him, working

Dull shears in one hand; & now believe me: The train

Is gone. The old woman is dead, & the boy. The iris curls,
On its stalk, in the shade

Of those elms: Where something like the icy & bitter fragrance

In the wake of a woman who's just swept past you on her way
Home

& you remain.

PAULA MEEHAN

Child Burial

Your coffin looked unreal,
fancy as a wedding cake.

I chose your grave clothes with care,
your favourite stripey shirt,

your blue cotton trousers.
They smelt of woodsmoke, of October,

your own smell there too.
I chose a gansy of handspun wool,

warm and fleecy for you. It is
so cold down in the dark.

No light can reach you and teach you
the paths of wild birds,

the names of the flowers,
the fishes, the creatures.

Ignorant you must remain
of the sun and its work,

my lamb, my calf, my eaglet,
my cub, my kid, my nestling,

my suckling, my colt. I would spin
time back, take you again

within my womb, your amniotic lair,
and further spin you back

through nine waxing months
to the split seeding moment

you chose to be made flesh
word within me.

I'd cancel the love feast
the hot night of your making.

I would travel alone
to a quiet mossy place,

you would spill from me into the earth
drop by bright red drop.

ROSANNA WARREN

Song

A yellow coverlet
in the greenwood:
spread the corners wide to the dim, stoop-shouldered pines.
Let blank sky
be your canopy.
Fringe the bedspread with the wall of lapsing stones.
Here faith has cut
in upright granite
"Meet me in Heaven" at the grave of each child
lost the same year,
three, buried here,
a century ago. Roots and mosses hold
in the same bed
mother, daughter, dead
together, in one day. "Lord, remember the poor,"
their crumbling letters pray.
I turn away.
I shall meet you nowhere, in no transfigured hour.

On soft, matted soil
blueberry bushes crawl,
each separate berry a small, hot globe of tinctured sun.
Crushed on the tongue
it releases a pang
of flesh. Tender flesh, slipped from its skin
preserves its blue heat
down my throat.

The Pastoral

Overview

The pastoral is central to poetry. In a simplified definition, it is that mode of poetry that sought to imitate and celebrate the virtues of rural life. Arcadia was once a real place, a small Greek area that developed a pastoral civilization in 400 B.C. But it quickly became a fiction. In Greece the fictive possibilities of the pastoral were written by Theocritus in his *Idylls,* in Rome by Virgil in his *Eclogues.*

In 1504, the Italian poet Jacopo Sannazzaro published *L'Arcadia,* renewing the fashion and visibility of the pastoral. His plot, about a heartbroken shepherd who finds comfort in the simplicity and shelter of a rural place spoke to a deep European unease about power, urbanization, and the demands made for a new centralization. Philip Sidney confirmed this renewal in England with his publication of what is now called "The Old Arcadia" in 1590. In the Elizabethan court the pastoral glowed as an oblique political comment on power: a poetry in which a perspective of grief and yearning is taken on and rural manners and customs are idealized from the vantage point of a corrupt and treacherous court.

By the end of the sixteenth century, and the start of the seventeenth, the pastoral convention had become one of the true intellectual engines of poetry. On the surface, it appeared to be about an ornamental and sometimes fictional view of the rural and bucolic life. But huge questions lurked below that clear surface. In the pastoral mode poets could experiment with these questions, some of which verged on a philosophical subversion of traditional religious themes in poetry. Was man made for nature or nature for man? Was the natural world to enter the poem as a realistic object or as a fictive projection of inner feelings? Would the natural world always enter the poem shadowed by the religious myths of the Garden of Eden and man's fall?

Throughout the seventeenth and eighteenth centuries, the pastoral convention was a constant in poetry. Shepherdesses and tidy rural constructs abounded. The pastoral was still both an escape and an idea. Then in the Romantic movement, within a period of thirty years, this historic convention suddenly cracked open. And there at its center—troubled, troubling, compelling, and crucial—the embryo of the contemporary nature poem.

It's not surprising that the pastoral broke apart in the early nineteenth century. The Industrial Revolution had, quite simply, destroyed its habitat. A poet's imagination could no longer find that easy rest in an ever-present countryside that was a communal as well as an imaginative possession. In this incarnation, the wounded pastoral became a seismic reader of the relation between the poet and society. When cold, fast streams were harnessed just above Manchester in the first years of the nineteenth century, and the mill wheels began to turn, the pastoral was both challenged and renewed. In the nineteenth century, the Industrial Revolution replaced the court as a place from which to mourn for and celebrate rural life. The pastoral mode proved its resilience and some of the compelling poems of that century are there to prove it.

Perhaps the best reason for including the pastoral mode here is its enduring presence—both tested and contested—in the nature poem and the importance of recognizing its old force in the newer forms. In this section we have moved as quickly as possible to the exciting contemporary negotiation with the pastoral that is to be found in our time. This convention, this mode can be recognized throughout the twentieth century, echoing in laments about urban intrusion, celebrations of urban hubris, speculations about the future of the physical world, right up to the new eco-poetry. We have deliberately chosen these poems to reflect the provocative unsettled relation with the old pastoral that contemporary poets state and restate. Whether looking west in California, or staring at Australian broad beans, the contemporary poet remains haunted by that strange mix of sweet dream and rude awakening that the pastoral convention has always offered.

What is particularly interesting is that the speaking parts of the pastoral—the inhabitants of its silent and idyllic neighborhoods of the past—have been assigned in our time to new actors. From Charles Wright's dark view of Laguna Beach to Jane Kenyon's dark "Let Evening Come" poets show their need and their ability to shatter the idyll of the pastoral while still making reference to it, just as Larkin's shadows and distances make up the violated pastoral of "The Explosion." The twentieth-century poets here continue a sparkling, subversive argument with all the old ideas once stored within this concept.

In the twentieth century the pastoral is often the almost invisible distance in the nature poem. A nature poem in which the dream becomes a nightmare—like Hughes's "The Thought-Fox"—or in which the idyll is restated with a new pessimism by a poet like James Wright.

CHRISTOPHER MARLOWE

The Passionate Shepherd to His Love

Come live with me and be my love,
And we will all the pleasures prove
That valleys, groves, hills, and fields,
Woods, or steepy mountain yields.

And we will sit upon the rocks,
Seeing the shepherds feed their flocks,
By shallow rivers to whose falls
Melodious birds sing madrigals.

And I will make thee beds of roses
And a thousand fragrant posies,
A cap of flowers, and a kirtle
Embroidered all with leaves of myrtle;

A gown made of the finest wool
Which from our pretty lambs we pull;

Fair-linèd slippers for the cold,
With buckles of the purest gold;

A belt of straw and ivy buds,
With coral clasps and amber-studs:
And if these pleasures may thee move,
Come live with me, and be my love.

The shepherd swains shall dance and sing
For thy delight each May morning:
If these delights thy mind may move,
Then live with me and be my love.

WILLIAM SHAKESPEARE

from *Love's Labor's Lost* (V.ii. 912–929)

When icicles hang by the wall
And Dick the shepherd blows his nail
And Tom bears logs into the hall,
    And milk comes frozen home in pail.
When blood is nipped and ways be foul,
Then nightly sings the staring owl,
                Tu-who;
Tu-whit, tu-who: a merry note,
While greasy Joan doth keel the pot.

When all aloud the wind doth blow,
And coughing drowns the parson's saw,
And birds sit brooding in the snow,
    And Marian's nose looks red and raw,
When roasted crabs hiss in the bowl,
Then nightly sings the staring owl,
                Tu-who;
Tu-whit, tu-who: a merry note,
While greasy Joan doth keel the pot.

ANDREW MARVELL

The Garden

How vainly men themselves amaze
To win the palm, the oak, or bays,

And their incessant labors see
Crowned from some single herb, or tree,
Whose short and narrow-vergèd shade
Does prudently their toils upbraid;
While all flowers and all trees do close
To weave the garlands of repose!

    Fair Quiet, have I found thee here,
And Innocence, thy sister dear?
Mistaken long, I sought you then
In busy companies of men.
Your sacred plants, if here below,
Only among the plants will grow;
Society is all but rude
To this delicious solitude.

    No white nor red was ever seen
So amorous as this lovely green.
Fond lovers, cruel as their flame,
Cut in these trees their mistress' name:
Little, alas, they know or heed
How far these beauties hers exceed!
Fair trees, wheresoe'er you barks I wound,
No name shall but your own be found.

    When we have run our passion's heat,
Love hither makes his best retreat.
The gods, that mortal beauty chase,
Still in a tree did end their race:
Apollo hunted Daphne so,
Only that she might laurel grow;
And Pan did after Syrinx speed,
Not as a nymph, but for a reed.

    What wondrous life is this I lead!
Ripe apples drop about my head;
The luscious clusters of the vine
Upon my mouth do crush their wine;
The nectarine, and curious peach
Into my hands themselves do reach;

Stumbling on melons, as I pass,
Insnared with flowers, I fall on grass.

Meanwhile the mind, from pleasure less,
Withdraws into its happiness;
The mind, that ocean where each kind
Does straight its own resemblance find;
Yet it creates, transcending these,
Far other worlds and other seas,
Annihilating all that's made
To a green thought in a green shade.

Here at the fountain's sliding foot,
Or at some fruit tree's mossy root,
Casting the body's vest aside,
My soul into the boughs does glide:
There, like a bird, it sits and sings,
Then whets and combs its silver wings,
And, till prepared for longer flight,
Waves in its plumes the various light.

Such was that happy garden-state,
While man there walked without a mate:
After a place so pure and sweet,
What other help could yet be meet!
But 'twas beyond a mortal's share
To wander solitary there:
Two paradises 'twere in one
To live in paradise alone.

How well the skilful gardener drew
Of flowers and herbs this dial new,
Where, from above, the milder sun
Does through a fragrant zodiac run;
And as it works, th' industrious bee
Computes its time as well as we!
How could such sweet and wholesome hours
Be reckoned but with herbs and flowers?

WILLIAM WORDSWORTH
To My Sister

It is the first mild day of March:
Each minute sweeter than before
The redbreast sings from the tall larch
That stands beside our door.

There is a blessing in the air,
Which seems a sense of joy to yield
To the bare trees, and mountains bare,
And grass in the green field.

My sister! ('tis a wish of mine)
Now that our morning meal is done,
Make haste, your morning task resign;
Come forth and feel the sun.

Edward will come with you;—and, pray,
Put on with speed your woodland dress;
And bring no book: for this one day
We'll give to idleness.

No joyless forms shall regulate
Our living calendar:
We from to-day, my Friend, will date
The opening of the year.

Love, now a universal birth,
From heart to heart is stealing,
From earth to man, from man to earth:
—It is the hour of feeling.

One moment now may give us more
Than years of toiling reason:
Our minds shall drink at every pore
The spirit of the season.

Some silent laws our hearts will make,
Which they shall long obey:
We for the year to come may take
Our temper from to-day.

And from the blessed power that rolls
About, below, above,
We'll frame the measure of our souls:
They shall be tuned to love.

Then come, my Sister! come, I pray,
With speed put on your woodland dress;
And bring no book: for this one day
We'll give to idleness.

JOHN KEATS

Ode on a Grecian Urn

I

Thou still unravished bride of quietness,
    Thou foster child of silence and slow time,
Sylvan historian, who canst thus express
    A flowery tale more sweetly than our rhyme:
What leaf-fringed legend haunts about thy shape
    Of deities or mortals, or of both,
        In Tempe or the dales of Arcady?
    What men or gods are these? What maidens loath?
What mad pursuit? What struggle to escape?
        What pipes and timbrels? What wild ecstasy?

II

Heard melodies are sweet, but those unheard
    Are sweeter; therefore, ye soft pipes, play on;
Not to the sensual ear, but, more endeared,
    Pipe to the spirit ditties of no tone:
Fair youth, beneath the trees, thou canst not leave
    Thy song, nor ever can those trees be bare;
        Bold Lover, never, never canst thou kiss,
Though winning near the goal—yet, do not grieve;
    She cannot fade, though thou hast not thy bliss,
        For ever wilt thou love, and she be fair!

III

Ah, happy, happy boughs! that cannot shed
    Your leaves, nor ever bid the Spring adieu;

And, happy melodist, unweariéd,
    Forever piping songs forever new;
More happy love! more happy, happy love!
    Forever warm and still to be enjoyed,
      Forever panting, and for ever young;
All breathing human passion far above,
    That leaves a heart high-sorrowful and cloyed,
      A burning forehead, and a parching tongue.

IV

Who are these coming to the sacrifice?
    To what green altar, O mysterious priest,
Lead'st thou that heifer lowing at the skies,
    And all her silken flanks with garlands dressed?
What little town by river or sea shore,
    Or mountain-built with peaceful citadel,
      Is emptied of its folk, this pious morn?
And, little town, thy streets forevermore
    Will silent be; and not a soul to tell
      Why thou art desolate, can e'er return.

V

O Attic shape! Fair attitude! with brede
    Of marble men and maidens overwrought,
With forest branches and the trodden weed;
    Thou, silent form, dost tease us out of thought
As doth eternity: Cold Pastoral!
    When old age shall this generation waste,
      Thou shalt remain, in midst of other woe
Than ours, a friend to man, to whom thou say'st,
    "Beauty is truth, truth beauty,"—that is all
      Ye know on earth, and all ye need to know.

A. E. HOUSMAN

Loveliest of Trees

Loveliest of trees, the cherry now
Is hung with bloom along the bough,

And stands about the woodland ride
Wearing white for Eastertide.

Now, of my threescore years and ten,
Twenty will not come again,
And take from seventy springs a score,
It only leaves me fifty more.

And since to look at things in bloom
Fifty springs are little room,
About the woodlands I will go
To see the cherry hung with snow.

FRANCIS LEDWIDGE

The Wife of Llew

And Gwydion said to Math, when it was Spring:
"Come now and let us make a wife for Llew."
And so they broke broad boughs yet moist with dew,
And in a shadow made a magic ring:
They took the violet and the meadow-sweet
To form her pretty face, and for her feet
They built a mound of daisies on a wing,
And for her voice they made a linnet sing
In the wide poppy blowing for her mouth.
And over all they chanted twenty hours.
And Llew came singing from the azure south
And bore away his wife of birds and flowers.

BABETTE DEUTSCH

Urban Pastoral

More domestic than elegant, leaves and pigeons
Hedge the dazzle beyond. Green, dust,
A purple strutting, screen the river's march.
The walks are for pigeons and ladies
Like parched pigeons, avoiding the bench where a tramp
Rustily sleeps. The carriages in the park
Are babies' now; children make all the traffic.

Spring brightly traveling, summer half awake,
Here the afternoon city plays at being
A dream of summer's: gaiety in repose,
Lazily festive as poster holidays,
A dream. Crossed by the tramp, rousing.
On paths where sparrows edge to snatch the bread
Crumbed for the humbled pigeons, the holiday
Is broken and scattered. Yet a strong green still
Throngs the boughs; and the river, preened, goes twinkling
Past all these birds, on to the salt sea.

JANET LEWIS

Remembered Morning

The axe rings in the wood
And the children come,
Laughing and wet from the river;
And all goes on as it should.
I hear the murmur and hum
Of their morning, forever.

The water ripples and slaps
The white boat at the dock;
The fire crackles and snaps.
The little noise of the clock
Goes on and on in my heart,
Of my heart parcel and part.

O happy early stir!
A girl comes out on the porch,
And the door slams after her.
She sees the wind in the birch,
And then the running day
Catches her into its way.

TED HUGHES

The Thought-Fox

I imagine this midnight moment's forest:
Something else is alive

Beside the clock's loneliness
And this blank page where my fingers move.

Through the window I see no star:
Something more near
Though deeper within darkness
Is entering the loneliness:

Cold, delicately as the dark snow,
A fox's nose touches twig, leaf;
Two eyes serve a movement, that now
And again now, and now, and now

Sets neat prints into the snow
Between trees, and warily a lame
Shadow lags by stump and in hollow
Of a body that is bold to come

Across clearings, an eye,
A widening deepening greenness,
Brilliantly, concentratedly,
Coming about its own business

Till, with a sudden sharp hot stink of fox
It enters the dark hole of the head.
The window is starless still; the clock ticks,
The page is printed.

PHILIP LARKIN

The Explosion

On the day of the explosion
Shadows pointed towards the pithead:
In the sun the slagheap slept.

Down the lane came men in pitboots
Coughing oath-edged talk and pipe-smoke,
Shouldering off the freshened silence.

One chased after rabbits; lost them;
Came back with a nest of lark's eggs;
Showed them; lodged them in the grasses.

So they passed in beards and moleskins,
Fathers, brothers, nicknames, laughter,
Through the tall gates standing open.

At noon, there came a tremor; cows
Stopped chewing for a second; sun,
Scarfed as in a heat-haze, dimmed.

The dead go on before us, they
Are sitting in God's house in comfort,
We shall see them face to face—

Plain as lettering in the chapels
It was said, and for a second
Wives saw men of the explosion

Larger than in life they managed—
Gold as on a coin, or walking
Somehow from the sun towards them,

One showing the eggs unbroken.

JAMES WRIGHT

Lying in a Hammock at William Duffy's Farm in Pine Island, Minnesota

Over my head, I see the bronze butterfly,
Asleep on the black trunk,
Blowing like a leaf in green shadow.
Down the ravine behind the empty house,
The cowbells follow one another
Into the distances of the afternoon.
To my right,
In a field of sunlight between two pines,
The droppings of last year's horses
Blaze up into golden stones.
I lean back, as the evening darkens and comes on.
A chicken hawk floats over, looking for home.
I have wasted my life.

DEREK WALCOTT

Midsummer, Tobago

Broad sun-stoned beaches.

White heat.
A green river.

A bridge,
scorched yellow palms

from the summer-sleeping house
drowsing through August.

Days I have held,
days I have lost,

days that outgrow, like daughters,
my harbouring arms.

GALWAY KINNELL

The Bear

1

In late winter
I sometimes glimpse bits of steam
coming up from
some fault in the old snow
and bend close and see it is lung-colored
and put down my nose
and know
the chilly, enduring odor of bear.

2

I take a wolf's rib and whittle
it sharp at both ends
and coil it up
and freeze it in blubber and place it out
on the fairway of the bears.

And when it has vanished
I move out on the bear tracks,

roaming in circles
until I come to the first, tentative, dark
splash on the earth.

And I set out
running, following the splashes
of blood wandering over the world.
At the cut, gashed resting places
I stop and rest,
at the crawl-marks
where he lay out on his belly
to overpass some stretch of bauchy ice
I lie out
dragging myself forward with bear-knives in my fists.

3

On the third day I begin to starve,
at nightfall I bend down as I knew I would
at a turd sopped in blood,
and hesitate, and pick it up,
and thrust it in my mouth, and gnash it down,
and rise
and go on running.

4

On the seventh day,
living by now on bear blood alone,
I can see his upturned carcass far out ahead, a scraggled,
steamy hulk,
the heavy fur riffling in the wind.

I come up to him
and stare at the narrow-spaced, petty eyes,
the dismayed
face laid back on the shoulder, the nostrils
flared, catching
perhaps the first taint of me as he
died.

I hack
a ravine in his thigh, and eat and drink,

and tear him down his whole length
and open him and climb in
and close him up after me, against the wind,
and sleep.

5

And dream
of lumbering flatfooted
over the tundra,
stabbed twice from within,
splattering a trail behind me,
splattering it out no matter which way I lurch,
no matter which parabola of bear-transcendence,
which dance of solitude I attempt,
which gravity-clutched leap,
which trudge, which groan.

6

Until one day I totter and fall—
fall on this
stomach that has tried so hard to keep up,
to digest the blood as it leaked in,
to break up
and digest the bone itself: and now the breeze
blows over me, blows off
the hideous belches of ill-digested bear blood
and rotted stomach
and the ordinary, wretched odor of bear,

blows across
my sore, lolled tongue a song
or screech, until I think I must rise up
and dance. And I lie still.

7

I awaken I think. Marshlights
reappear, geese
come trailing again up the flyway.
In her ravine under old snow the dam-bear

lies, licking
lumps of smeared fur
and drizzly eyes into shapes
with her tongue. And one
hairy-soled trudge struck out before me,
the next groaned out,
the next,
the next,
the rest of my days I spend
wandering: wondering
what, anyway,
was that sticky infusion, that rank flavor of blood, that
    poetry, by which I lived?

AMY CLAMPITT

Fog

A vagueness comes over everything,
as though proving color and contour
alike dispensable: the lighthouse
extinct, the islands' spruce-tips
drunk up like milk in the
universal emulsion; houses
reverting into the lost
and forgotten; granite
subsumed, a rumor
in a mumble of ocean.
               Tactile
definition, however, has not been
totally banished: hanging
tassel by tassel, panicled
foxtail and needlegrass,
dropseed, furred hawkweed,
and last season's rose-hips
are vested in silenced
chimes of the finest,
clearest sea-crystal.
               Opacity

opens up rooms, a showcase
for the hueless moonflower
corolla, as Georgia
O'Keeffe might have seen it,
of foghorns; the nodding
campanula of bell buoys;
the ticking, linear
filigree of bird voices.

JANE KENYON

Let Evening Come

Let the light of late afternoon
shine through chinks in the barn, moving
up the bales as the sun moves down.

Let the cricket take up chafing
as a woman takes up her needles
and her yarn. Let evening come.

Let dew collect on the hoe abandoned
in long grass. Let the stars appear
and the moon disclose her silver horn.

Let the fox go back to its sandy den.
Let the wind die down. Let the shed
go black inside. Let evening come.

To the bottle in the ditch, to the scoop
in the oats, to air in the lung
let evening come.

Let it come, as it will, and don't
be afraid. God does not leave us
comfortless, so let evening come.

PHILIP LEVINE

Smoke

Can you imagine the air filled with smoke?
It was. The city was vanishing before noon

or was it earlier than that? I can't say because
the light came from nowhere and went nowhere.

This was years ago, before you were born, before
your parents met in a bus station downtown.
She'd come on Friday after work all the way
from Toledo, and he'd dressed in his only suit.

Back then we called this a date, sometimes
a blind date, though they'd written back and forth
for weeks. What actually took place is now lost.
It's become part of the mythology of a family,

the stories told by children around the dinner table.
No, they aren't dead, they're just treated that way,
as objects turned one way and then another
to catch the light, the light overflowing with smoke.

Go back to the beginning, you insist. Why
is the air filled with smoke? Simple. We had work.
Work was something that thrived on fire, that without
fire couldn't catch its breath or hang on for life.

We came out into the morning air, Bernie, Stash,
Williams, and I, it was late March, a new war
was starting up in Asia or closer to home,
one that meant to kill us, but for a moment

the air held still in the gray poplars and elms
undoing their branches. I understood the moon
for the very first time, why it came and went, why
it wasn't there that day to greet the four of us.

Before the bus came a small black bird settled
on the curb, fearless or hurt, and turned its beak up
as though questioning the day. "A baby crow,"
someone said. Your father knelt down on the wet cement,

his lunchbox balanced on one knee and stared quietly
for a long time. "A grackle far from home," he said.
One of the four of us mentioned *tenderness,*
a word I wasn't used to, so it wasn't me.

The bus must have arrived. I'm not there today.
The windows were soiled. We swayed this way and that
over the railroad tracks, across Woodward Avenue,
heading west, just like the sun, hidden in smoke.

ROBERT HASS

Meditation at Lagunitas

All the new thinking is about loss.
In this it resembles all the old thinking.
The idea, for example, that each particular erases
the luminous clarity of a general idea. That the clown-
faced woodpecker probing the dead sculpted trunk
of that black birch is, by his presence,
some tragic falling off from a first world
of undivided light. Or the other notion that,
because there is in this world no one thing
to which the bramble of *blackberry* corresponds,
a word is elegy to what it signifies.
We talked about it late last night and in the voice
of my friend, there was a thin wire of grief, a tone
almost querulous. After a while I understood that,
talking this way, everything dissolves: *justice,
pine, hair, woman, you* and *I.* There was a woman
I made love to and I remembered how, holding
her small shoulders in my hands sometimes,
I felt a violent wonder at her presence
like a thirst for salt, for my childhood river
with its island willows, silly music from the pleasure boat,
muddy places where we caught the little orange-silver fish
called *pumpkinseed.* It hardly had to do with her.
Longing, we say, because desire is full
of endless distances. I must have been the same to her.
But I remember so much, the way her hands dismantled bread,
the thing her father said that hurt her, what
she dreamed. There are moments when the body is as numinous
as words, days that are the good flesh continuing.

Such tenderness, those afternoons and evenings,
saying *blackberry, blackberry, blackberry.*

JOHN KOETHE

From the Porch

The stores were bright, and not too far from home.
The school was only half a mile from downtown,
A few blocks from the Oldsmobile dealer. In the sky,
The airplanes came in low towards Lindbergh Field,
Passing overhead with a roar that shook the windows.
How *inert* the earth must look from far away:
The morning mail, the fantasies, the individual days
Too intimate to see, no matter how you tried;
The photos in the album of the young man leaving home.
Yet there was always time to visit them again
In a roundabout way, like the figures in the stars,
Or a life traced back to its imaginary source
In an adolescent reverie, a forgotten book—
As though one's childhood were a small midwestern town
Some forty years ago, before the elm trees died.
September was a modern classroom and the latest cars,
That made a sort of futuristic dream, circa 1955.
The earth was still uncircled. You could set your course
On the day after tomorrow. And children fell asleep
To the lullaby of people murmuring softly in the kitchen,
While a breeze rustled the pages of *Life* magazine,
And the wicker chairs stood empty on the screened-in porch.

ALFRED CORN

A Walrus Tusk from Alaska

Arp might have done a version in white marble,
the model held aloft, in approximate awe:
this tough cross-section oval of tusk,
dense and cool as fossil cranium—

preliminary bloodshed condonable
if Inupiat hunters on King Island may
follow as their fathers did the bark of a husky,
echoes ricocheted from roughed-up eskers

on the glacier, a resonance salt cured
and stained deep green by Arctic seas, whose tilting floor
mirrors the mainland's snowcapped amphitheater.
Which of his elders set Mike Saclamana the task

and taught him to decide, in scrimshaw, what was so?
Netted incisions black as an etching
saw a way to scratch in living infinitives
known since the Miocene to have animated

the Bering Strait: one humpbacked whale, plump,
and bardic; an Orca caught on the ascending arc,
salt droplets flung from a flange of soot-black fin. . . .
Farther along the bone conveyor belt a small

ringed seal will never not be swimming, part-time
landlubber, who may feel overshadowed by the donor
walrus ahead. And by his scribal tusk, which stands
in direct correspondence with the draughtsman's burin,

skillful enough to score their tapeloop ostinato,
no harp sonata, but, instead, the humpbacked whale's
yearning bassoon (still audible if you cup
the keepsake to your ear and let it sound the depths).

CHARLES WRIGHT

Looking West from Laguna Beach at Night

I've always liked the view from my mother-in-law's house at night,
Oil rigs off Long Beach
Like floating lanterns out in the smog-dark Pacific,
Stars in the eucalyptus,
Lights of airplanes arriving from Asia, and town lights
Littered like broken glass around the bay and back up the hill.

In summer, dance music is borne up
On the sea winds from the hotel's beach deck far below,
"Twist and Shout," or "Begin the Beguine."
It's nice to think that somewhere someone is having a good time,
And pleasant to picture them down there
Turned out, tipsy and flushed, in their white shorts and their
    turquoise shirts.

Later, I like to sit and look up
At the mythic history of Western civilization,
Pinpricked and clued through the zodiac.
I'd like to be able to name them, say what's what and how who got
    where,
Curry the physics of metamorphosis and its endgame,
But I've spent my life knowing nothing.

LES MURRAY

The Broad Bean Sermon

Beanstalks, in any breeze, are a slack church parade
without belief, saying *trespass against us* in unison,
recruits in mint Air Force dacron, with unbuttoned leaves.

Upright with water like men, square in stem-section
they grow to great lengths, drink rain, keel over all ways,
kink down and grow up afresh, with proffered new greenstuff.

Above the cat-and-mouse floor of a thin bean forest
snails hang rapt in their food, ants hurry through several
    dimensions:
spiders tense and sag like little black flags in their cordage.

Going out to pick beans with the sun high as fence-tops, you find
plenty, and fetch them. An hour or a cloud later
you find shirtfulls more. At every hour of daylight

appear more than you missed: ripe, knobbly ones, fleshy-sided,
thin-straight, thin-crescent, frown-shaped, bird-shouldered, boat-
    keeled ones,

beans knuckled and single-bulged, minute green dolphins at suck,

beans upright like lecturing, outstretched like blessing fingers
in the incident light, and more still, oblique to your notice
that the noon glare or cloud-light or afternoon slants will uncover

till you ask yourself Could I have overlooked so many, or
do they form in an hour? unfolding into reality
like templates for subtly broad grins, like unique caught
   expressions,

like edible meanings, each sealed around with a string
and affixed to its moment, an unceasing colloquial assembly,
the portly, the stiff, and those lolling in pointed green slippers . . .

Wondering who'll take the spare bagfulls, you grin with happiness
—it is your health—you vow to pick them all
even the last few, weeks off yet, misshapen as toes.

LUCIE BROCK-BROIDO

Of the Finished World

Open the final book: November spills
Its lamplit light, the clenched astronomer hunched

At table, considering his vexed celestial
Map, illegible as the flinch

Of needles falling on the blanched
Rye fields in pentagrams.

The harvest is done with itself, its ransack
Done. The wild coated horses bunch

In the clot of darkness that falls on the land.
In the thrice-ploughed field, picked

Clean, what is left of the bottle-gourds
Will freeze by night, a ruined hour

From here. On the freighted road, laden with
Old hunger & apocrypha, a heaven sloughs

Its midden things, things left of the unfinished
World, its most hideous & permanent

Impermanence. As long as I am, I am
Hither—here—a little mob of Spoon

& Ladle, Sugar-Trough, a clinched antimony
Of will. I was not awake for any war to speak

Of. Suddenly I cannot see anymore in the dark
Where the grains amass in their silo stacks.

In the finished world, I will be wind-awry,
Will be out of mind, in asylum

Of the quiet that fell on a clotted room
Where even the astronomer can no longer

Attend to the tenebrous world undone.
How have I lived here so long?

THYLIAS MOSS

Tornados

Truth is, I envy them
not because they dance; I out jitterbug them
as I'm shuttled through and through legs
strong as looms, weaving time. They
do black more justice than I, frenzy
of conductor of philharmonic and electricity, hair
on end, result of the charge when horns and strings release
the pent up Beethoven and Mozart. Ions played

instead of notes. The movement
is not wrath, not hormone swarm because
I saw my first forming above the church a surrogate
steeple. The morning of my first baptism and
salvation already tangible, funnel for the spirit
coming into me without losing a drop, my black
guardian angel come to rescue me before all the words

get out, *I looked over Jordan and what did I see coming for
to carry me home. Regardez,* it all comes back, even the first
grade French, when the tornado stirs up the past, bewitched spoon
lost in its own spin, like a roulette wheel that won't
be steered, like the world. They drove me underground,
tornado watches and warnings, atomic bomb drills. Adult
storms so I had to leave the room. Truth is

the tornado is a perfect nappy curl, tightly wound,
spinning wildly when I try to tamper with its nature, shunning
the hot comb and pressing oil even though if absolutely straight
I'd have the longest hair in the world. Bouffant tornadic
crown taking the royal path on a trip to town, stroll down
Tornado Alley where it intersects Memory Lane. Smoky spirit-
clouds, shadows searching for what cast them.

C. K. WILLIAMS

Loss

In this day and age Lord
you are like one of those poor farmers
who burns the forests off
and murders his lands and then
can't leave and goes sullen and lean
among the rusting yard junk, the scrub
and the famished stock.

Lord I have felt myself raked
into the earth like manure,
harrowed and plowed under,
but I am still enough like you
to stand on the porch
chewing a stalk or drinking
while tall weeds come up dead
and the house dogs, snapping
their chains like moths, howl
and point towards the withering
meadows at nothing.

TIMOTHY STEELE

Waiting for the Storm

Breeze sent a wrinkling darkness
Across the bay. I knelt
Beneath an upturned boat,
And moment by moment, felt

The sand at my feet grow colder,
The damp air chill and spread.
Then the first raindrops sounded
On the hull over my head.

MARY KINZIE

An Engraving of Blake

From the ceiling near the roof
Runs the smoke of star and field:
The father brings his weather proof
That he will try, and we will yield.
The boly unwinds into the dark;
His beard is blowing in the dark.

About his eyes, no energy.
The climate falls into his hand.
We cast about us as we sleep
And see, that this is as he planned—
That we should know his earth, his air
For rocks of tears and rivers of hair.

EILÉAN NÍ CHUILLEANÁIN

Pygmalion's Image

Not only her stone face, laid back staring in the ferns,
But everything the scoop of the valley contains begins to move
(And beyond the horizon the trucks beat the highway.)

A tree inflates gently on the curve of the hill;
An insect crashes on the carved eyelid;

Grass blows westward from the roots,
As the wind knifes under her skin and ruffles it like a book.

The crisp hair is real, wriggling like snakes;
A rustle of veins, tick of blood in the throat;
The lines of the face tangle and catch, and
A green leaf of language comes twisting out of her mouth.

LOUISE GLÜCK

Mock Orange

It is not the moon, I tell you.
It is these flowers
lighting the yard.

I hate them.
I hate them as I hate sex,
the man's mouth
sealing my mouth, the man's
paralyzing body—

and the cry that always escapes,
the low, humiliating
premise of union—

In my mind tonight
I hear the question and pursuing answer
fused in one sound
that mounts and mounts and then
is split into the old selves,
the tired antagonisms. Do you see?
We were made fools of.
And the scent of mock orange
drifts through the window.

How can I rest?
How can I be content
while there is still
that odor in the world?

MARY OLIVER

The Black Walnut Tree

My mother and I debate:
we could sell
the black walnut tree
to the lumberman,
and pay off the mortgage.
Likely some storm anyway
will churn down its dark boughs,
smashing the house. We talk
slowly, two women trying
in a difficult time to be wise.
Roots in the cellar drains,
I say, and she replies
that the leaves are getting heavier
every year, and the fruit
harder to gather away.
But something brighter than money
moves in our blood—an edge
sharp and quick as a trowel
that wants us to dig and sow.
So we talk, but we don't do
anything. That night I dream
of my fathers out of Bohemia
filling the blue fields
of fresh and generous Ohio
with leaves and vines and orchards.
What my mother and I both know
is that we'd crawl with shame
in the emptiness we'd made
in our own and our fathers' backyard.
So the black walnut tree
swings through another year
of sun and leaping winds,
of leaves and bounding fruit,
and, month after month, the whip-
crack of the mortgage.

MEDBH McGUCKIAN

Gateposts

A man will keep a horse for prestige,
But a woman ripens best underground.
He settles where the wind
Brings his whirling hat to rest,
And the wind decides which door is to be used.

Under the hip-roofed thatch,
The bed-wing is warmed by chimney breast;
On either side the keeping-holes
For his belongings, hers.

He says it's unlucky to widen the house
And leaves the gateposts holding up the fairies.
He lays his lazy-beds and burns the river,
He builds turf-castles,
And sprigs the corn with apple-mint.

She spreads heather on the floor
And sifts the oatmeal ark for thin-bread farls:
All through the blue month, July,
She tosses stones in basins to the sun,
And watches for the trout in the holy well.

SUSAN PROSPERE

Heart of the Matter

How forlorn and lost
they must have looked, the mahogany deer
carved on the cabinet,
peering forth from the trailing
vines and foliage, antlers
intertwined, their bodies forever
suspended, frozen
as if jacklighted, as if having come
so far to the edge
of the forest,
they couldn't bear to enter

the room, with its stale air,
the claw-footed sofa. Coaxed
from the wood, whittled,
these fallow deer, clustered
around the keyhole, guardians
of some mortal secret. . . .

It was a woman's hand, I think,
that turned the key
to lock away some token, hidden perhaps
in her underclothes, lying under
her corset, its hooks
and eyes open. I like to believe
it was she, needing
consequence, image, passion,
who placed the china figurines
in the curio cabinet, almost touching,
the shepherdess and the sweep,
vivified, at least for a moment,
by closeness. Once they were slip
in a single bowl, poured
into molds of equal measure,
and set on the topmost
shelf together—she with a rose
pinned to her bosom, a gilded crook
beside her, but no sheep walk
to cross, no flock to tend to,
and he in pitch black clothes,
holding ladder and broom,
his face glowing,
having swept, as yet, no nooks,
no hearth, no ingles.

Day after day, lifted up, dusted,
placed on the shelf closer
and closer, the shadow of one
sometimes falling across the other,
they felt the shape
that love can take—the form of one

lying darkly upon the other—
and though you might say
they were only dolls, their features
glazed, their bodies rigid,
they, too, are of the earth, and I,
for one, have come to believe
in the primal sadness
of a divided substance. Oh, come
to me now, toting your ladder,
and we'll go, as they once did,
past the opening night
at the doll's theater,
past the one-act play of star-crossed lovers,
past the household creatures—
the potpourri jar
exuding sweetness, the captured knight
and the ivory castle,
the knave of hearts
doubling with self-love—
and I'll take you with me over the doused embers
into the dark heart
of the stove,
where we'll climb together towards the stars
bracketed inside the chimney,
past firebrick and flue
into the stratosphere.

MARY O'MALLEY

Shoeing the Currach

Seventeen feet of canvas
Stretched across the supple hoops of her
And with one deft push of a shoe
She'd spin into his hands
And lightly he'd lift and turn her.

That's how it was with them
Until the balance shifted.

The foot smashed down,
An awkward turn, he can't hold her,
Now she's torn and useless on the sand.

Disgusted, he walks away,
His big hands useless
And no words for what is done.

The Ode

Overview

From its origins in classical antiquity, the ode was a solemn, heroic, and elevated form. It elevated the person, the object, the occasion. In ancient times, in the Pindaric ode, athletes were praised, statesmen were applauded. Therefore the early examples of the ode are full of flatteries, exaggerations, and claims for the excellence and high standing of the subject.

The ode might have remained a static and historic form. But the Romantic movement galvanized it. Suddenly these poets, struggling with their new and volatile arrangements of the inner and outer world, discovered themselves in this form.

In the nineteenth century, the ode transited from its old heroic mode and became a form that examined and exalted lyric crisis. In this form Keats celebrated the nightingale, the Grecian urn, and the darkening weather of Autumn. In this form also, Shelley wrote his powerful "Ode to the West Wind."

But the ode, like the pastoral and elegy, was part convention, part mode, and all opportunity. Modern poets have taken the spirit of the ode—its address, its decorum—and widened it to include a much more panoramic landscape of reference and celebration.

In the nineteenth century, when Shelley wrote "Ode to the West Wind" or Keats "To Autumn," two things are obvious: The ode is no longer a ceremonial form, and the writing of the sonnet has influenced the structure of the ode. Shelley's "Ode To The West Wind" is largely made of sonnets, but Wordsworth's defining "Ode on the Intimations of Immortality" is irregular, exuberant, shifting from long lines to short, and from epigrammatic to philosophical statements.

For poets in this century, the ode was almost a lost form. Its straight-faced and unswerving elevation of objects and persons no longer seems so possible in an age of lost faith and broken images. But, as in Robert Pinsky's dark and witty meditation on its power, the ode still casts a long shadow over the contemporary poet.

PERCY BYSSHE SHELLEY
Ode to the West Wind

I

O wild West Wind, thou breath of Autumn's being,
Thou, from whose unseen presence the leaves dead
Are driven, like ghosts from an enchanter fleeing,

Yellow, and black, and pale, and hectic red,
Pestilence-stricken multitudes: O thou,
Who chariotest to their dark wintry bed

The wingéd seeds, where they lie cold and low,
Each like a corpse within its grave, until
Thine azure sister of the Spring shall blow

Her clarion o'er the dreaming earth, and fill
(Driving sweet buds like flocks to feed in air)
With living hues and odors plain and hill:

Wild Spirit, which art moving everywhere;
Destroyer and preserver; hear, oh, hear!

II

Thou on whose stream, mid the steep sky's commotion,
Loose clouds like earth's decaying leaves are shed,
Shook from the tangled boughs of Heaven and Ocean,

Angels of rain and lightning: there are spread
On the blue surface of thine aëry surge,
Like the bright hair uplifted from the head

Of some fierce Maenad, even from the dim verge
Of the horizon to the zenith's height,
The locks of the approaching storm. Thou dirge

Of the dying year, to which this closing night
Will be the dome of a vast sepulcher,
Vaulted with all thy congregated might

Of vapors, from whose solid atmosphere
Black rain, and fire, and hail will burst: oh, hear!

III

Thou who didst waken from his summer dreams
The blue Mediterranean, where he lay,
Lulled by the coil of his crystalline streams,

Beside a pumice isle in Baiae's bay,
And saw in sleep old palaces and towers
Quivering within the wave's intenser day,

All overgrown with azure moss and flowers
So sweet, the sense faints picturing them! Thou
For whose path the Atlantic's level powers

Cleave themselves into chasms, while far below
The sea-blooms and the oozy woods which wear
The sapless foliage of the ocean, know

Thy voice, and suddenly grow gray with fear,
And tremble and despoil themselves: oh, hear!

IV

If I were a dead leaf thou mightest bear;
If I were a swift cloud to fly with thee;
A wave to pant beneath thy power, and share

The impulse of thy strength, only less free
Than thou, O uncontrollable! If even
I were as in my boyhood, and could be

The comrade of thy wanderings over Heaven,
As then, when to outstrip thy skyey speed
Scarce seemed a vision; I would ne'er have striven

As thus with thee in prayer in my sore need.
Oh, lift me as a wave, a leaf, a cloud!
I fall upon the thorns of life! I bleed!

A heavy weight of hours has chained and bowed
One too like thee: tameless, and swift, and proud.

V

Make me thy lyre, even as the forest is:
What if my leaves are falling like its own!
The tumult of thy mighty harmonies

Will take from both a deep, autumnal tone,
Sweet though in sadness. Be thou, Spirit fierce,
My spirit! Be thou me, impetuous one!

Drive my dead thoughts over the universe
Like withered leaves to quicken a new birth!
And, by the incantation of this verse,

Scatter, as from an unextinguished hearth
Ashes and sparks, my words among mankind!
Be through my lips to unawakened earth

The trumpet of a prophecy! O Wind,
If Winter comes, can Spring be far behind?

JOHN KEATS

To Autumn

I

Season of mists and mellow fruitfulness,
    Close bosom-friend of the maturing sun;
Conspiring with him how to load and bless
    With fruit the vines that round the thatch-eaves run;
To bend with apples the mossed cottage-trees,
    And fill all fruit with ripeness to the core;
        To swell the gourd, and plump the hazel shells
    With a sweet kernel; to set budding more,
And still more, later flowers for the bees,

Until they think warm days will never cease,
    For Summer hast o'er-brimmed their clammy cells.

II

Who hath not seen thee oft amid thy store?
    Sometimes whoever seeks abroad may find
Thee sitting careless on a granary floor,
    Thy hair soft-lifted by the winnowing wind;
Or on a half-reaped furrow sound asleep,
    Drowsed with the fume of poppies, while thy hook
        Spares the next swath and all its twinéd flowers:
And sometimes like a gleaner thou dost keep
    Steady thy laden head across a brook;
    Or by a cider-press, with patient look,
        Thou watchest the last oozings hours by hours.

III

Where are the songs of Spring? Aye, where are they?
    Think not of them, thou hast thy music too—
While barréd clouds bloom the soft-dying day,
    And touch the stubble-plains with rosy hue;
Then in a wailful choir the small gnats mourn
    Among the river sallows, borne aloft
        Or sinking as the light wind lives or dies;
And full-grown lambs loud bleat from hilly bourn;
    Hedge crickets sing; and now with treble soft
    The redbreast whistles from a garden-croft;
        And gathering swallows twitter in the skies.

HENRY TIMROD

Ode

**Sung on the occasion of decorating the graves of the Confederate dead at
Magnolia Cemetery, Charleston, S.C., 1867**

Sleep sweetly in your humble graves,
    Sleep, martyrs of a fallen cause;
Though yet no marble column craves
    The pilgrim here to pause.

In seeds of laurels in the earth
    The bloom of your fame is blown,
And somewhere, waiting for its birth,
    The shaft is in the stone!

Meanwhile, behalf the tardy years
    Which keep in trust your storied tombs,
Behold! your sisters bring their tears,
    And these memorial blooms.

Small tributes! but your shades will smile
    More proudly on these wreaths to-day,
Than when some cannon-moulded pile
    Shall overlook this bay.

Stoop, angels, hither from the skies!
    There is no holier spot of ground
Than where defeated valor lies,
    By mourning beauty crowned!

HENRY WADSWORTH LONGFELLOW
The Fire of Driftwood
Devereux Farm near Marblehead

We sat within the farmhouse old,
    Whose windows, looking o'er the bay,
Gave to the sea-breeze damp and cold,
    An easy entrance, night and day.

Not far away we saw the port,
    The strange, old-fashioned, silent town,
The lighthouse, the dismantled fort,
    The wooden houses, quaint and brown.

We sat and talked until the night,
    Descending, filled the little room;
Our faces faded from the sight,
    Our voices only broke the gloom.

We spake of many a vanished scene,
    Of what we once had thought and said,

Of what had been, and might have been,
        And who was changed, and who was dead;

And all that fills the hearts of friends,
        When first they feel, with secret pain,
Their lives thenceforth have separate ends,
        And never can be one again;

The first slight swerving of the heart,
        That words are powerless to express,
And leave it still unsaid in part,
        Or say it in too great excess.

The very tones in which we spake
        Had something strange, I could but mark;
The leaves of memory seemed to make
        A mournful rustling in the dark.

Oft died the words upon our lips,
        As suddenly, from out the fire
Built of the wreck of stranded ships,
        The flames would leap and then expire.

And, as their splendor flashed and failed,
        We thought of wrecks upon the main,
Of ships dismasted, that were hailed
        And sent no answer back again.

The windows, rattling in their frames,
        The ocean, roaring up the beach,
The gusty blast, the bickering flames,
        All mingled vaguely in our speech;

Until they made themselves a part
        Of fancies floating through the brain,
The long-lost ventures of the heart,
        That send no answers back again.

O flames that glowed! O hearts that yearned!
        They were indeed too much akin,
The driftwood fire without that burned,
        The thoughts that burned and glowed within.

HART CRANE

from *The Bridge*

Proem: to Brooklyn Bridge

How many dawns, chill from his rippling rest
The seagull's wings shall dip and pivot him,
Shedding white rings of tumult, building high
Over the chained bay waters Liberty—

Then, with inviolate curve, forsake our eyes
As apparitional as sails that cross
Some page of figures to be filed away;
—Till elevators drop us from our day . . .

I think of cinemas, panoramic sleights
With multitudes bent toward some flashing scene
Never disclosed, but hastened to again,
Foretold to other eyes on the same screen;

And Thee, across the harbor, silver-paced
As though the sun took step of thee, yet left
Some motion ever unspent in thy stride—
Implicitly thy freedom staying thee!

Out of some subway scuttle, cell or loft
A bedlamite speeds to thy parapets,
Tilting there momently, shrill shirt ballooning,
A jest falls from the speechless caravan.

Down Wall, from girder into street noon leaks,
A rip-tooth of the sky's acetylene,
All afternoon the cloud-flown derricks turn . . .
Thy cables breathe the North Atlantic still.

And obscure as that heaven of the Jews,
Thy guerdon . . . Accolade thou dost bestow
Of anonymity time cannot raise:
Vibrant reprieve and pardon thou dost show.

O harp and altar, of the fury fused,
(How could mere toil align thy choiring strings!)

Terrific threshold of the prophet's pledge,
Prayer of pariah, and the lover's cry—

Again the traffic lights that skim thy swift
Unfractioned idiom, immaculate sigh of stars,
Beading thy path—condense eternity:
And we have seen night lifted in thine arms.

Under thy shadow by the piers I waited;
Only in darkness is thy shadow clear.
The City's fiery parcels all undone,
Already snow submerges an iron year . . .

O Sleepless as the river under thee,
Vaulting the sea, the prairies' dreaming sod,
Unto us lowliest sometime sweep, descend
And of the curveship lend a myth to God.

MARIANNE MOORE
The Paper Nautilus

For authorities whose hopes
are shaped by mercenaries?
    Writers entrapped by
    teatime fame and by
commuters' comforts? Not for these
    the paper nautilus
    constructs her thin glass shell.

Giving her perishable
souvenir of hope, a dull
    white outside and smooth-
    edged inner surface
glossy as the sea, the watchful
    maker of it guards it
    day and night; she scarcely

    eats until the eggs are hatched.
Buried eightfold in her eight
    arms, for she is in
    a sense a devil-

fish, her glass ram's-horn-cradled freight
   is hid but is not crushed;
   as Hercules, bitten

   by a crab loyal to the hydra,
was hindered to succeed,
   the intensively
   watched eggs coming from
the shell free it when they are freed—
   leaving its wasp-nest flaws
   of white on white, and close-

   laid Ionic chiton-folds
like the lines in the mane of
   a Parthenon horse,
   round which the arms had
wound themselves as if they knew love
   is the only fortress
   strong enough to trust to.

JUDITH WRIGHT

Australia 1970

Die, wild country, like the eaglehawk,
dangerous till the last breath's gone,
clawing and striking. Die
cursing your captor through a raging eye.

Die like the tigersnake
that hisses such pure hatred from its pain
as fills the killer's dreams
with fear like suicide's invading stain.

Suffer, wild country, like the ironwood
that gaps the dozer-blade.
I see your living soil ebb with the tree
to naked poverty.

Die like the soldier-ant
mindless and faithful to your million years.

Though we corrupt you with our torturing mind,
stay obstinate; stay blind.

For we are conquerors and self-poisoners
more than scorpion or snake
and dying of the venoms that we make
even while you die of us.

I praise the scoring drought, the flying dust,
the drying creek, the furious animal,
that they oppose us still;
that we are ruined by the thing we kill.

CHARLES SIMIC

Miracle Glass Co.

Heavy mirror carried
Across the street,
I bow to you
And to everything that appears in you,
Momentarily
And never again the same way:

This street with its pink sky,
Row of gray tenements,
A lone dog,
Children on rollerskates,
Woman buying flowers,
Someone looking lost.

In you, mirror framed in gold
And carried across the street
By someone I can't even see,
To whom, too, I bow.

HOWARD NEMEROV

The Blue Swallows

Across the millstream below the bridge
Seven blue swallows divide the air

In shapes invisible and evanescent,
Kaleidoscopic beyond the mind's
Or memory's power to keep them there.

"History is where tensions were,"
"Form is the diagram of forces."
Thus, helplessly, there on the bridge,
While gazing down upon those birds—
How strange, to be above the birds!—
Thus helplessly the mind in its brain
Weaves up relation's spindrift web,
Seeing the swallows' tails as nibs
Dipped in invisible ink, writing . . .

Poor mind, what would you have them write?
Some cabalistic history
Whose authorship you might ascribe
To God? to Nature? Ah, poor ghost,
You've capitalized your Self enough.
That villainous William of Occam
Cut out the feet from under that dream
Some seven centuries ago.
It's taken that long for the mind
To waken, yawn and stretch, to see
With opened eyes emptied of speech
The real world where the spelling mind
Imposes with its grammar book
Unreal relations on the blue
Swallows. Perhaps when you will have
Fully awakened, I shall show you
A new thing: even the water
Flowing away beneath those birds
Will fail to reflect their flying forms,
And the eyes that see become as stones
Whence never tears shall fall again.

O swallows, swallows, poems are not
The point. Finding again the world,
That is the point, where loveliness

Adorns intelligible things
Because the mind's eye lit the sun.

ROBERT CREELEY

America

America, you ode for reality!
Give back the people you took.

Let the sun shine again
on the four corners of the world

you thought of first but do not
own, or keep like a convenience.

People are your own word, you
invented that locus and term.

Here, you said and say, is
where we are. Give back

what we are, these people you made,
us, and nowhere but you to be.

ROBERT PINSKY

Ode to Meaning

Dire one and desired one,
Savior, sentencer—

In an old allegory you would carry
A chained alphabet of tokens:

Ankh Badge Cross.
Dragon,
Engraved figure guarding a hallowed intaglio,
Jasper kinema of legendary Mind,
Naked omphalos pierced
By quills of rhyme or sense, torah-like: unborn
Vein of will, xenophile
Yearning out of Zero.

Untrusting I court you. Wavering
I seek your face, I read
That Crusoe's knife
Reeked of you, that to defile you
The soldier makes the rabbi spit on the torah.
"I'll drown my book" says Shakespeare.

Drowned walker, revenant.
After my mother fell on her head, she became
More than ever your sworn enemy. She spoke
Sometimes like a poet or critic of forty years later.
Or she spoke of the world as Thersites spoke of the heroes,
"I think they have swallowed one another. I
Would laugh at that miracle."

You also in the laughter, warrior angel:
Your helmet the zodiac, rocket-plumed
Your spear the beggar's finger pointing to the mouth
Your heel planted on the serpent Formulation
Your face a vapor, the wreath of cigarette smoke crowning
Bogart as he winces through it.

You not in the words, not even
Between the words, but a torsion,
A cleavage, a stirring.

You stirring even in the arctic ice,
Even at the dark ocean floor, even
In the cellular flesh of a stone.
Gas. Gossamer. My poker friends
Question your presence
In a poem by me, passing the magazine
One to another.

Not the stone and not the words, you
Like a veil over Arthur's headstone,
The passage from Proverbs he chose
While he was too ill to teach
And still well enough to read, *I was*
Beside the master craftsman

Delighting him day after day, ever
*At play in his presence—*you

A soothing veil of distraction playing over
Dying Arthur playing in the hospital,
Thumbing the Bible, fuzzy from medication,
Ever courting your presence,
And you the prognosis,
You in the cough.

Gesturer, when is your spur, your cloud?
You in the airport rituals of greeting and parting.
Indicter, who is your claimant?
Bell at the gate. Spiderweb iron bridge.
Cloak, video, aroma, rue, what is your
Elected silence, where was your seed?

What is Imagination
But your lost child born to give birth to you?

Dire one. Desired one.
Savior, sentencer—

Absence,
Or presence ever at play:
Let those scorn you who never
Starved in your dearth. If I
Dare to disparage
Your harp of shadows I taste
Wormwood and motor oil, I pour
Ashes on my head. You are the wound. You
Be the medicine.

JOY HARJO

Perhaps the World Ends Here

The world begins at a kitchen table. No matter what, we must eat
to live.

The gifts of earth are brought and prepared, set on the table. So it
has been since creation, and it will go on.

We chase chickens or dogs away from it. Babies teethe at the corners. They scrape their knees under it.

It is here that children are given instructions on what it means to be human. We make men at it, we make women.

At this table we gossip, recall enemies and the ghosts of lovers.

Our dreams drink coffee with us as they put their arms around our children. They laugh with us at our poor falling-down selves and as we put ourselves back together once again at the table.

This table has been a house in the rain, an umbrella in the sun.

Wars have begun and ended at this table. It is a place to hide in the shadow of terror. A place to celebrate the terrible victory.

We have given birth on this table, and have prepared our parents for burial here.

At this table we sing with joy, with sorrow. We pray of suffering and remorse. We give thanks.

Perhaps the world will end at the kitchen table, while we are laughing and crying, eating of the last sweet bite.

IV

Open Forms

Overview

You can see them from far away. Men and women at the back
of poetry readings or lectures on poetry. Not young. Hesi-
tant to come to the front and talk to the speaker or the poet.
But ready to do it after all. And ready with a question that is almost
always the same question. "What happened?" they will say. Or "I
grew up reading poetry and liking it." And then a pause. "But some-
thing happened."

These are the men and women—or used to be—who saw it hap-
pen: who saw the great disjunction, or at least the apparent disjunc-
tion, between the poetic forms they had grown up knowing, reading,
remembering, and loving and a sudden influx of different shapes on
the page. Who learned to think of poetry as one thing. And then
were told it was another. No wonder they felt as if something had cut
them off. Had left them stranded without the comforts and props
they had known.

But it is the contention of this book that, however understandable
their confusion and discomfort, the disjunction was not a disjunction:
It was a dialogue in disguise. The powerful fractures of form and
convention that the modernist poets initiated in the second decade of
the twentieth century were not wilful abandonments of what had
gone before. They were in fact a passionate dialogue with it.

And so the question "Is form a fiction?"—the question Eliot

and Pound and Williams and poets right up to Rich and Ashbery have asked in our time—is a question that goes to the heart of what form is. But it is also a question that goes to the heart of what form was.

This dialogue, this powerful and contentious discussion about the relation of reality to expression, far from being a headstrong rejection of the past, is one of the glories of this century's literature. The problem is to catch it and listen to it, in all its power and diversity. And, of course, in that sense it does not show itself as a discussion of rhythms and rhymes and stanzas only. But also of their source: the powerful feelings and confusions about identity, expression, and subject matter that have prompted poets of all kinds in this century to voice their feelings.

We have included here those poems that we feel give a temporary, poignant shelter to both past and future: that both strain at the bonds of the customs and conventions of historic form and yet, paradoxically, renew them by engaging them so thoroughly. Therefore, Yeats is here and also Plath, using somewhat traditional stanzas and yet, at the same time, reversing their containments with argument, tension, and vision. Adrienne Rich, Allen Ginsberg, T. S. Eliot are here, and also Langston Hughes, giving the lyric a new future by the strength of his voice. We have called this section Open Forms to suggest and confirm our view that poetic form is a continuum, and not a finished product.

W. B. YEATS

The Circus Animals' Desertion

I

I sought a theme and sought for it in vain,
I sought it daily for six weeks or so.
Maybe at last, being but a broken man,
I must be satisfied with my heart, although
Winter and summer till old age began
My circus animals were all on show,
Those stilted boys, that burnished chariot,
Lion and woman and the Lord knows what.

II

What can I but enumerate old themes?
First that sea-rider Oisin led by the nose
Through three enchanted islands, allegorical dreams,
Vain gaiety, vain battle, vain repose,
Themes of the embittered heart, or so it seems,
That might adorn old songs or courtly shows;
But what cared I that set him on to ride,
I, starved for the bosom of his faery bride?

And then a counter-truth filled out its play,
The Countess Cathleen was the name I gave it;
She, pity-crazed, had given her soul away,
But masterful Heaven had intervened to save it.
I thought my dear must her own soul destroy,
So did fanaticism and hate enslave it,
And this brought forth a dream and soon enough
This dream itself had all my thought and love.

And when the Fool and Blind Man stole the bread
Cuchulain fought the ungovernable sea;
Heart-mysteries there, and yet when all is said
It was the dream itself enchanted me:
Character isolated by a deed
To engross the present and dominate memory.
Players and painted stage took all my love,
And not those things that they were emblems of.

III

Those masterful images because complete
Grew in pure mind, but out of what began?
A mound of refuse or the sweepings of a street,
Old kettles, old bottles, and a broken can,
Old iron, old bones, that raving slut
Who keeps the till. Now that my ladder's gone,
I must lie down where all the ladders start,
In the foul rag-and-bone shop of the heart.

T. S. ELIOT

The Love Song of J. Alfred Prufrock

S'io credesse che mia risposta fosse
A persona che mai tornasse al mondo,
Questa fiamma staria senza piu scosse.
Ma perciocche giammai di questo fondo
Non torno vivo alcun, s'i'odo il vero,
Senza tema d'infamia ti rispondo.

Let us go then, you and I,
When the evening is spread out against the sky
Like a patient etherised upon a table;
Let us go, through certain half-deserted streets,
The muttering retreats
Of restless nights in one-night cheap hotels
And sawdust restaurants with oyster-shells:
Streets that follow like a tedious argument
Of insidious intent
To lead you to an overwhelming question . . .
Oh, do not ask, "What is it?"
Let us go and make our visit.

In the room the women come and go
Talking of Michelangelo.

The yellow fog that rubs its back upon the window-panes,
The yellow smoke that rubs its muzzle on the window-panes
Licked its tongue into the corners of the evening,
Lingered upon the pools that stand in drains,
Let fall upon its back the soot that falls from chimneys,
Slipped by the terrace, made a sudden leap,
And seeing that it was a soft October night,
Curled once about the house, and fell asleep.

And indeed there will be time
For the yellow smoke that slides along the street,
Rubbing its back upon the window-panes;
There will be time, there will be time
To prepare a face to meet the faces that you meet;
There will be time to murder and create,

And time for all the works and days of hands
That lift and drop a question on your plate;
Time for you and time for me,
And time yet for a hundred indecisions,
And for a hundred visions and revisions,
Before the taking of a toast and tea.

      In the room the women come and go
      Talking of Michelangelo.

      And indeed there will be time
To wonder, "Do I dare?" and, "Do I dare?"
Time to turn back and descend the stair,
With a bald spot in the middle of my hair—
[They will say: "How his hair is growing thin!"]
My morning coat, my collar mounting firmly to the chin,
My necktie rich and modest, but asserted by a simple pin—
[They will say: "But how his arms and legs are thin!"]
Do I dare
Disturb the universe?
In a minute there is time
For decisions and revisions which a minute will reverse.

      For I have known them all already, known them all—
Have known the evenings, mornings, afternoons,
I have measured out my life in coffee spoons;
I know the voices dying with a dying fall
Beneath the music from a farther room.
      So how should I presume?

      And I have known the eyes already, known them all—
The eyes that fix you in a formulated phrase,
And when I am formulated, sprawling on a pin,
When I am pinned and wriggling on the wall,
Then how should I begin
To spit out all the butt-ends of my days and ways?
      And how should I presume?

      And I have known the arms already, known them all—
Arms that are braceleted and white and bare

[But in the lamplight, downed with light brown hair!]
Is it perfume from a dress
That makes me so digress?
Arms that lie along a table, or wrap about a shawl.
  And should I then presume?
  And how should I begin?

. . . . .

Shall I say, I have gone at dusk through narrow streets
And watched the smoke that rises from the pipes
Of lonely men in shirt-sleeves, leaning out of windows? . . .

  I should have been a pair of ragged claws
Scuttling across the floors of silent seas.

. . . . .

  And the afternoon, the evening, sleeps so peacefully!
Smoothed by long fingers,
Asleep . . . tired . . . or it malingers,
Stretched on the floor, here beside you and me.
Should I, after tea and cakes and ices,
Have the strength to force the moment to its crisis?
But though I have wept and fasted, wept and prayed,
Though I have seen my head [grown slightly bald] brought in
upon a platter,
I am no prophet—And here's no great matter;
I have seen the moment of my greatness flicker,
And I have seen the eternal Footman hold my coat, and snicker,
And in short, I was afraid.

  And would it have been worth it, after all,
After the cups, the marmalade, the tea,
Among the porcelain, among some talk of you and me,
Would it have been worth while,
To have bitten off the matter with a smile,
To have squeezed the universe into a ball
To roll it toward some overwhelming question,
To say: "I am Lazarus, come from the dead,
Come back to tell you all, I shall tell you all"—

If one, settling a pillow by her head,
    Should say: "That is not what I meant at all.
    That is not it, at all."

    And would it have been worth it, after all,
Would it have been worth while,
After the sunsets and the dooryards and the sprinkled streets,
After the novels, after the teacups, after the skirts that trail along
the floor—
And this, and so much more?—
It is impossible to say just what I mean!
But as if a magic lantern threw the nerves in patterns on a screen:
Would it have been worth while
If one, settling on a pillow or throwing off a shawl,
And turning toward the window, should say:
    "That is not it at all,
    That is not what I meant, at all."

. . . . .

No! I am not Prince Hamlet, nor was meant to be;
Am an attendant lord, one that will do
To swell a progress, start a scene or two,
Advise the prince; no doubt, an easy tool,
Deferential, glad to be of use,
Politic, cautious, and meticulous;
Full of high sentence, but a bit obtuse;
At times, indeed, almost ridiculous—
Almost, at times, the Fool.

    I grow old . . . I grow old . . .
I shall wear the bottoms of my trousers rolled.

    Shall I part my hair behind? Do I dare to eat a peach?
I shall wear white flannel trousers, and walk upon the beach.
I have heard the mermaids singing, each to each.

    I do not think that they will sing to me.

    I have seen them riding seaward on the waves
Combing the white hair of the waves blown back
When the wind blows the water white and black.

We have lingered in the chambers of the sea
By sea-girls wreathed with seaweed red and brown
Till human voices wake us, and we drown.

LANGSTON HUGHES

I, Too

I, too, sing America.

I am the darker brother.
They send me to eat in the kitchen
When company comes,
But I laugh,
And eat well,
And grow strong.

Tomorrow,
I'll be at the table
When company comes.
Nobody'll dare
Say to me,
"Eat in the kitchen,"
Then.

Besides,
They'll see how beautiful I am
And be ashamed—

I, too, am America.

WALLACE STEVENS

The Idea of Order at Key West

She sang beyond the genius of the sea.
The water never formed to mind or voice,
Like a body wholly body, fluttering
Its empty sleeves; and yet its mimic motion
Made constant cry, caused constantly a cry,
That was not ours although we understood,
Inhuman, of the veritable ocean.

The sea was not a mask. No more was she.
The song and water were not medleyed sound
Even if what she sang was what she heard,
Since what she sang was uttered word by word.
It may be that in all her phrases stirred
The grinding water and the gasping wind;
But it was she and not the sea we heard.

For she was the maker of the song she sang.
The ever-hooded, tragic-gestured sea
Was merely a place by which she walked to sing.
Whose spirit is this? we said, because we knew
It was the spirit that we sought and knew
That we should ask this often as she sang.

If it was only the dark voice of the sea
That rose, or even colored by many waves;
If it was only the outer voice of sky
And cloud, of the sunken coral water-walled,
However clear, it would have been deep air,
The heaving speech of air, a summer sound
Repeated in a summer without end
And sound alone. But it was more than that,
More even than her voice, and ours, among
The meaningless plungings of water and the wind,
Theatrical distances, bronze shadows heaped
On high horizons, mountainous atmospheres
Of sky and sea.

           It was her voice that made
The sky acutest at its vanishing.
She measured to the hour its solitude.
She was the single artificer of the world
In which she sang. And when she sang, the sea,
Whatever self it had, became the self
That was her song, for she was the maker. Then we,
As we beheld her striding there alone,
Knew that there never was a world for her
Except the one she sang and, singing, made.

Ramon Fernandez, tell me, if you know,
Why, when the singing ended and we turned
Toward the town, tell why the glassy lights,
The lights in the fishing boats at anchor there,
As the night descended, tilting in the air,
Mastered the night and portioned out the sea,
Fixing emblazoned zones and fiery poles,
Arranging, deepening, enchanting night.

Oh! Blessed rage for order, pale Ramon,
The maker's rage to order words of the sea,
Words of the fragrant portals, dimly-starred,
And of ourselves and of our origins,
In ghostlier demarcations, keener sounds.

WILLIAM CARLOS WILLIAMS

Spring and All

By the road to the contagious hospital
under the surge of the blue
mottled clouds driven from the
northeast—a cold wind. Beyond, the
waste of broad, muddy fields
brown with dried weeds, standing and fallen

patches of standing water
the scattering of tall trees

All along the road the reddish
purplish, forked, upstanding, twiggy
stuff of bushes and small trees
with dead, brown leaves under them
leafless vines—

Lifeless in appearance, sluggish
dazed spring approaches—

They enter the new world naked,
cold, uncertain of all
save that they enter. All about them
the cold, familiar wind—

Now the grass, tomorrow
the stiff curl of wildcarrot leaf

One by one objects are defined—
It quickens: clarity, outline of leaf

But now the stark dignity of
entrance—Still, the profound change
has come upon them: rooted, they
grip down and begin to awaken

ALLEN GINSBERG

America

America I've given you all and now I'm nothing.
America two dollars and twentyseven cents January 17, 1956.
I can't stand my own mind.
America when will we end the human war?
Go fuck yourself with your atom bomb.
I don't feel good don't bother me.
I won't write my poem till I'm in my right mind.
America when will you be angelic?
When will you take off your clothes?
When will you look at yourself through the grave?
When will you be worthy of your million Trotskyites?
America why are your libraries full of tears?
America when will you send your eggs to India?
I'm sick of your insane demands.
When can I go into the supermarket and buy what I need with my
good looks?
America after all it is you and I who are perfect not the next world.
Your machinery is too much for me.
You made me want to be a saint.
There must be some other way to settle this argument.
Burroughs is in Tangiers I don't think he'll come back it's sinister.
Are you being sinister or is this some form of practical joke?
I'm trying to come to the point.
I refuse to give up my obsession.
America stop pushing I know what I'm doing.
America the plum blossoms are falling.

I haven't read the newspapers for months, everyday somebody goes
 on trial for murder.
America I feel sentimental about the Wobblies.
America I used to be a communist when I was a kid I'm not sorry.
I smoke marijuana every chance I get.
I sit in my house for days on end and stare at the roses in the closet.
When I go to Chinatown I get drunk and never get laid.
My mind is made up there's going to be trouble.
You should have seen me reading Marx.
My psychoanalyst thinks I'm perfectly right.
I won't say the Lord's Prayer.
I have mystical visions and cosmic vibrations.
America I still haven't told you what you did to Uncle Max after he
 came over from Russia.
I'm addressing you.
Are you going to let your emotional life be run by Time Magazine?
I'm obsessed by Time Magazine.
I read it every week.
Its cover stares at me every time I slink past the corner candystore.
I read it in the basement of the Berkeley Public Library.
It's always telling me about responsibility. Businessmen are serious.
Movie producers are serious. Everybody's serious but me.
It occurs to me that I am America.
I'm talking to myself again.

Asia is rising against me.
I haven't got a chinaman's chance.
I'd better consider my national resources.
My national resources consist of two joints of marijuana millions of
 genitals an unpublishable private literature that
 jetplanes 1400 miles an hour and twentyfive-
 thousand mental institutions.
I say nothing about my prisons nor the millions of underprivileged
 who live in my flowerpots under the light of five
 hundred suns.
I have abolished the whorehouses of France, Tangiers is the next to
 go.
My ambition is to be President despite the fact that I'm a Catholic.

America how can I write a holy litany in your silly mood?

I will continue like Henry Ford my strophes are as individual as
         his automobiles more so they're all different sexes.
America I will sell you strophes $2500 apiece $500 down on your
         old strophe
America free Tom Mooney
America save the Spanish Loyalists
America Sacco & Vanzetti must not die
America I am the Scottsboro boys.
America when I was seven momma took me to Communist Cell
         meetings they sold us garbanzos a handful per
         ticket a ticket costs a nickel and the speeches were
         free everybody was angelic and sentimental about
         the workers it was all so sincere you have no idea
         what a good thing the party was in 1835 Scott
         Nearing was a grand old man a real mensch
         Mother Bloor the Silk-strikers' Ewig-Weibliche
         made me cry I once saw the Yiddish orator Israel
         Amter plain. Everybody must have been a spy.
America you don't really want to go to war.
America it's them bad Russians.
Them Russians them Russians and them Chinamen. And them
         Russians.
The Russia wants to eat us alive. The Russia's power mad. She
         wants to take our cars from out our garages.
Her wants to grab Chicago. Her needs a Red *Reader's Digest* Her
         wants our auto plants in Siberia. Him big
         bureaucracy running our fillingstations.
That no good. Ugh. Him make Indians learn read. Him need big
         black niggers. Hah. Her make us all work sixteen
         hours a day. Help.
America this is quite serious.
America this is the impression I get from looking in the television
         set.
America is this correct?
I'd better get right down to the job.
It's true I don't want to join the Army or turn lathes in precision
         parts factories, I'm nearsighted and psychopathic
         anyway.
         America I'm putting my queer shoulder to the wheel.

FRANK O'HARA

Ave Maria

Mothers of America
           let your kids go to the movies!
get them out of the house so they won't know what you're up to
it's true that fresh air is good for the body
                        but what about the soul
that grows in darkness, embossed by silvery images
and when you grow old as grow old you must
                        they won't hate you
they won't criticize you they won't know
                  they'll be in some
                    glamorous country
they first saw on a Saturday afternoon or playing hookey
they may even be grateful to you
                for their first sexual experience
which only cost you a quarter
                and didn't upset the peaceful home
they will know where candy bars come from
                  and gratuitous bags of
                  popcorn
as gratuitous as leaving the movie before it's over
with a pleasant stranger whose apartment is in the Heaven on
    Earth Bldg
near the Williamsburg Bridge
                oh mothers you will have made the
                little tykes
so happy because if nobody does pick them up in the movies
they won't know the difference
                and if somebody does it'll be sheer
              gravy
and they'll have been truly entertained either way
instead of hanging around the yard
              or up in their room
                hating you
prematurely since you won't have done anything horribly mean
    yet

except keeping them from the darker joys
> it's unforgivable the
> latter
so don't blame me if you won't take this advice
> and the family
> breaks up
and your children grow old and blind in front of a TV set
> seeing
movies you wouldn't let them see when they were young

DENISE LEVERTOV

Uncertain Oneiromancy

I spent the entire night leading a blind man
through an immense museum
so that (by internal bridges, or tunnels?
somehow!) he could avoid the streets,
the most dangerous avenues, all the swift
chaotic traffic . . .   I persuaded him
to allow my guidance, through to the other
distant doors, though once inside, labyrinthine corridors,
steps, jutting chests and chairs and stone arches
bewildered him as I named them at each swerve,
and were hard for me to manoeuver him
around and between. As he could perceive nothing,
I too saw only the obstacles, the objects
with sharp corners: not one painting, not one carved
credenza or limestone martyr.   We did at last
emerge, however, into that part of the city
he had been headed for when I took over;
he raised his hat in farewell, and went on, uphill,
tapping his stick. I stood looking after him,
watching as the street enfolded him, wondering
if he would make it, and after I woke, wondering still
what in me he was, and who
the *I* was that took that long short-cut with him
through room after room of beauty his blindness
hid from me as if it had never been.

SYLVIA PLATH

Daddy

You do not do, you do not do
Any more, black shoe
In which I have lived like a foot
For thirty years, poor and white,
Barely daring to breathe or Achoo.

Daddy, I have had to kill you.
You died before I had time—
Marble-heavy, a bag full of God,
Ghastly statue with one gray toe
Big as a Frisco seal

And a head in the freakish Atlantic
Where it pours bean green over blue
In the waters off beautiful Nauset.
I used to pray to recover you.
Ach, du.

In the German tongue, in the Polish town
Scraped flat by the roller
Of wars, wars, wars.
But the name of the town is common.
My Polack friend

Says there are a dozen or two.
So I never could tell where you
Put your foot, your root,
I never could talk to you.
The tongue stuck in my jaw.

It stuck in a barb wire snare.
Ich, ich, ich, ich,
I could hardly speak.
I thought every German was you.
And the language obscene

An engine, an engine
Chuffing me off like a Jew.
A Jew to Dachau, Auschwitz, Belsen.

I began to talk like a Jew.
I think I may well be a Jew.

The snows of the Tyrol, the clear beer of Vienna
Are not very pure or true.
With my gipsy ancestress and my weird luck
And my Taroc pack and my Taroc pack
I may be a bit of a Jew.

I have always been scared of *you*,
With your Luftwaffe, your gobbledygoo.
And your neat mustache
And your Aryan eye, bright blue.
Panzer-man, panzer-man, O You—

Not God but a swastika
So black no sky could squeak through.
Every woman adores a Fascist,
The boot in the face, the brute
Brute heart of a brute like you.

You stand at the blackboard, daddy,
In the picture I have of you,
A cleft in your chin instead of your foot
But no less a devil for that, no not
Any less the black man who

Bit my pretty red heart in two.
I was ten when they buried you.
At twenty I tried to die
And get back, back, back to you.
I thought even the bones would do.

But they pulled me out of the sack,
And they stuck me together with glue.
And then I knew what to do.
I made a model of you,
A man in black with a Meinkampf look

And a love of the rack and the screw.
And I said I do, I do.

So daddy, I'm finally through.
The black telephone's off at the root,
The voices just can't worm through.

If I've killed one man, I've killed two—
The vampire who said he was you
And drank my blood for a year,
Seven years, if you want to know.
Daddy, you can lie back now.

There's a stake in your fat black heart
And the villagers never liked you.
They are dancing and stamping on you.
They always *knew* it was you.
Daddy, daddy, you bastard, I'm through.

ADRIENNE RICH

Diving into the Wreck

First having read the book of myths,
and loaded the camera,
and checked the edge of the knife-blade,
I put on
the body-armor of black rubber
the absurd flippers
the grave and awkward mask.
I am having to do this
not like Cousteau with his
assiduous team
aboard the sun-flooded schooner
but here alone.

There is a ladder.
The ladder is always there
hanging innocently
close to the side of the schooner.
We know what it is for,
we who have used it.
Otherwise

it's a piece of maritime floss
some sundry equipment.

I go down.
Rung after rung and still
the oxygen immerses me
the blue light
the clear atoms
of our human air.
I go down.
My flippers cripple me,
I crawl like an insect down the ladder
and there is no one
to tell me when the ocean
will begin.

First the air is blue and then
it is bluer and then green and then
black I am blacking out and yet
my mask is powerful
it pumps my blood with power
the sea is another story
the sea is not a question of power
I have to learn alone
to turn my body without force
in the deep element.

And now: it is easy to forget
what I came for
among so many who have always
lived here
swaying their crenellated fans
between the reefs
and besides
you breathe differently down here.

I came to explore the wreck.
The words are purposes.
The words are maps.
I came to see the damage that was done

and the treasures that prevail.
I stroke the beam of my lamp
slowly along the flank
of something more permanent
than fish or weed

the thing I came for:
the wreck and not the story of the wreck
the thing itself and not the myth
the drowned face always staring
toward the sun
the evidence of damage
worn by salt and sway into this threadbare beauty
the ribs of the disaster
curving their assertion
among the tentative haunters.

This is the place.
And I am here, the mermaid whose dark hair
streams black, the merman in his armored body
We circle silently
about the wreck
we dive into the hold.
I am she: I am he

whose drowned face sleeps with open eyes
whose breasts still bear the stress
whose silver, copper, vermeil cargo lies
obscurely inside barrels
half-wedged and left to rot
we are the half-destroyed instruments
that once held to a course
the water-eaten log
the fouled compass

We are, I am, you are
by cowardice or courage
the one who find our way
back to this scene

carrying a knife, a camera
a book of myths
in which
our names do not appear.

LUCILLE CLIFTON

move

On May 13, 1985 Wilson Goode, Philadelphia's first Black mayor, authorized the
bombing of 6221 Osage Avenue after the complaints of neighbors, also Black, about
the Afrocentric back-to-nature group headquartered there and calling itself Move. All
the members of the group wore dreadlocks and had taken the surname Africa. In the
bombing eleven people, including children, were killed and sixty-one homes in the
neighborhood were destroyed.

they had begun to whisper
among themselves hesitant
to be branded neighbor to the wild
haired women the naked children reclaiming a continent
away

move

he hesitated
then turned his smoky finger
toward africa toward the house
he might have lived in might have
owned or saved had he not turned
away

move

the helicopter rose at the command
higher at first then hesitating
then turning toward the center
of its own town only a neighborhood
away

move

she cried as the child stood
hesitant in the last clear sky

he would ever see the last
before the whirling blades the whirling smoke
and sharp debris carried all clarity
away

move

if you live in a mind
that would destroy itself
to comfort itself
if you would stand fire
rather than difference
do not hesitate move
away

SHARON OLDS

The Language of the Brag

I have wanted excellence in the knife-throw,
I have wanted to use my exceptionally strong and accurate arms
and my straight posture and quick electric muscles
to achieve something at the center of a crowd,
the blade piercing the bark deep,
the haft slowly and heavily vibrating like the cock.

I have wanted some epic use for my excellent body,
some heroism, some American achievement
beyond the ordinary for my extraordinary self,
magnetic and tensile, I have stood by the sandlot
and watched the boys play.

I have wanted courage, I have thought about fire
and the crossing of waterfalls, I have dragged around

my belly big with cowardice and safety,
my stool black with iron pills,
my huge breasts oozing mucus,
my legs swelling, my hands swelling,
my face swelling and darkening, my hair
falling out, my inner sex

stabbed again and again with terrible pain like a knife.
I have lain down.

I have lain down and sweated and shaken
and passed blood and feces and water and
slowly alone in the center of a circle I have
passed the new person out
and they have lifted the new person free of the act
and wiped the new person free of that
language of blood like praise all over the body.

I have done what you wanted to do, Walt Whitman,
Allen Ginsberg, I have done this thing,
I and the other women this exceptional
act with the exceptional heroic body,
this giving birth, this glistening verb,
and I am putting my proud American boast
right here with the others.

CAROLYN FORCHÉ

The Colonel

What you have heard is true. I was in his house. His wife carried
a tray of coffee and sugar. His daughter filed her nails, his son went
out for the night. There were daily papers, pet dogs, a pistol on the
cushion beside him. The moon swung bare on its black cord over
the house. On the television was a cop show. It was in English.
Broken bottles were embedded in the walls around the house to
scoop the kneecaps from a man's legs or cut his hands to lace. On
the windows there were gratings like those in liquor stores. We
had dinner, rack of lamb, good wine, a gold bell was on the table
for calling the maid. The maid brought green mangoes, salt, a type
of bread. I was asked how I enjoyed the country. There was a brief
commercial in Spanish. His wife took everything away. There was
some talk then of how difficult it had become to govern. The
parrot said hello on the terrace. The colonel told it to shut up, and
pushed himself from the table. My friend said to me with his eyes:
say nothing. The colonel returned with a sack used to bring
groceries home. He spilled many human ears on the table. They

were like dried peach halves. There is no other way to say this. He
took one of them in his hands, shook it in our faces, dropped it into
a water glass. It came alive there. I am tired of fooling around he
said. As for the rights of anyone, tell your people they can go fuck
themselves. He swept the ears to the floor with his arm and held
the last of his wine in the air. Something for your poetry, no? he
said. Some of the ears on the floor caught this scrap of his voice.
Some of the ears on the floor were pressed to the ground.

A I

The German Army, Russia, 1943

For twelve days,
I drilled through Moscow ice
to reach paradise,
that white tablecloth, set with a plate
that's cracking bit by bit
like the glassy air, like me.
I know I'll fly apart soon,
the pieces of me so light they float.
The Russians burned their crops,
rather than feed our army.
Now they strike us against each other like dry rocks
and set us on fire with a hunger
nothing can feed.
Someone calls me and I look up.
It's Hitler.
I imagine eating his terrible, luminous eyes.
Brother, he says.
I stand up, tie the rags tighter around my feet.
I hear my footsteps running after me,
but I am already gone.

YUSEF KOMUNYAKAA

Starlight Scope Myopia

Gray-blue shadows lift
shadows onto an oxcart.

Making night work for us,
the starlight scope brings
men into killing range.

The river under Vi Bridge
takes the heart away

like the Water God
riding his dragon.
Smoke-colored

Viet Cong
move under our eyelids,

lords over loneliness
winding like coral vine through
sandalwood & lotus,

inside our lowered heads
years after this scene

ends. The brain closes
down. What looks like
one step into the trees,

they're lifting crates of ammo
& sacks and rice, swaying

under their shared weight.
Caught in the infrared,
what are they saying?

Are they talking about women
or calling the Americans

beaucoup dien cai dau?
One of them is laughing.
You want to place a finger

to his lips & say "shhhh."
You try reading ghost talk

on their lips. They say
"up-up we go," lifting as one.
This one, old, bowlegged,

you feel you could reach out
& take him into your arms. You

peer down the sights of your M-16,
seeing the full moon
loaded onto an oxcart.

JORIE GRAHAM

Reading Plato

This is the story
    of a beautiful
lie, what slips
    through my fingers,
your fingers. It's winter,
    it's far

in the lifespan
    of man.
Bareheaded, in a soiled
    shirt,
speechless, my friend
    is making

lures, his hobby. Flies
    so small
he works with tweezers and
    a magnifying glass.
They must be
    so believable

they're true—feelers,
    antennae,
quick and frantic
    as something
drowning. His heart
    beats wildly
in his hands. It is
    blinding
and who will forgive him

        in his tiny
   garden? He makes them
        out of hair,

deer hair, because it's hollow
       and floats.
Past death, past sight,
       this is
his good idea, what drives
       the silly days

together. Better than memory. Better
       than love.
Then they are done, a hook
       under each pair
of wings, and it's Spring,
       and the men

wade out into the riverbed
       at dawn. Above,
the stars still connect-up
       their hungry animals.
Soon they'll be satisfied
       and go. Meanwhile

upriver, downriver, imagine, quick
       in the air,
in flesh, in a blue
       swarm of
flies, our knowledge of
       the graceful

deer skips easily across
       the surface.
Dismembered, remembered,
       it's finally
alive. Imagine
       the body

they were all once
       a part of,

these men along the lush
green banks
trying to slip in
and pass

for the natural world.

Close-Up of Open Forms

"DIVING INTO THE WRECK"

by Adrienne Rich

PHOTO © ROBERT GIARD, *PARTICULAR VOICES*; COURTESY
W. W. NORTON & COMPANY

Adrienne Rich was born in Baltimore, Maryland, in the early summer of 1929. Her father was a pathologist at Johns Hopkins University and Jewish. Her mother was Southern and Gentile. She went to Radcliffe, married and already had three young sons when this poem was written. Throughout her career, her work has addressed contradictions, tensions, paradoxes, in both ethics and craft.

As a young poet Rich was influenced by the ethos of the American mid-century. Her first book won the Yale Younger Poets Award, and she wrote in forms. "In those years" she wrote in an essay called "When We Dead Awaken" "formalism was part of the strategy— like asbestos gloves it allowed me to handle materials I couldn't pick up barehanded."

"Diving into the Wreck" employs subtle yet fierce arguments with the poetic tradition, while elaborating on and subverting the shadows, plays, and past of canonical power. The speaker has the authoritative tone of a speaker in the grand tradition. But the enterprise is entirely different. Whereas poets of the past meditated on the power and eloquence of expression, this poem—with its open weave of phrase, stanza, vernacular, and off-kilter music—puts that voice at the service of powerlessness and silence. The form challenges the past while adding to it: This is a poem that mixes a panorama of the narrative, the lyric, and the dream convention to achieve its powerful conclusion.

A Brief Glossary

accentual-syllabic meter This is the usual method of measuring **meter** in English. It is the basis for the iambic meters that form a great deal of English poetry. Both the number of syllables and accents are measured in this type of meter. Accents may be variable in this meter, but syllables are strictly counted.

alliteration Repetition of sounds, usually first letters of consonants, e.g., *silver shoon.*

assonance The use of matching vowels in consecutive words. These may be used with or against different consonants. An example from the title of an old pop song would be: *Going loco down in Acupulco.*

ballad A narrative poem usually in quatrains with a distinctive and memorable rhythm. The characteristic ballad **meter** uses **iambic tetrameter** for the first and third lines, and **iambic trimeter** for the second and fourth.

blank verse **Iambic pentameter** that is not rhymed. Widely used in Elizabethan and Jacobean drama and in *Paradise Lost* by Milton.

caesura The break in a metrical line. It can come after the second or third beat.

Arnaut Daniel Twelfth-century **troubadour** poet. He invented the **sestina,** then called the *sixtine.* Master of the *trobar clus,* or high style of troubadour poetry.

distich A strophic unit of two lines.

elegy A formal lament, either for a dead person, or as an expression of a tragic sense of life. In England, *Lycidas* by Milton set the classic elegiac convention of an elevated lament. Not since classical times—when the elegy was formulated as a *distich* with a hexameter followed by a pentameter—has the elegy been associated with any fixed metrical pattern.

enjambment   Carrying on of sense from one line to another.

envoi   A brief ending, usually not more than four lines long—most often to the **ballad,** but also to the **sestina**—which contains a summary and rounding off of the subject and argument of the poem.

heroic couplet   Two rhyming **iambic pentameter** lines. As a vehicle for epigram and statement, the couplet flourished in and came to define the mode of a great deal of eighteenth-century poetry.

heterometric stanza   A stanza using lines of differing lengths.

iamb   A unit of measure in poetry: a short syllable followed by a long, e.g., *I am.*

iambic pentameter   Pentameter is Greek for *five measures.* This line has five measures and ten syllables. It is the measure used in the **villanelle** and **sestina** and is the signature **meter** in **blank verse.**

iambic tetrameter   An accentual-syllabic **meter** with eight syllables and four stresses to the line. It is the backbone of the **ballad** form.

iambic trimeter   A line with three stresses. Often used in **ballad** meter, or with longer lines in **lyric** stanzas, for instance, from Whittier's poem *The Changeling: For the fairest maid of Hampton/The needed not to search.*

isometric stanza   A stanza using lines of the same length.

lyric   An ancient subdivision of poetry. One of poetry's three categories, the others being narrative and dramatic.

meter   Measurable patterns associated with verse composition. In English, the more usual **meter** is called **accentual-syllabic.**

octave   The name given to the first eight-line section of the **Petrarchan sonnet.** The second section is the **sestet.**

ode   A formal, ceremonious lyric poem, often used to address a person on a public or state occasion. In modern times the ode has also addressed private states of crisis or emblematic objects. Although the early Greek Pindaric ode had a set form, odes in the English language vary in length and structure.

ottava rima   A **stanza** of eight iambic lines usually rhyming *abababcc.* A fast narrative stanza, Byron used it for *Don Juan.*

pantoum   A poetic form that is not of fixed length—so it may be long or short—and is composed of quatrains in which the second and fourth lines of each **stanza** serve as the first and third lines of the next until the last stanza when the first line of the poem reappears as the last.

pastoral   A convention that celebrated the virtues of rural life and largely idealized them. This idealization became an important part of poetry's perspective on itself as a value system seeking to recover a lost golden age. With the Industrial Revolution in England the pastoral fell into disuse. But it remains a shadow behind nature poetry to this day.

Petrarchan sonnet   The first and very influential form of the **sonnet** set by the Italian poet Francesco Petrarca in the fourteenth century. His sonnet has an **octave** and a **sestet.** The rhyme scheme is *abbaabba* and *cdecde.*

quasi-stanzaic   A loose grouping of lines and paragraphs within a poem.

sestet   The last six iambic lines of the Italian or **Petrarchan sonnet.** Often the octet states the proposition and the sestet answers it.

sestina   A form of thirty-nine lines and six **stanzas,** with a three-line **envoi** at the end. There are no rhymes. The form works by repetition of end-words, six in all, which are repeated throughout the poem in a shifting order with a fixed pattern.

Shakespearian sonnet   The sonnet form evolved in England, and used by Shakespeare—though not invented by him. Howard, Earl of Surrey (1517–1547), developed it. It consists of three quatrains and a couplet—*abab cdcd efef gg*—which suited the rhyme-poor English language better than the Italian model of **octave** and **sestet.**

sonnet   A fourteen-line poem in **iambic pentameter** with a variable rhyme scheme. There are two types of traditional sonnets: the first the **Petrarchan with** an **octave** and **sestet.** The second the Shakespearian with three **quatrains** and a rhyming couplet.

stanza   Literally "station" or "stopping place." A structural unit in a poem with a pattern of rhyme and **meter** that is repeated throughout the poem.

trochee   An important unit of **meter** in which a long foot is followed by a short one. At the start of a line this produces a distinct effect. Yeats's *Sailing to Byzantium* begins with a trochee: *THAT is no country for old men.*

troubadours   Poets of the twelfth century from the Occitan region of France. One of them, Arnaut Daniel, invented the *sixtine,* or **sestina.**

villanelle   A closed form of nineteen lines. It has five **stanzas.** Each of these are three lines long, with a final stanza of four lines. The first line of the first stanza is repeated as the last line of the second and fourth stanzas.

Biographies and Further Reading

Ai (1947–)

Born in Texas, educated at the University of Arizona and the University of California, Irvine. Her second book, *Killing Floor* (1979), received the James Laughlin Poetry Award from the Academy of American Poets. She has published five books of poetry and has received fellowships from the Guggenheim Foundation, the NEA, and Radcliffe, among others. She lives in Boulder, Colorado.

Selected publications: *Fate: New Poems* (1991); *Greed* (1993); *Vice: New and Selected Poems* (1999).

Matthew Arnold (1822–1888)

Born in England, educated at Oxford. Became an inspector of schools and was professor of poetry at Oxford from 1857 to 1867. His social and literary criticism was both celebrated and influential in Victorian England.

Selected publications: *The Poems of Matthew Arnold*, Kenneth Allott, ed. (1979); *The Letters of Matthew Arnold*, Cecil Lang, ed. (1996). Biographical and critical works: *A Life of Matthew Arnold*, Nicholas Murray (1997).

John Ashbery (1927–)

Born in Rochester, New York. Educated at Harvard. His *Self Portrait in a Convex Mirror* (1976) won three major poetry prizes. Among his awards are fellowships from the Academy of American Poets, and the Fulbright, MacArthur, and Guggenheim foundations.

Selected publications: *Selected Poems* (1985); *Hotel Lautrémont* (1992); *And the Stars Were Shining* (1994); *Can You Hear, Bird* (1995); *Wakefulness* (1998); *Girls on the Run: A Poem* (1999). Biographical and critical works: *Five Temperaments: Elizabeth Bishop, Robert Lowell, James Merrill, Adrienne Rich, John Ashbery*, David Kalstone (1977); *The Tribe of John Ashbery and Contemporary Poetry*, Susan M. Schultz, ed. (1995).

W. H. Auden (1907–1973)

Born in York, England. Educated in private schools and at Oxford. Received the Queen's Gold Medal for Poetry at an early age. After the outbreak of World War II, he made his home in the United States. He was also a noted librettist.

Selected publications: *The Dyer's Hand and Other Essays* (1962); *Collected Poems* (1976); *The English Auden: Poems, Essays and Dramatic Writings 1927–1939* (1977).

George Barker (1913–   )

Born in Essex, England. Attended Regent Street Polytechnic in London. His first book of verse was *Thirty Preliminary Poems* (1933). His early work has been described as "lyrical, intensely personal, and tragic." He moved to the United States in 1940, but returned to England three years later. Won *Poetry* magazine's Levinson Prize in 1966.

Selected publications: *Collected Poems,* Robert Fraser, ed. (1987); *Street Ballads* (1992). Biographical and critical works: *George Barker,* Martha Fodaski (1969).

Barnabe Barnes (1569–1609)

Educated at Brasenose College, Oxford, he was a prolific writer of verse. In addition to *Parthenophil and Parthenophe, Sonnetts, Madrigals, Elegies and Odes,* first published in 1593, he also wrote *A Divine Centurie of Spirituall Sonnets* (1595) and an anti-popish tragedy, *The Devil's Charter.*

Selected publications: *Parthenophil and Parthenophe,* Victor A. Doyno, ed. (1971); *The Devil's Charter,* Jim Pogue, ed. (1980). Biographical and critical works: *Lyric Forms in the Sonnet Sequences of Barnabe Barnes,* Philip E. Blank (1974).

John Berryman (1914–1972)

Born in Oklahoma. Educated at Columbia and Cambridge. *Homage to Mistress Bradstreet* (1956) won him wide acclaim. *77 Dream Songs* (1964) showed him to be a daring and innovative formalist.

Selected publications: *Selected Poems 1938–1968* (1972); *Collected Poems 1937–1971* (1989). Biographical and critical works: *The Freedom of the Poet* (1976); *Dream Song: The Life of John Berryman,* Paul L. Mariani (1990).

John Betjeman (1906–1984)

Born in London. Educated at Oxford where he met Auden. Apart from his poetry, he wrote a series of regional guidebooks and studies of Oxford and of the English landscape. He was appointed Poet Laureate of Great Britain in 1972.

Selected publications: *Collected Poems* (1970); *Metro-land: Verses* (1977); *Uncollected Poems* (1982). Biographical and critical works: *John Betjeman: His Life and Work,* Patrick Taylor-Martin (1983).

Frank Bidart (1939–   )

Born in Bakersfield, California. Educated at the University of California at

Riverside and Harvard, where he became a close friend of both Elizabeth Bishop and Robert Lowell. His many honors include the Lila Wallace–Reader's Digest Foundation Writer's Award, the Morton Dauwen Zabel Award given by the American Academy of Arts and Letters, the Shelley Award of the Poetry Society of America, and the *Paris Review*'s first Bernard F. Connor Prize.

Selected publications: *Golden State* (1973); *Book of the Body* (1977); *In the Western Night, Collected Poems 1965–1990* (1990); *Desire* (1997).

Elizabeth Bishop (1911–1979)

Born in Worcester, Massachusetts. Educated at Vassar. Lived in Key West and, later, in Brazil. In the last years of her life she taught at Harvard. Her distinctive voice was admired by her contemporaries, including Lowell and Jarrell. Her use and renewal of closed forms is among the most exemplary in the century.

Selected publications: *The Complete Poems 1927–1979* (1983); *The Collected Prose,* Robert Giroux, ed. (1984); *One Art: Letters of Elizabeth Bishop,* Robert Giroux, ed. (1994). Biographical and critical works: *Becoming a Poet,* David Kalstone (1989); *Elizabeth Bishop: The Biography of a Poetry,* Lorrie Goldensohn (1992).

William Blake (1757–1827)

Born in London. He attended art school and was apprenticed as an engraver to the Society of Antiquaries. In 1789 he engraved and published *Songs of Innocence. Songs of Experience* appeared in 1794.

Selected publications: *The Poetry and Prose of William Blake,* David V. Erdman and Harold Bloom, eds. (1982). Biographical and critical works: *William Blake,* Martin K. Nurmi (1976); *Blake,* Peter Ackroyd (1995).

Louise Bogan (1897–1970)

Born in Maine. Educated at the Girl's Latin School in Boston and at Boston University. She was the poetry critic of *The New Yorker* for many years. In addition to her poetry she published a prose book, *Achievement in American Poetry: 1900–1950.*

Selected publications: *Collected Poems 1923–1953* (1954); *Selected Criticism: Poetry and Prose* (1955); *The Blue Estuaries: Poems 1923–1968* (1977). Biographical and critical works: *Louise Bogan: A Portrait,* Elizabeth Frank (1986).

Anne Bradstreet (c. 1612–1672)

Born in England. Emigrated to Massachusetts in 1630. Her volume of poems, *The Tenth Muse, Lately Sprung Up in America,* was published in England in 1650 and in Boston in 1678.

Selected publications: *Works of Anne Bradstreet in Prose and Verse* (1867); *The Complete Works of Anne Bradstreet* (1981). Biographical and critical works: *Anne Bradstreet: The Tenth Muse,* Elizabeth W. White (1971); *The Norton Anthology of Literature by Women: The Tradition in English,* Sandra Gilbert and Susan Gubar, eds. (1985); *Anne Bradstreet Revisited,* Rosamond Rosenmeier (1991).

Lucie Brock-Broido (1956–   )

She has taught at Harvard University, at the Bennington Writing Seminars, and at Princeton University, and is now director of poetry in Columbia's Writing Division. In addition to numerous awards, she is the recipient of an NEA Poetry Fellowship. She lives in New York City and in Cambridge, Massachusetts.

Selected publications: *A Hunger* (1988); *The Master Letters* (1995).

Emily Brontë (1818–1848)

Born in Yorkshire, the sister of Charlotte and Anne. Using the pseudonym Ellis Bell she published the novel *Wuthering Heights* in 1847. She also wrote poetry and short fiction, but her early death prevented a larger output.

Selected publications: *The Complete Poems* (1941). Biographical and critical works: *The Madwoman in the Attic,* Sandra M. Gilbert and Susan Gubar (1979).

Gwendolyn Brooks (1917–   )

Born in Topeka, Kansas. Grew up in Chicago where she attended Englewood High School and Wilson Junior College. She succeeded Carl Sandburg as Poet Laureate of Illinois. Her volume *Annie Allen* (1949) received the Pulitzer Prize.

Selected publications: *A Street in Bronzeville* (1945); *Aloneness* (1971); *Report from Part One: An Autobiography* (1972); *The Near-Johannesburg Boy and Other Poems* (1986); *Report from Part Two* (1996); *Selected Poems* (1999). Biographical and critical works: *A Life of Gwendolyn Brooks,* George E. Kent (1990).

Sterling A. Brown (1901–1989)

Born in Washington, D.C. Educated at Williams College and Harvard. Taught at Virginia Seminary College and Howard. A committed folklorist, he was profoundly interested in African-American music and dialect as a source for his own work.

Selected publications: *Southern Road* (1932); *The Last Ride of Wild Bill and Eleven Narrative Poems* (1975); *The Collected Poems of Sterling Brown*

(1980); *A Son's Return: Selected Essays of Sterling A. Brown,* Mark A. Sanders, ed. (1996).

Elizabeth Barrett Browning (1806–1861)

Born in Herefordshire, England. Lived as an invalid until she eloped to Italy with Robert Browning. She lived mostly in Italy where she became an advocate for Italian unification, and died in Florence.

Selected publications: *Complete Works of Elizabeth Barrett Browning,* Helen A. Clarke and Charlotte Porter, eds. (1900). Biographical and critical works: *The Life of Elizabeth Barrett Browning,* Gardner B. Taplin (1957); *Aurora Leigh: Authoritative Text, Backgrounds and Contexts,* Margaret Reynolds, ed. (1995).

Robert Browning (1812–1889)

Born in Camberwell, London. Lived in Italy in later years. In 1846 he married Elizabeth Barrett. After her death, he returned to London.

Selected publications: *The Complete Works of Robert Browning* (1969). Biographical and critical works: *Dared and Done: The Marriage of Elizabeth Barrett and Robert Browning,* Julia Markus (1995).

George Gordon, Lord Byron (1788–1824)

Born in Scotland. Educated at Cambridge. Inherited title when he was ten years old. The first part of *Childe Harold* was published in 1812 to great acclaim. Died at Missolonghi in struggle for Greek freedom.

Selected publications: *Complete Poetical Works* (1905). Biographical and critical works: *Byron: Child of Passion, Fool of Fame,* Benita Eisler (1999).

Hayden Carruth (1921–)

Born in Connecticut, educated at Chapel Hill and the University of Chicago. He has won the National Book Critics Circle Award and the National Book Award for Poetry.

Selected publications: *Collected Shorter Poems, 1946–1991* (1992); *Collected Longer Poems* (1993). Biographical and critical works: *Reluctantly: Autobiographical Essays* (1998).

Geoffrey Chaucer (c. 1343–1400)

Born in London. Was both a courtier and a diplomat. His openness to French and Italian literature, and its effect on his own work, allowed him to influence and change the usage of the English language in poetry.

Selected publications: *The Riverside Chaucer,* Larry D. Benson, ed. (1987). Biographical and critical works: *Chaucer and His Readers: Imagining the Author in Late-Medieval England,* Seth Lerer (1993).

Eiléan Ní Chuilleanáin (1942–)
Born in Cork. Educated at University College Cork. She teaches at Trinity College Dublin. In addition to her poetry she is an editor of the magazine *Cyphers.*

Selected publications: *The Second Voyage: Selected Poems* (1986); *The Magdalene Sermon* (1989); *The Brazen Serpent* (1995).

Amy Clampitt (1920–1994)
Born in New Providence, Iowa. Educated at Grinnell College. Worked for Oxford University Press, then as a freelance author and editor. First poetry collection, *Multitudes, Multitudes,* was published in 1974. Among her many awards was a MacArthur Fellowship.

Selected publications: *The Kingfisher* (1983); *What the Light Was Like* (1985); *Archaic Figures* (1987); *The Collected Poems of Amy Clampitt* (1997).

Lucille Clifton (1936–)
Born in Depew, New York. She has served as Poet Laureate for the State of Maryland. Her many awards include the Shelley Award and the "Discovery"/*The Nation* Award, as well as an Emmy Award from the American Academy of Television Arts and Sciences.

Selected publications: *Next: New Poems* (1987); *Good Woman: Poems and a Memoir 1969–1980* (1987); *Quilting, Poems 1987–1990* (1991); *The Book of Light* (1993); *The Terrible Stories: Poems* (1996).

Henri Cole (1956–)
Born in Fukuoka, Japan, reared in Virginia. Attended William and Mary, the University of Wisconsin at Milwaukee, and Columbia. He has taught poetry at Harvard and now teaches at Brandeis. His books have received many awards, including the Rome Fellowship in Literature from the American Academy of Arts and Letters. He was executive director of the Academy of American Poets from 1982 to 1988, and has taught at Columbia, Reed College, Yale, and the University of Maryland.

Selected publications: *The Marble Queen* (1986), *The Zoo Wheel of Knowledge* (1989); *The Look of Things* (1995); *Visible Man* (1998).

Jane Cooper (1924–)
Born in Atlantic City, New Jersey. She is the author of four books of poetry. *The Weather of Six Mornings* (1969) won the James Laughlin Poetry Award from the Academy of American Poets. She has received an Award in Literature from the American Academy of Arts and Letters, the Shelley Award, and fellowships from the Bunting Institute of Radcliffe College, the Guggenheim Foundation, the Ingram Merrill Foundation, and the NEA.

She taught for many years at Sarah Lawrence College and was the 1996–97 New York State Poet. She lives in New York City.

Selected publications: *Maps and Windows* (1974); *Scaffolding: Selected Poems* (1993); *Green Notebook, Winter Road* (1994); *The Flashboat: Poems Collected and Reclaimed* (1999).

Wendy Cope (1945–)
Born in Kent, England. Educated at Oxford. Her first book, *Making Cocoa for Kingsley Amis* (1986), was notable for its parodies of classical and contemporary forms. She has taught primary school and music and was an editor at *Contact* magazine.

Selected publications: *Serious Concerns* (1992).

Alfred Corn (1943–)
Born in Georgia but a longtime resident of New York City. Educated at Emory and Columbia. First collection, *All Roads at Once,* was published in 1976. Has won many awards, including a fellowship from the Academy of American Poets. In addition to his poetry he has published *The Metamorphoses of Metaphor,* a collection of critical essays. He has taught at Columbia, Yale, and CUNY, among others.

Selected publications: *Notes from a Child of Paradise* (1984); *The West Door* (1988); *Autobiographies: Poems* (1992); *The Poem's Heartbeat: A Manual of Prosody* (1997); *Stake: Poems, 1972–1992* (1999).

Hart Crane (1899–1932)
Born in Garretsville, Ohio. When his parents divorced he dropped out of high school and moved to New York without finishing high school. His major poem, *The Bridge,* was published in 1930. On a return voyage from Mexico to the United States he committed suicide by jumping into the sea.

Selected publications: *The Complete Poems and Selected Letters and Prose* (1966); *The Poems of Hart Crane,* Marc Simon, ed. (1986). Biographical and critical works: *The Broken Tower: A Life of Hart Crane,* Paul Mariani (1999).

Douglas Crase (1944–)
Born in Michigan. A widely anthologized poet, essayist, and critic. His volume of poetry, *The Revisionist* (1981), earned nominations for the National Book Critics Circle Award and the American Book Award in poetry. He has received an Ingram Merrill Award, a Whiting Writer's Award, and fellowships from the MacArthur and Guggenheim foundations and the American Academy and Institute of Arts and Letters.

Selected publications: *Amerifil.txt: A Commonplace Book* (compiled by Douglas Crase) (1996).

Robert Creeley (1926–   )
Born in Arlington, Massachusetts. Educated at Harvard but left to join the American Field Service in India and Burma. Taught at Black Mountain College and took an additional degree from the University of New Mexico. He is the founder-editor of the *Black Mountain Review*.

Selected publications: *The Collected Poems of Robert Creeley 1945–1975* (1982); *Mirrors* (1983); *The Collected Prose of Robert Creeley* (1984); *Memory Gardens* (1986); *Windows* (1990); *Selected Poems, 1945–1990* (1991); *Life & Death* (1993).

Countee Cullen (1903–1946)
Born in Louisville, Kentucky, he was raised by an Episcopal minister in New York City, and educated at New York University. Completed his master's degree at Harvard. He spent much of his life teaching in New York schools until his early death.

Selected publications: *Color* (1925); *Copper Sun* (1927); *The Ballad of the Brown Girl* (1928); *The Black Christ and Other Poems* (1929); *The Medea and Some Other Poems* (1935); *My Soul's High Song: The Collected Writings of Countee Cullen, Voice of the Harlem Renaissance,* Gerald Early, ed. (1991). Biographical and critical works: *Bio-bibliography of Countee P. Cullen,* Margaret Perry, ed. (1971).

E. E. Cummings (1894–1962)
Born in Cambridge, Massachusetts. Educated at Harvard. In 1916, he volunteered to go to France as a member of an ambulance corps. He was interned in a prison camp by the French for his outspoken pacifism and criticism of the Allied efforts, which became the basis of his semi-fictional *The Enormous Room* (1922).

Selected publications: *E. E. Cummings: Complete Poems 1904–1962* (1980). Biographical and critical works: *Dreams in the Mirror: A Biography of E. E. Cummings,* Richard S. Kennedy (1980).

Babette Deutsch (1895–1982)
Born in New York City. Educated at Barnard and Columbia. In addition to numerous book of poetry, she published novels, literary criticism, and children's books. She also translated several poetry books. She taught at Columbia for over twenty years.

Selected publications: *Honey Out of the Rock* (1925); *Animal, Vegetable, Mineral* (1954); *The Collected Poems of Babette Deutsch* (1969).

Emily Dickinson (1830–1886)
Born in Amherst, Massachusetts. She lived an intense imaginative life within a small circle of family and friends and did not publish widely in her

lifetime. *The Complete Poems of Emily Dickinson* was first published in 1924. Selected publications: *Poems* (1955). Biographical and critical works: *Letters*, Thomas H. Johnson and Theodora Ward, eds. (1958); *Emily Dickinson: The Mind of the Poet*, Al Gelpi (1965); *The Life of Emily Dickinson*, Richard B. Sewall (1974).

Austin Dobson (1840–1921)

Born in England. Educated at Beaumaris Grammar School and worked for many years in the Board of Trade. He was an accomplished writer of light verse and also wrote a number of important literary biographies.

Selected publications: *Complete Poetical Works of Austin Dobson* (1923). Biographical and critical works: *Bibliography of Austin Dobson*, F. E. Murray (1968).

John Donne (1572–1631)

Born in London. Studied law. Worked as a political secretary. Became Dean of St. Paul's later in life and was a celebrated preacher.

Selected publications: *Complete Poetry*, John T. Shawcross, ed. (1967). Biographical and critical works: *Life and Letters of John Donne*, Edmund Gosse (1899); *John Donne: A Life*, R. C. Bald (1970).

Mark Doty (1953–   )

Born in Tennessee. Educated at Drake University and Goddard College. Among his awards are fellowships from the Guggenheim, Ingram Merrill, Rockefeller, and Whiting foundations. He lives in Provincetown, Massachusetts, and Salt Lake City, where he teaches at the University of Utah.

Selected publications: *Atlantis* (1995); *Heaven's Coast: A Memoir* (1996); *Sweet Machine* (1998).

Ernest Dowson (1867–1900)

Born in Kent, England. Educated at Oxford. He supported himself as a translator until his early death. A founding member of the Rhymers' Club with Yeats.

Selected publications: *Poetical Works of Ernest Dowson* (1967); *The Letters of Ernest Dowson*, Desmond Flower and Henry Maas, eds. (1967). Biographical and critical works: *Ernest Dowson*, Mark Longaker (1967); *Eight Late Victorian Poets Shaping the Artistic Sensibility of an Age*, Jean R. Halladay (1993).

Michael Drayton (1563–1631)

Born in Warwickshire, England. He was an influential writer of religious verse and of odes, sonnets, and satire. His topographical poem on England, *Polyolbion*, was completed in 1622.

Selected publications: *The Works of Michael Drayton,* J. William Hebel, ed. (1931). Biographical and critical works: *Michael Drayton and His Circle,* B. H. Newdigate, ed. (1941).

John Dryden (1631–1700)

Born in England. Educated at Westminster and Cambridge. Noted for his satiric verse and command of the dramatic couplet. He was appointed Poet Laureate in 1668 and wrote extensively for the theater. He also translated Virgil.

Selected publications: *The Poetry of John Dryden,* Van Doren, ed. (1920). Biographical and critical works: *John Dryden: A Literary Life,* Paul Hammond (1953).

Carol Ann Duffy (1955–   )

Born in Glasgow. Educated at University of Liverpool. Her first book, *Standing Female Nude,* was published in 1985. Has received a Lannan Award for poetry and the Forward Prize. She is poetry editor of *Ambit* magazine.

Selected publications: *Selling Manhattan* (1987); *The Other Country* (1990); *Mean Time* (1993); *Meeting Midnight* (1999).

William Dunbar (c. 1460–c. 1525)

Born in Scotland. Little is known of his life. He may have been a Franciscan friar. Was a courtier as well as a cleric, traveled widely, and was receptive to the new cultures of poetry in Europe.

Selected publications: *Poems of William Dunbar* (1932).

T. S. Eliot (1888–1965)

Born in St. Louis. Educated at Harvard and Oxford. In 1910 he wrote "The Love Song of J. Alfred Prufrock." Shortly afterward, he moved to London. *The Waste Land* was published in 1922. His last important poems were *The Four Quartets.* He founded an important new review, the *Criterion.* He wrote a number of commercially successful verse plays and many influential critical essays. In 1948 he was awarded the Nobel Prize for Literature.

Selected publications: *The Complete Poems and Plays* (1969); *Selected Prose of T. S. Eliot,* Frank Kermode, ed. (1975). Biographical and critical works: *The Invisible Poet: T. S. Eliot,* Hugh Kenner (1959); *T. S. Eliot,* Peter Ackroyd (1984).

William Empson (1906–1984)

Born in Yorkshire, England, educated at Cambridge. A professor of English, his poems and criticisms reflect his engagement with the many layers of language.

Selected publications: *Seven Types of Ambiguity* (1930, rev. 1947); *Collected Poems* (1955). Biographical and critical works: *Critical Essays on William Empson,* John Constable, ed. (1993).

Anne Finch, Countess of Winchilsea (1661–1720)

Born in Berkshire, England. She was a maid of honor in the Stuart Court where she met her husband, Heneage Finch, future Earl of Winchilsea. Her admirers and friends included Jonathan Swift and Alexander Pope, both of whom encouraged her to write and publish. Her early poems were published anonymously; however, in 1713, *Miscellany Poems, on Several Occasions* appeared in print. She is significant as one of the earliest published women poets in England. Her poetry sparkles with witty commentary and playful humor.

Selected publications: *Selected Poems of Anne Finch, Countess of Winchilsea,* Katharine M. Rogers, ed. (1979); *The Wellesley Manuscript Poems of Anne, Countess of Winchilsea,* Jean M. Ellis D'Allessandro, ed. (1988). Biographical and critical works: *Anne Finch and Her Poetry: A Critical Biography,* Barbara McGovern (1992).

Carolyn Forché (1950–)

Born in Detroit, Michigan, and earned degrees from Michigan State University and Bowling Green State University. She won the Yale Series of Younger Poets Award for *Gathering the Tribes* (1976). She is a Lannan Foundation Fellow and has received fellowships from the Guggenheim Foundation and the NEA.

Selected publications: *The Country Between Us* (1981); *Against Forgetting: Twentieth Century Poetry of Witness,* Carolyn Forché, ed. (1993); *The Angel of History* (1994).

Robert Frost (1874–1963)

Born in San Francisco and lived there for eleven years. He went to Dartmouth but dropped out in the first semester. In 1912 he moved with his family to England. He returned to the United States in 1915 and, in the decades that followed, became one of America's most celebrated poets.

Selected publications: *Complete Poems* (1949); *The Poetry of Robert Frost* (1969); *Robert Frost: Poetry and Prose* (1972). Biographical and critical works: *Homage to Robert Frost,* Joseph Brodsky et al., eds. (1996); *Robert Frost: A Life,* Jay Parini (1999).

Allen Ginsberg (1926–1997)

Born in Newark, New Jersey. Studied at Columbia University in the 1940s, where he began the friendships and associations that resulted in the grouping known as the Beat Generation. His first book of poems, *Howl* (1956), was a radical focus of new energies in American poetry.

Selected publications: *Siesta in Xbalba and Return to the States* (1956); *Empty Mirror: Early Poems* (1961); *Kaddish and Other Poems, 1958–1960* (1961); *Cosmopolitan Greetings: Poems, 1986–1992* (1994); *Journals Mid-Fifties 1954–1958* (1995); *Selected Poems 1947–1995* (1996). Biographical and critical works: *Towards a New American Poetics: Essays and Interviews*, Ekbert Faas, ed. (1978); *Ginsberg*, Barry Miles (1989).

Louise Glück (1943–)
Born in New York City. Educated at Sarah Lawrence and Columbia. Her first collection, *Firstborn*, was published in 1968. She won the National Book Critics Circle Award in 1985. *The Wild Iris* (1992) received the Pulitzer Prize and the Poetry Society of America's William Carlos Williams Award. She teaches poetry at Williams College and lives in Cambridge.

Selected publications: *Descending Figure* (1980); *The Triumph of Achilles* (1985); *Ararat* (1990); *Proofs and Theories: Essays on Poetry* (1994); *The First Four Books of Poems* (1995); *Vita Nova* (1999). Biographical and critical works: *The Veiled Mirror and the Woman Poet: H. D., Louise Bogan, Elizabeth Bishop, and Louise Glück*, Elizabeth Dodd (1992).

Oliver Goldsmith (1730–1774)
Born in Ireland. Educated at Trinity College, Dublin. He wrote extensively for *London* magazine. *The Deserted Village* was published in 1770.

Selected publications: *Collected Works* (1966). Biographical and critical works: *The True Genius of Oliver Goldsmith*, R. H. Hopkins (1969).

Edmund Gosse (1849–1928)
Born in England and became a transcriber at the British Museum. A critic, essayist, and journalist, he was also Librarian at the House of Lords.

Selected publications: *Collected Poems of Edmund Gosse* (1911). Biographical and critical works: *Edmund Gosse: A Literary Landscape, 1849–1928*, Ann Thwaite (1984).

Jorie Graham (1951–)
Born in Italy. Educated at the Sorbonne, Columbia, and University of Iowa. Among her many awards and fellowships are a MacArthur Fellowship and the Pulitzer Prize. She teaches at the Iowa Writers' Workshop.

Selected publications: *Hybrids of Plants and of Ghosts* (1980); *Erosion* (1983); *Region of Unlikeness* (1992); *The Dream of the Unified Field: Selected Poems 1974–1994* (1995). Biographical and critical works: *The Breaking of Style: Hopkins, Heaney, Graham*, Helen Vendler (1995).

Thomas Gray (1716–1771)

Born in London. Educated at Eton and Cambridge. He refused the Poet Laureateship in 1757. Appointed Regius Professor of Modern History at Cambridge in 1768. *Elegy in a Country Churchyard* was finished in 1750.

Selected publications: *Poems of Thomas Gray*, William Collins et al., eds. (1969). Biographical and critical works: *Thomas Gray: The Progress of a Poet*, B. Eugene McCarthy (1997).

Thom Gunn (1929–   )

Born in Gravesend, England. Educated at Cambridge and Stanford. He has won the Lenore Marshall Poetry Prize of the Academy of American Poets, as well as a MacArthur Fellowship. He lives in San Francisco.

Selected publications: *Collected Poems* (1993); *Shelf Life: Essays, Memoirs, and an Interview* (1993); *Frontiers of Gossip* (1998).

Ivor Gurney (1890–1937)

Born in Gloucester. Attended the Royal College of Music. At the outset of World War I he was posted to the front, where he was gassed and wounded. He was committed briefly to a hospital for shell shock, where he wrote his first book of poetry, *Severne and Somme* (1917). In 1922 he was diagnosed with schizophrenia and committed to a London hospital, where he died.

Selected publications: *Poems of Ivor Gurney* (1973). Biographical and critical works: *Ivor Gurney*, George Walter (1998).

Marilyn Hacker (1942–   )

Born in New York City, she was educated at New York University and the Arts Student League. She has worked as an antiquarian bookseller and as the editor of both books and magazines. She has won many awards, including the James Laughlin Poetry Award from the Academy of American Poets and a National Book Award.

Selected publications: *Love, Death, and the Changing of the Seasons* (1986); *Selected Poems, 1965–1990* (1994); *Winter Numbers* (1994); *Squares and Courtyards* (2000).

Thomas Hardy (1840–1928)

Born in Dorset, England. Early in his life he practiced as an architect. Better known as a novelist in his lifetime, he has become increasingly influential as a poet since his death.

Selected publications: *The Complete Poems*, James Gibson, ed. (1976). Biographical and critical works: *Thomas Hardy: A Literary Life*, James Gibson (1996).

Joy Harjo (1951–)
Born in Tulsa, Oklahoma. *In Mad Love and War* (1990) received an American Book Award and the Delmore Schwartz Memorial Award. Her many honors include the William Carlos Williams Award and fellowships from the Arizona Commission on the Arts, the Witter Bynner Foundation, and the National Endowment for the Arts. She also performs her poetry and plays saxophone with her band, Poetic Justice. She lives in Albuquerque, New Mexico.

Selected publications: *What Moon Drove Me to This?* (1979); *She Had Some Horses* (1983); *Secrets from the Center of the World* (1989); *The Woman Who Fell From the Sky* (1994); *A Map to the Next World* (2000).

Gwen Harwood (1920–1995)
Born and educated in Brisbane, Australia. She also wrote critical essays, fiction, and libretti.

Selected publications: *The Lion's Bride* (1981); *Bone Scan* (1988); *Collected Poems* (1991). Biographical and critical works: *Gwen Harwood*, Stephanie Trigg (1994).

Robert Hass (1941–)
Born in San Francisco. Educated at St. Mary's College and at Stanford University. He won the 1972 Yale Series of Younger Poets Award for *Field Guide* (1973) and the National Book Critics Circle Award for *Sun Under Wood* (1996). He was Poet Laureate of the United States from 1995 to 1997.

Selected publications: *Praise* (1979); *Twentieth Century Pleasures: Prose on Poetry* (essays) (1984); *Human Wishes* (1989). Biographical and critical works: *Regions of Unlikeness: Explaining Contemporary Poetry*, Thomas Gardner (1999).

Robert Hayden (1913–1980)
Born Asa Bundy Sheffey in Detroit. Studied with Auden at the University of Michigan. First book, *Heart-Shape in the Dust*, was published in 1940. He won the Hopwood Award for Poetry on two occasions and the Grand Prize for Poetry at the Dakar Festival of the Arts. Became Consultant in Poetry to the Library of Congress (the forerunner of the U.S. Poet Laureatship) in 1976.

Selected publications: *American Journal* (1978); *Collected Poems* (1985). Biographical and critical works: *Robert Hayden*, Fred M. Fetrow (1984).

Seamus Heaney (1939–)
Born in County Derry, Northern Ireland. Educated at Queen's University. He has held a professorship at Harvard, was Oxford Professor of Poetry in

1989, and was awarded the Nobel Prize for Literature in 1995. In addition to his poetry he has written critical essays and drama.

Selected publications: *Selected Poems 1965–1975* (1980); *Government of the Tongue* (1988); *The Redress of Poetry* (1995); *Opened Ground: Poems 1966–1996* (1998). Biographical and critical works: *Seamus Heaney,* Helen Vendler (1998).

Anthony Hecht (1923–   )

Born in New York City. After graduating from Bard College, he joined the U.S. Army and served in both Europe and Japan. His second book, *The Hard Hours* (1967), was awarded the Pulitzer Prize. He has taught at Rochester and Georgetown.

Selected publications: *Millions of Strange Shadows* (1977); *The Venetian Vespers* (1979); *Transparent Man* (1990); *Collected Earlier Poems* (1990); *Flight Among the Tombs* (1996). Biographical and critical works: *The Burdens of Formality: Essays on the Poetry of Anthony Hecht,* Sydney Lea, ed. (1989).

George Herbert (1593–1633)

Born in Wales. Educated at Westminster and Cambridge. He took orders and served in the parish of Bemerton until his death. Most of his verse was included in *The Temple,* a collection of poems on religious themes.

Selected publications: *The Temple,* F. E. Hutchinson, ed. (1939). Biographical and critical works: *George Herbert and the Seventeenth-Century Religious Poets,* Mario A. Di Cesare, ed. (1978).

Mary Sidney Herbert, Countess of Pembroke (1561–1621)

Born in Worcestershire, into an aristocratic family. She was well educated for her time—she knew Latin, as well as French and Italian. Her most enduring literary accomplishment was a continuation of the English version of the Psalms her brother had begun before his death.

Selected publications: *The Psalms of Sir Philip Sidney and the Countess of Pembroke,* J. C. A. Rathmell, ed. (1963); *The Triumph of Death and Other Uncollected Poems,* G. F. Waller, ed. (1977). Biographical and critical works: *Mary Sidney Herbert, Countess of Pembroke: A Critical Study of Her Writings and Literary Milieu,* G. F. Waller (1979).

Daryl Hine (1936–   )

Born near Vancouver. Attended McGill University, received his doctorate from University of Chicago. He was editor of *Poetry* magazine from 1968 to 1978. He received a MacArthur Fellowship in 1986.

Selected publications: *In and Out* (1975); *Ovid's Heroines* (verse translation, 1991); *The Devil's Picture Book* (1960).

Edward Hirsch (1950–)
Born in Chicago and educated at Grinnell and the University of Pennsylvania. Among his honors, he has received the National Book Critics Circle Award, the Lavan Younger Poets Award, and the Delmore Schwartz Memorial Award from New York University. He also received a MacArthur Fellowship.

Selected publications: *For the Sleepwalkers* (1981); *Wild Gratitude* (1986); *The Night Parade* (1989); *Earthly Measures* (1994); *On Love* (1998).

John Hollander (1929–)
Born in New York City. Educated at Columbia and Indiana University. His first book, *A Crackling of Thorns* (1958), was chosen for the Yale Series of Younger Poets with an introduction by W. H. Auden. A powerful advocate and practitioner of poetic form, his book *Rhyme's Reason* (1981) is a classic of lucid and witty exposition. His many awards include a MacArthur Fellowship. He has taught at Harvard, Columbia, and Yale.

Selected publications: *Types of Shape* (1969); *Spectral Emanations* (1978); *The Figure of Echo* (1981); *Powers of Thirteen* (1983); *Melodious Guile* (1988); *Harp Lake* (1988); *Tesserae* (1993); *Selected Poetry* (1993); *The Work of Poetry* (1997).

Garrett Hongo (1951–)
Born in Volcano, Hawaii. His honors include fellowships from the Guggenheim Foundation and the NEA. His second book won the James Laughlin Poetry Award from the Academy of American Poets.

Selected publications: *Yellow Light* (1982); *The River of Heaven* (1988); *The Open Boat: Poems from Asian America* (editor) (1993); *Volcano: A Memoir of Hawai'i* (1995).

Gerard Manley Hopkins (1844–1889)
Born in Stratford, England. Educated at Oxford. He converted to Catholicism in 1866 and was an ordained priest. In 1884 he was appointed to the Chair of Greek at Dublin University. Little of his poetry was published during his lifetime.

Selected publications: *Poems* (1970); *Poems and Prose of Gerard Manley Hopkins,* W. H. Gardner, ed. (1990). Biographical and critical works: *Gerard Manley Hopkins: A Very Private Life,* Robert Bernard Martin (1991).

A. E. Housman (1859–1936)
Born in Worcestershire and educated at Oxford. Despite the fact that he failed at his Honors degree examination he became a leading classical scholar and served for many years as professor of Latin at Cambridge. His *Shropshire Lad* (1896) is a model of the dark lyric sequence.

Selected publications: *Last Poems* (1922); *Collected Poems* (1939); *Letters,* H. Maas, ed. (1971). Biographical and critical works: *A. E. Housman Revisited,* Terence Allan Hoagwood (1995).

Henry Howard, Earl of Surrey (c. 1517–1547)

He was the son of Thomas Howard, later Duke of Norfolk. With Thomas Wyatt he brought the sonnet form from Italy to England and introduced the use of blank verse in his translation of the *Aeneid.* Executed at the age of thirty for treason.

Selected publications: *Silver Poets of the Sixteenth Century* (1947); *Poems* (1964). Biographical and critical works: *Henry Howard, Earl of Surrey,* E. Casaday (1938).

Richard Howard (1929–)

Born in Cleveland, Ohio, and educated at Columbia and at the Sorbonne. His first collection of poems, *Untitled Subjects* (1969), was awarded the Pulitzer Prize in 1970. Among his many honors is a MacArthur Fellowship. He has served as poetry editor for the *New Republic* and the *Paris Review,* among others. He lives in New York City and Houston. In addition to his poetry he is a distinguished translator.

Selected publications: *Alone with America: Essays on the Art of Poetry in the United States since 1950* (1969); *Lining Up* (1983); *No Traveller* (1989); *Like Most Revelations: New Poems* (1994); *Trappings* (1999).

Langston Hughes (1902–1967)

Born in Joplin, Missouri, and grew up in Kansas, Ohio, and Illinois. He attended Columbia University but dropped out after a year and visited South America and France. He was a central figure in the Harlem Renaissance and a defining figure in American poetry.

Selected publications: *I Wonder As I Wander: An Autobiographical Journey* (1956); *The Collected Poems of Langston Hughes* (1994). Biographical and critical works: *The Life of Langston Hughes,* Arnold Rampersad (1986–88).

Ted Hughes (1930–1998)

Born in Yorkshire, England. After national service he studied at Cambridge. In 1956 he married American poet Sylvia Plath. His first book, *The Hawk in the Rain,* was published in 1957. Published many collections of poetry as well as plays, translations, and books for children. Succeeded Sir John Betjeman as Poet Laureate of Great Britain in 1984.

Selected publications: *New Selected Poems, 1957–1994* (1995); *Tales from Ovid* (1997); *Birthday Letters* (1998). Biographical and critical works: *Critical Essays on Ted Hughes,* Leonard M. Scigaj, ed. (1992).

Denis Johnson (1949–   )
Born in Munich, Germany, raised in Tokyo, Manila, and the suburbs of Washington, D.C. He received his BA and MFA from University of Iowa. He has published five books of poetry and four novels, as well as short stories. Among his awards are fellowships from the NEA, the Guggenheim, Whiting, and Lannan Foundations, an Award for Literature from the American Academy of Arts and Letters, and the Robert Frost Award.

Selected publications: *The Man Among the Seals* (1969); *Inner Weather* (1976); *The Incognito Lounge* (1982); *The Veil* (1987); *The Throne of the Third Heaven of the Nations Millennium General Assembly: Poems Collected and New* (1995).

Samuel Johnson (1709–1784)
Born in Lichfield, England. Educated at Lichfield Grammar School and at Oxford. In London, he contributed extensively to *The Gentleman's Magazine*. In 1749 he published *The Vanity of Human Wishes,* his longest and generally regarded as his finest poem. His *Dictionary* was published in 1755 and his *Journey to the Western Islands of Scotland* in 1775.

Selected publications: *Poems* (1810); *Journey to the Western Islands of Scotland,* Peter Levi, ed. (1993). Biographical and critical works: *The Cambridge Companion to Samuel Johnson,* Greg Clingham, ed. (1997).

Ben Jonson (1572–1637)
Born in London, in the same year as Donne. Educated in Westminster School. His play, *Every Man in His Humour,* with Shakespeare in the cast, was performed in 1598. His erudite and powerful poetry was deeply influential on later English poets.

Selected publications: *The Complete Poetry of Ben Jonson,* William Hunter, ed. (1963); *The Complete Masques,* Stephen Orgel, ed. (1969). Biographical and critical works: *Ben Jonson,* Richard Allen Cave (1991).

Donald Justice (1925–   )
Born in Miami. Educated at Miami, North Carolina, and Iowa, where he taught for many years at the Iowa Writers' Workshop. He is a distinctive, wry, and often powerfully ironic formalist. His many awards include the Pulitzer (1980) and the Bollingen (1991) prizes.

Selected publications: *The Sunset Maker* (1987); *A Donald Justice Reader* (1991); *New and Selected Poems* (1995). Biographical and critical works: *Certain Solitudes: On the Poetry of Donald Justice, Dana Gioia and William Logan,* eds. (1997).

Patrick Kavanagh (1905–1967)
Born in County Monaghan, Ireland, and educated locally. Moved to Dublin

in 1939. Published his own magazine, called *Kavanagh's Weekly*. His poem *The Great Hunger* was a landmark in Irish poetry.

Selected publications: *Collected Prose* (1967); *The Complete Poems* (1984). Biographical and critical works: *Patrick Kavanagh: Man and Poet*, Peter Kavanagh, ed. (1986).

John Keats (1795–1821)

Born in London. He was apprenticed to an apothecary, then studied to be a surgeon. He passed his examinations but abandoned this career in favor of poetry. His sonnet on Chapman's *Homer* was published in 1816. He died of tuberculosis.

Selected publications: *Selected Letters*, Lionel Trilling, ed. (1951); *Poetical Works* (1958). Biographical and critical works: *Keats*, J. M. Murry (1955); *John Keats*, W. J. Bate (1963); *Keats*, Andrew Motion (1998).

Weldon Kees (1914–1955)

Born in Nebraska, educated at Doane College and the University of Missouri. Worked for the Federal Writer's Project in Lincoln. Became a journalist in New York in the forties. His work shows an openness to both dark lyrics and narrative form and exhibits the strong influence of modernism.

Selected publications: *The Collected Poems of Weldon Kees*, Donald Justice, ed. (1975, rev. 1992); *Weldon Kees and the Midcentury Generation: Letters, 1935–1955*, Robert Knoll, ed. (1986).

Jane Kenyon (1947–1995)

Born in Ann Arbor, Michigan. Graduated from University of Michigan. Lived in New Hampshire, whose landscape enters her poems. Worked as a translator as well as a poet. She received a Guggenheim Fellowship and was nominated Poet Laureate of New Hampshire a few months before her untimely death.

Selected publications: *Otherwise: From Room to Room* (1978); *The Boat of Quiet Hours* (1986); *Let Evening Come* (1990); *New and Selected Poems* (1996). Biographical and critical works: *Bright Unequivocal Eye: Poems, Papers, and Remembrances from the First Jane Kenyon Conference*, Bert G. Hornback, ed. (2000).

Galway Kinnell (1927–   )

Born in Providence, Rhode Island. Educated at Princeton and Rochester. His first collection of poetry, *What a Kingdom It Was*, was published in 1960. *Selected Poems* (1982) was awarded the Pulitzer Prize. He has taught at University of California, Pittsburgh, Sarah Lawrence, and most recently at NYU. He lives in Vermont and New York City.

Selected publications: *Body Rags* (1968); *The Past* (1985); *Imperfect Thirst*

(1994). Biographical and critical works: *Critical Essays on Galway Kinnell,* Nancy Lewis Tuten, ed. (1996).

Thomas Kinsella (1928–   )

Born in Dublin. Served for many years in the Irish Civil Service. Taught at Southern Illinois University and later at Temple University. Owns and manages the Peppercanister Press. In addition to his own poetry, he has translated extensively from Irish.

Selected publications: *The Táin* (1970); *An Duanaire 1600–1900: Poems of the Dispossessed* (translator) (1981); *Collected Poems* (1996); *The Dual Tradition: An Essay on Poetry and Politics in Ireland* (1995). Biographical and critical works: *The Whole Matter: The Poetic Evolution of Thomas Kinsella,* Thomas H. Jackson (1995).

Mary Kinzie (1944–   )

Born in Montgomery, Alabama. Educated at Johns Hopkins. Has received a Guggenheim Fellowship. She is director of the Creative Writing Program at Northwestern.

Selected publications: *Summers of Vietnam* (1990); *Autumn Eros* (1991); *Ghost Ship* (1996).

Rudyard Kipling (1865–1936)

Born in Bombay, India, the son of English parents. At the age of six he was sent back to be educated in England. In 1882 he returned to India as a journalist. He won the Nobel Prize for Literature in 1907. Used poetic forms with gusto and oracular power.

Selected publications: *A Choice of Kipling's Verse,* T. S. Eliot, ed. (1941); *Early Verse by Rudyard Kipling, 1879–1889,* Andrew Rutherford, ed. (1986). Biographical and critical works: *Unforgiving Minute: A Life of Rudyard Kipling,* Harry Ricketts (1999).

Carolyn Kizer (1925–   )

Born in Spokane, Washington. Educated at Sarah Lawrence, Columbia, and University of Washington. Served as the first director of literary programs at the National Endowment for the Arts. Her awards include an American Academy of Arts and Letters Award, the Frost Medal, the John Masefield Memorial Award, and the Theodore Roethke Memorial Poetry Award. Her 1984 volume *Yin* won the Pulitzer Prize.

Selected publications: *Midnight Was My Cry: New and Selected Poems* (1971); *Mermaids in the Basement: Poems for Women* (1984); *The Nearness of You* (1986); *Harping On: Poems 1985–1995* (1996). Biographical and critical works: *An Answering Music: On the Poetry of Carolyn Kizer,* David Rigsbee, ed. (1990).

John Koethe (1945–)

Born in San Diego. He has received the Frank O'Hara Award and the Bernard F. Connor Award from the *Paris Review,* as well as a Guggenheim Fellowship. He is a professor of philosophy at the University of Wisconsin at Milwaukee.

Selected publications: *Blue Vents* (1969); *Domes* (1973); *The Late Wisconsin Spring* (1984); *The Constructor* (1999).

Yusef Komunyakaa (1947–)

Born in Bogalusa, Louisiana. He received his MFA from University of California. Was awarded the Bronze Star for his service in Vietnam, where he was a correspondent and managing editor of the *Southern Cross.* He has received the Thomas Forcade Award, the Hanes Poetry Prize, and the Pulitzer Prize. He teaches at Princeton and lives in New York City.

Selected publications: *I Apologize for the Eyes in My Head* (1986); *Magic City* (1992); *Neon Vernacular: New and Selected Poems: 1977–1989* (1993).

Aemilia Lanyer (1569–1645)

Little is known of her life. She was the daughter of a Jewish-Italian musician at the English Court. Her only volume of poetry, *Salve Deus Rex Judaorum,* is dedicated to and praises her patronesses. Her prose is feminist in attitude and content. Some historians have suggested she could be Shakespeare's "Dark Lady."

Selected publications: *Salve Deus Rex Judaorum* (1611); *The Norton Anthology of Literature by Women: The Tradition in English,* Sandra Gilbert and Susan Gubar, eds. (1985); *Poems of Aemilia Lanyer,* Suzanne Woods, ed. (1992).

Philip Larkin (1922–1985)

Born in Coventry. Educated at Oxford. Served for many years as Librarian of Hull University. His first collection, *The North Ship,* appeared in 1945. He also published two novels and a book on jazz.

Selected publications: *The Less Deceived* (1955); *The Whitsun Weddings* (1964); *High Windows* (1974); *Collected Poems* (1988). Biographical and critical works: *Philip Larkin: A Writer's Life,* Andrew Motion (1993).

Francis Ledwidge (1887–1917)

Born in County Meath, Ireland. He worked at a variety of jobs, from miner to grocer's clerk. He served in World War I and was killed in battle. His poetry is rich in nature imagery; his lines are full of color, in the manner of Keats, and unaffectedly melodious.

Selected publications: *The Complete Poems of Francis Ledwidge* (1944);

Francis Ledwidge, Selected Poems, Dermot Bolger, ed. (1992). Biographical and critical works: *Francis Ledwidge: A Life of the Poet, 1887–1917,* Alice Curtayne (1972).

Denise Levertov (1923–1997)

Born in Essex, and educated at home. In 1948 she moved to the United States and was immediately drawn to experimental poetry. She became associated with the Black Mountain school of poetry; her poetry reflects her involvement in anti-war activism.

Selected publications: *To Stay Alive* (1971); *Footprints* (1972); *Candles in Babylon* (1982); *Sands of the Well* (1996). Biographical and critical works: *Denise Levertov: Selected Criticism,* Albert Gelpi, ed. (1993); *Tesserae: Memories and Suppositions* (1995); *Letters of Denise Levertov and William Carlos Williams,* Christopher MacGowan, ed. (1998).

Philip Levine (1928–   )

Born in Detroit. Attended Wayne State University, where he studied with John Berryman, and University of Iowa. His first book, *On the Edge,* was published in 1963. In 1980 he won both the National Book Critics Circle Award and the American Book Award. He has received the Ruth Lilly Poetry Award, the Harriet Monroe Memorial Prize for Poetry, the Frank O'Hara Award, and two Guggenheim Foundation fellowships. *The Simple Truth* (1994) won the Pulitzer Prize. He taught for many years at California State.

Selected publications: *Ashes: Poems New and Old* (1979); *What Work Is* (1991); *New Selected Poems* (1991); *The Bread of Time: Toward an Autobiography* (1994); *The Mercy* (1999).

Janet Lewis (1899–1998)

Born near Chicago. Educated at University of Chicago. She spent time in Paris before contracting tuberculosis, which forced her to return to the United States. She spent five years in a New Mexico sanitarium before moving to Los Atos, California. She taught creative writing at Stanford. Her poems are collected in *Poems Old and New, 1918–78* (1981). She also wrote a libretto based on her bestselling novel *The Wife of Martin Guerre* (1967).

Selected publications: *Indian in the Woods* (1922); *Ancient Ones* (1979); *Morning Devotion* (1995). Biographical and critical works: *Janet Lewis,* Charles Crow (1980).

Henry Wadsworth Longfellow (1807–1882)

Born in Portland, Maine, and educated at Bowdoin, where Hawthorne was a fellow student. His prose romance *Hyperion* was published in 1839. *Bal-*

lads and Other Poems appeared in 1841. It was followed by many other collections, including *Poems on Slavery* and *Ultima Thule.*

Selected publications: *The Complete Poetical Works of Longfellow* (1922). Biographical and critical works: *Longfellow: His Life and Work,* Newton Arvin (1963).

Robert Lowell (1917–1977)

Born in Boston. Educated at St. Mark's School, Harvard, and Kenyon College. His first poetry collection, *Land of Unlikeness,* was published in 1944. He received the Pulitzer for his second, *Lord Weary's Castle,* in 1947.

Selected publications: *Life Studies* (1959); *For the Union Dead* (1964); *Day by Day* (1977). Biographical and critical works: *Five Temperaments: Elizabeth Bishop, Robert Lowell, James Merrill, Adrienne Rich, John Ashbery,* David Kalstone (1977); *Robert Lowell,* Ian Hamilton (1982).

Louis MacNeice (1907–1963)

Born in Belfast, educated at Oxford. He lived in England most of his life, and was associated with the thirties' generation of politically committed poets in England.

Selected publications: *The Strings Are False: An Unfinished Autobiography* (1965); *Collected Poems* (1966). Biographical and critical works: *Louis MacNeice,* Jon Stallworthy (1995).

Walter de la Mare (1873–1956)

Born in Charlton, Kent. Became a bookkeeper for Standard Oil and worked there for eighteen years. His first book of poetry, *Song of Childhood,* was published in 1902.

Selected publications: *Collected Poems of Walter de la Mare* (1979). Biographical and critical works: *Walter de la Mare: A Biography and Critical Study,* R. L. Mégroz (1924).

Christopher Marlowe (1564–1593)

Born in Canterbury, England, and educated at Cambridge. *Tamburlaine* marked a new direction in blank verse. His plays include *Tragedy of Dr. Faustus, The Jew of Malta,* and *Edward II.* A controversial political figure, he was killed in a tavern brawl at an early age.

Selected publications: *Complete Poems and Translations,* Stephen Orgel, ed. (1971). Biographical and critical works: *Christoper Marlowe,* Thomas Healey (1996).

Andrew Marvell (1621–1678)

Born in Yorkshire, England. Educated at Hull Grammar School and Cambridge. In 1653 he became tutor to Cromwell's ward, William Dutton, and, in 1657, assistant to Milton in the Latin secretaryship. After the Restoration he entered Parliament and wrote many satires and pamphlets.

Selected publications: *The Poems and Letters of Andrew Marvell,* H. M. Margoliouth, ed. (1963). Biographical and critical works: *Andrew Marvell,* Augustine Birrell (1973); *Andrew Marvell Companion,* Robert Ray (1998).

J. D. McClatchy (1945–   )
Born in Bryn Mawr, Pennsylvania. A witty, assured writer of forms, he is also an inventive ironist. He is the recipient of the Witter Bynner Award for Poetry from the American Academy of Arts and Letters, and fellowships from the Guggenheim Foundation and the NEA.

Selected publications: *Scenes from Another Life* (1981); *Stars Principal* (1986); *The Rest of the Way* (1992); *Ten Commandments* (1998).

Medbh McGuckian (1950–   )
Born in Belfast. Educated at Queen's University, Belfast. Her first collection, *The Flower Master,* was published in 1982.

Selected publications: *On Ballycastle Beach* (1988); *Marconi's Cottage* (1991); *Captain Lavender* (1995); *Selected Poems* (1997); *Shelmalier* (1998). Biographical and critical works: *Women Creating Women: Contemporary Irish Women Poets,* Patricia Boyle Haberstroh (1996).

Claude McKay (1890–1948)
Born in Jamaica. Emigrated to the United States where he studied at the Tuskegee Institute and at Kansas State College. He edited the radical newspapers *The Liberator* and *The Masses.* A central figure in the Harlem Renaissance, his most important book, *Harlem Shadows,* was published in 1922.

Selected publications: *A Long Way from Home: An Autobiography,* (1937); *Selected Poems* (1953); *The Passion of Claude McKay: Selected Poetry and Prose 1912–1948* (1973).

Paula Meehan (1955–   )
Born in Dublin. Educated at Trinity College and received her MFA from Eastern Washington University. She has been writer in residence at University College Dublin and Trinity College. She lives in Dublin.

Selected publications: *The Man Who Was Marked by Winter* (1991); *Pillow Talk* (1994).

James Merrill (1926–1995)
Born in New York City. Before graduating from Amherst, he served with the U.S. Army for a year at the end of World War II. He was awarded the

National Book Award, the Bollingen Prize, and the Pulitzer Prize, and is considered a commanding and innovative formalist.

Selected publications: *Water Street* (1962); *The Fire Screen* (1969); *The Changing Light at Sandover* (1982); *A Different Person* (1993). Biographical and critical works: *Five Temperaments,* David Kalstone, ed. (1977); *Critical Essays on James Merrill,* Guy Rotella, ed. (1996).

W. S. Merwin (1927–   )

Born in New York City. Educated at Princeton, where he studied with John Berryman. He was poetry editor at the *Nation* from 1951 to 1953. Has lived for many years in Hawaii. His honors include the Aiken Taylor Award for Modern American Poetry, the Bollingen Prize, a Ford Foundation grant, and the Governor's Award for Literature of the State of Hawaii. He was awarded the Pulitzer Prize in 1971. In addition to his poetry, he has written translations and several volumes of memoirs.

Selected publications: *The Rain in the Trees* (1988); *Selected Poems* (1988); *Travels* (1993); *The Second Four Books of Poems* (1993); *Flower and Hand: Poems 1977–1983* (1997); *The River Sound* (1999). Biographical and critical works: *W. S. Merwin,* Cheri Davis (1981).

Charlotte Mew (1869–1928)

Born in London to a family that, after the death of her father, became impoverished. She took on any odd writing jobs she could find to support the family. Her important, central collection, *The Farmer's Bride,* was not published until 1916. She committed suicide after being institutionalized in 1927.

Selected publications: *Collected Poems and Prose,* Val Warner, ed. (1981). Biographical and critical works: *Charlotte Mew and Her Friends,* Penelope Fitzgerald (1984).

Edna St. Vincent Millay (1892–1950)

Born in Rockland, Maine. Educated at Vassar. She lived in Greenwich Village after college, where she met other prominent writers and artists. Her first volume, *Renascence and Other Poems,* was published in 1917. She won the Pulitzer Prize in 1923.

Selected publications: *A Few Figs from Thistles* (1920); *Second April* (1921); *The Harp-Weaver and Other Poems* (1923); *Collected Sonnets* (1941). Biographical and critical works: *The Poet and Her Book,* Jean Gould (1969); *Edna St. Vincent Millay, 1892–1950,* Frances Mattson (1991); *Critical Essays on Edna St. Vincent Millay,* William B. Thesing (1993).

John Milton (1608–1674)

Born in London and educated at Cambridge. A vigorous polemicist for

Cromwell, he wrote a powerful prose of advocacy. He completed *Paradise Lost* in 1663. *Paradise Regained* and *Samson Agonistes* were published together in 1671.

Selected publications: *Complete Poems and Major Prose* (1957); *Poetical Works* (1965). Biographical and critical works: *The Living Milton,* Frank Kermode (1970).

Marianne Moore (1887–1972)

Born in Kirkwood, Missouri. Educated at the Metzger Institute and Bryn Mawr. In 1918 she moved to New York. Her first collection of poetry, *Poems* (1921), was published in England. For three years she was the editor of *The Dial.* Her many honors included the Bollingen Prize, the National Book Award, and the Pulitzer Prize.

Selected publications: *O to Be a Dragon* (1959); *The Arctic Fox* (1964); *Tell Me, Tell Me* (1966); *The Complete Poems of Marianne Moore* (1967); *The Selected Letters of Marianne Moore,* Bonnie Costello et al., eds. (1997). Biographical and critical works: *Becoming a Poet: Elizabeth Bishop with Marianne Moore and Robert Lowell,* David Kalstone (1989); *Marianne Moore: Questions of Authority,* Cristanne Miller (1995).

Thylias Moss (1954–   )

Born in Cleveland. Educated at Oberlin and University of New Hampshire. She has received a fellowship from the Guggenheim Foundation and the Witter Bynner Award. She is a professor of English at the University of Michigan.

Selected publications: *Hosiery Seams on a Bowlegged Woman* (1983); *Small Congregations: New and Selected Poems* (1993); *Tale of a Sky-Blue Dress* (memoir) (1998).

Les Murray (1938–   )

Born in Bunyah, New South Wales, educated at the University of Sydney. His first book was *The Ilex Tree,* published in 1965. He has edited several poetry anthologies and is literary editor of *Quadrant.* He lives in Australia.

Selected publications: *The Daylight Moon* (1988); *Translations from the Natural World* (1994); *Subhuman Redneck Poems* (1996); *Fredy Neptune: A Novel in Verse* (1999). Biographical and critical works: *Vivid Steady State: Les Murray and Australian Poetry,* Lawrence Bourke (1992).

Carol Muske (1945–   )

Born in St. Paul, Minnesota. Attended California State University at San Francisco. Has also written fiction. She has received a Guggenheim Fellowship and a National Endowment for the Arts Poetry Fellowship. She is a professor at the University of Southern California.

Selected publications: *Camouflage* (1975); *Red Trousseau* (1993); *An Octave Above Thunder: New and Selected Poems* (1997).

Ogden Nash (1902–1971)

Born in Rye, New York. Went briefly to Harvard, worked in advertising, and joined the staff of *The New Yorker* in 1929. Acclaimed for his witty, acerbic light verse.

Selected publications: *Selected Poetry of Ogden Nash* (1995). Biographical and critical works: *The Life and Rhymes of Ogden Nash,* David Stuart (1991).

Howard Nemerov (1920–1991)

Born in New York City. Educated at Harvard. During World War II, he served in the Royal Canadian Air Force and, later, the U.S. Air Force. He was appointed U.S. Poet Laureate twice, in 1963 and 1988. His *Collected Poems* (1977) was awarded the Pulitzer Prize and the National Book Award. He received the Bollingen Prize in 1981.

Selected publications: *War Stories* (1987); *The Oak in the Acorn: On Remembrance of Things Past, and on Teaching Proust, Who Will Never Learn.*

Frank O'Hara (1926–1966)

Born in Baltimore, Maryland, and grew up in Massachusetts. He served in the U.S. Navy during World War II. Studied at Harvard where he majored in music and began his association with John Ashbery. Worked at the Museum of Modern Art in New York, and was a catalyst in both the painting and poetry worlds until his early death.

Selected publications: *A City Winter, and Other Poems* (1951); *Meditations in an Emergency* (1956); *Odes* (1960); *In Memory of My Feelings* (1967); *The Collected Poems of Frank O'Hara,* Donald Allen, ed. (1971). Biographical and critical works: *City Poet: The Life and Times of Frank O'Hara,* Brad Gooch (1993); *Frank O'Hara: Poet among Painters,* Marjorie Perloff (rev. ed., 1998).

Sharon Olds (1942–)

Born in San Francisco, and educated at Stanford University and Columbia University. Her first book, *Satan Says* (1980), received the inaugural San Francisco State University Poetry Center Book Award. She helps run the NYU workshop program at Goldwater Hospital on Roosevelt Island.

Selected publications: *The Dead and the Living* (1984); *The Father* (1992); *The Wellspring* (1996); *Blood, Tin, Straw* (1999).

Mary Oliver (1935–   )
Born in Cleveland, Ohio. Educated at Ohio State and Vassar. Won the Pulitzer Prize for *American Primitive* (1983).

Selected publications: *House of Light* (1990); *New and Selected Poems* (1992); *Blue Pastures* (1995); *West Wind: Poems and Prose Poems* (1997); *Winter Hours* (1999).

Mary O'Malley (1954–   )
Born in Connemara, County Galway, and educated at University College, Galway. Lived in Portugal for eight years. In addition to her poetry, she has edited a number of anthologies.

Selected publications: *A Consideration of Silk* (1990); *Where the Rocks Float* (1993); *The Knife in the Wave* (1997).

Jacqueline Osherow (1956–   )
Born in Philadelphia. Attended Princeton. Winner of the Poetry Society of America's 1995 Lucy Medwick Award and the 1993 John Masefield Memorial Award, as well as a Guggenheim Fellowship. She is director of creative writing at the University of Utah.

Selected publications: *Looking for Angels in New York* (1988); *Conversations with Survivors* (1994); *With a Moon in Transit* (1996).

Wilfred Owen (1893–1918)
Born in Oswestry, England. Educated at Birkenhead Institute and then the Technical School in Shrewesbury. He served in the British Army during World War I. He wrote extensively on anti-war themes while recuperating from shell shock, but returned to battle in 1918 and was killed one week before Armistice.

Selected publications: *Collected Poems* (1931, 1963, 1973); *Collected Letters,* Harold Owen and John Bell, eds. (1967).

Michael Palmer (1943–   )
Born in New York City. Educated at Harvard. He is the author of eight books of poetry. His honors include two grants from the NEA and a Guggenheim Foundation Fellowship. He lives in San Francisco.

Selected publications: *Blake's Newton* (1972); *The Circular Gates* (1974); *Notes for Echo Lake* (1981); *Sun* (1988); *At Passages* (1996); *The Lion Bridge: Selected Poems 1972–1995* (1998). Biographical and critical works: *Regions of Unlikeness: Explaining Contemporary Poetry,* Thomas Gardner (1999).

Katherine Philips (1632–1664)
Born in London, she was the daughter of a merchant. Went to school in

Hackney. Founded the Society of Friendship, a literary salon for the discussion of poetry, religion, and other topics. Known as "The Matchless Orinda." Her collected verses were published in 1667.

Selected publications: *The Norton Anthology of Literature by Women: The Tradition in English,* Sandra Gilbert and Susan Gubar, eds. (1985); *Collected Works of Katherine Philips,* Patrick Thomas, ed. (1990). Biographical and critical works: *Katherine Philips ("Orinda"),* Patrick Thomas (1988).

Robert Pinsky (1940–)

Born in New Jersey. Educated at Rutgers and Stanford. In addition to his poetry he has published *Mindwheel* (1987), a computer novel. Appointed U.S. Poet Laureate in 1997. Among his many honors are an American Academy of Arts and Letters award, *Poetry* magazine's Oscar Blumenthal Prize, and the William Carlos Williams Award. He teaches at Boston University.

Selected publications: *An Explanation of America* (1979); *History of My Heart* (1984); *The Want Bone* (1990); *The Inferno of Dante* (1994); *The Figured Wheel: New and Collected Poems 1966–1996* (1996).

Sylvia Plath (1932–1963)

Born in Boston. Educated at Smith and Cambridge, as a Fulbright Scholar. There she met her husband, Ted Hughes, whom she married in 1956. Her first volume, *The Colossus,* was published in 1960. Her second, *Ariel,* was published after her death in 1965. The years between the books show a remarkable technical growth and the daring and power of her gift.

Selected publications: *Crossing the Water* (1971); *Winter Trees* (1972); *Letters Home: Correspondence, 1950–1963,* Aurelia Schober Plath, ed. (1975); *The Collected Poems* (1981); *The Journals of Sylvia Plath,* Ted Hughes and Frances McCullough, eds. (1991). Biographical and critical works: *Revising Life: Sylvia Plath's Ariel Poems,* Susan Van Dyne (1993).

Alexander Pope (1688–1744)

Born in London. He was largely self-educated. The first edition of his collected works appeared in 1751. Celebrated in his day for his command of the couplet and his epigrammatic wit.

Selected publications: *Twickenham,* John Butt, ed. (1963). Biographical and critical works: *On the Poetry of Pope,* Geoffrey Tillotson (1950).

Ezra Pound (1885–1972)

Born in Hailey, Idaho. Educated at the University of Pennsylvania and Hamilton College. His reputation was established by the publication of

Hugh Selwyn Mauberley: Life and Contacts in 1920. A poet and editor of great influence, he radicalized the concept of renewing poetic forms, often through an eloquent subversion of traditional practice.

Selected publications: *The Cantos of Ezra Pound* (1921); *Personae: Collected Poems* (1926); *The Confucian Analects* (1951); *Literary Essays*, T. S. Eliot, ed. (1954); *Collected Early Poems* (1976); *Ezra and Dorothy Pound: Letters in Captivity, 1945–1946,* Omar Pound and Robert Spoo, eds. (1999). Biographical and critical works: *A Serious Character: The Life of Ezra Pound*, Humphrey Carpenter (1988); *The Cambridge Companion to Ezra Pound,* Ira B. Nadel, ed. (1999).

Susan Prospere (1952–)

Born in Starkville, Mississippi. Received the "Discovery"/*The Nation* Award, the PEN Southwest Houston Discovery Award, and an Ingram Merrill grant. She lives in Houston.

Selected publications: *Sub Rosa* (1992).

John Crowe Ransom (1888–1974)

Born in Pulaski, Tennessee. Educated at Vanderbilt and as a Rhodes Scholar at Oxford. Served as a lieutenant during the First World War. After many years at Vanderbilt he moved to Kenyon College in 1937 and founded the *Kenyon Review,* which he edited until 1959.

Selected publications: *Two Gentlemen in Bonds* (1926); *Selected Poems* (1945); *Poems and Essays* (1955). Biographical and critical works: *Gentleman in a Dustcoat: A Biography of John Crowe Ransom,* Thomas Daniel Young (1977).

Adrienne Rich (1929–)

Born in Baltimore, Maryland, she was educated at Radcliffe and won the Yale Series of Younger Poets Award for her first book. In 1997 she was awarded the Academy of American Poets' Tanning Prize for outstanding and proven mastery in the art of poetry. She has also received a MacArthur Fellowship, the Ruth Lilly Poetry Prize, and the Lenore Marshall Poetry Prize. She was active in the anti-war movement and edited the journal *Sinister Wisdom.*

Selected publications: *The Fact of a Doorframe: Poems Selected and New, 1950–1984* (1984); *An Atlas of the Difficult World: Poems 1988–1991* (1991); *Collected Early Poems: 1950–1970* (1993); *Adrienne Rich's Poetry and Prose: Poems, Prose, Reviews, and Criticism,* Albert Gelpi and Barbara Charlesworth Gelpi, eds. (1993); *Dark Fields of the Republic: Poems 1991–1995* (1995); *Midnight Salvage* (1999). Biographical and critical works: *Five Temperaments,* David Kalstone (1977).

Alberto Ríos (1952–)

Born in Nogales, Arizona, on the Mexican border. Went to the University of Arizona. Concepts of transitional places, people, and poetics enrich his work. He has won the Arizona Governor's Arts Award and fellowships from the Guggenheim Foundation and the NEA.

Selected publications: *Five Indiscretions: A Book of Poems* (1985); *The Lime Orchard Woman: Poems* (1988); *Teodora Luna's Two Kisses: Poems* (1990); *Pig Cookies and Other Stories* (1995); *Capirotada: A Nogales Memoir* (1999).

Edwin Arlington Robinson (1869–1935)

Born in Head Tide, Maine. Attended Harvard. New England was the theme of much of his work. He won the Pulitzer Prize three times—in 1922, 1925, and 1928.

Selected publications: *Collected Poems* (1922); *Selected Letters of Edwin Arlington Robinson* (1940); *Tilbury Town* (1953); *Uncollected Poetry and Prose,* Richard Cary, ed. (1975); *The Essential Robinson,* Donald Hall, ed. (1994); *The Poetry of E. A. Robinson,* Robert Mezey, ed. (1999).

Theodore Roethke (1908–1963)

Born in Saginaw, Michigan. Studied at the University of Michigan and Harvard. Taught in a number of colleges and universities. Often wrote in closed forms with a commanding rhetoric and distinctive cadence.

Selected publications: *The Far Field* (1964); *Collected Poems* (1966); *Selected Letters,* Ralph J. Mills, Jr., ed. (1968). Biographical and critical works: *A Concordance to the Poems of Theodore Roethke,* Gary Lane, ed. (1972); *Theodore Roethke: An American Romantic,* Jay Parini (1979).

Christina Rossetti (1830–1894)

Born in London. She was the daughter of an Italian patriot who came to England in 1824. Her early work was published under the pseudonym Ellen Alleyne. Her work encompasses poems of fantasy, verses for the young, and religious poetry. *Monna Innominata* is a sonnet series on unhappy love. A vivid lyric formalist.

Selected publications: *The Complete Poems of Christina Rossetti*, Rebecca Crump, ed. (1979). Biographical and critical works: *The Achievement of Christina Rossetti,* David A. Kent, ed. (1987).

Dante Gabriel Rossetti (1828–1882)

Born in London to an Italian patriot. Educated at Royal Academy Antique

School. A founding member, with Holman Hunt, John Everett Millais, and others, of the Pre-Raphaelite Brotherhood.

Selected publications: *Collected Works,* W. M. Rossetti, ed. (1897). Biographical and critical works: *Dante Gabriel Rossetti Revisited,* David Riede (1992); *Rossetti and His Circle,* Elizabeth Prettejohn (1997).

Muriel Rukeyser (1913–1980)

Born in New York City. Educated at Vassar and Columbia. Taught at the California Labor School in Berkeley. Her first volume, *Theory of Flight* (1935), was published in the Yale Series of Younger Poets. In addition to her own poetry she translated works by Octavio Paz. She was active in the anti-war movement in the sixties. She was a founding editor of the left-wing *Student Review.*

Selected publications: *The Gates* (1976); *Collected Poems of Muriel Rukeyser* (1978); *A Muriel Rukeyser Reader,* Jan Heller Levi, ed. (1994). Biographical and critical works: *The Poetic Vision of Muriel Rukeyser,* Louise Kertesz (1980).

David St. John (1949–   )

Born in Fresno, California. He received his MFA from Iowa. His awards include the "Discovery"/*The Nation* Award, the James D. Phelan Prize, and the Prix de Rome Fellowship in Literature.

Selected publications: *Hush* (1976); *No Heaven* (1985); *Study for the World's Body: New and Selected Poems* (1994); *Where the Angels Come Toward Us: Selected Essays, Reviews and Interviews* (1995).

Mary Jo Salter (1954–   )

Born in Michigan. She attended Harvard and Cambridge universities. In addition to publishing four books of poetry, she is a co-editor of the *Norton Anthology of Poetry.* She teaches at Mount Holyoke College.

Selected publications: *Heary Purcell in Japan* (1985); *Unfinished Painting* (1989); *Sunday Skaters* (1994); *A Kiss in Space* (1999).

Gjertrud Schnackenberg (1953–   )

Born in Tacoma, Washington. Educated at Mount Holyoke College. The recipient of a number of awards, she lived for two years at the American Academy in Rome. She lives in Boston.

Selected publications: *Portraits and Elegies* (1982); *The Lamplit Answer* (1985); *A Gilded Lapse of Time* (1992).

William Shakespeare (1564–1616)

Born in Stratford-on-Avon. Celebrated in the centuries after his death chiefly as a playwright, his early formal verse—from sonnets to lyrics—

deserves close attention. He was a powerful, emotive formalist. His work in the sonnet was profoundly influential on the development of the form.

Selected publications: *Love Poems and Sonnets of William Shakespeare* (1957); *Concordance,* Martin Spevack, ed. (1973). Biographical and critical works: *Shakespeare's Lives,* Samuel Schoenbaum (1970).

Percy Bysshe Shelley (1792–1822)

Born in Sussex, England, and educated at Eton and Oxford. He lived much of his life abroad. In 1819 he published *The Cenci* and his renowned drama *Prometheus Unbound.* Shortly afterward he wrote many of his most celebrated lyrics. He drowned while sailing near Spezia.

Selected publications: *Complete Poems of Percy Bysshe Shelley* (1994). Biographical and critical works: *Shelley: The Pursuit,* Richard Holmes (1975).

Philip Sidney (1554–1586)

Born in Kent, England. Educated at Shrewesbury and at Oxford. An innovative and exemplary sonneteer, he was also interested in putting classic meters into verse.

Selected publications: *The Poems of Sir Philip Sidney,* William Ringler, ed. (1962); *An Apology for Poetry* (1965). Biographical and critical works: *Life of Sir Philip Sidney,* Fulke Greville (1971); *The Making of Sir Philip Sidney,* Edward Berry (1998).

Charles Simic (1938–   )

Born in Yugoslavia. Educated at University of Chicago and NYU. His family moved to the United States in 1949. *The World Doesn't End* (1989) was awarded the Pulitzer Prize. He served with the U.S. Army and has taught at California State College and University of New Hampshire.

Selected publications: *Selected Poems: 1963–1983* (1985); *The Uncertain Certainty: Essays and Interviews* (1985); *Walking the Black Cat* (1996); *Orphan Factory: Essays and Memoirs,* (1997); *Jackstraws: Poems* (1999).

Charlotte Smith (1749–1806)

Born in London and raised in Sussex, England. She married Benjamin Smith, the extravagant son of a London merchant, who was eventually sent to debtor's prison. She began to write to support her family. Her many novels include *Emmeline* (1788) and *The Old Manor House* (1793). Her *Elegiac Sonnets and Other Poems* (1784) was immensely popular and was still in print forty-five years after her death.

Selected Publications: *Beachy Head* (1807). Biographical and critical works: *Charlotte Smith, Poet and Novelist,* Florence Hillbish (1941); *Before Their Time,* Katharine M. Rogers, ed. (1979).

Stevie Smith (1902–1971)
Born in Yorkshire, England. Her first book, a novel, was published in 1936. Her first collection of poetry was published the following year. In 1969 she was awarded the Queen's Gold Medal for Poetry.

Selected publications: *A Good Time Was Had by All* (1937); *Not Waving but Drowning* (1957); *Scorpion and Other Poems* (1972); *Collected Poems* (1976). Biographical and critical works: *Stevie Smith,* Frances Spalding (1988).

Edmund Spenser (c. 1552–1599)
Born in London and educated at Merchant Taylor's School and at Cambridge. Lived for some years in Ireland. He began work on *The Faerie Queen* in 1579. It was published in three volumes in 1590.

Selected publications: *Edmund Spenser's Poetry,* Hugh Maclean, ed. (1979). Biographical and critical works: *Spenser and Literary Pictorialism,* John Bender (1972).

Timothy Steele (1948–)
Born in Vermont. Educated at Stanford and Brandeis. His awards include a Guggenheim Fellowship and a Lavan Younger Poets Award. He is professor of English at California State University.

Selected publications: *Sapphics Against Anger and Other Poems* (1986); *The Color Wheel* (1994); *Sapphics and Uncertainties: Poems 1970–1986* (1995).

Wallace Stevens (1879–1955)
Born in Reading, Pennsylvania. Educated at Harvard. He entered New York Law School and practiced, unsuccessfully, at the New York Bar. He joined the legal staff of an insurance firm and eventually became a vice-president of the Hartford Accident and Indemnity Company. His first collection of poetry, *Harmonium,* appeared in 1923.

Selected publications: *Collected Poems* (1954); *Letters of Wallace Stevens* (1966); *The Palm at the End of the Mind: Selected Poems and a Play,* Holly Stevens, ed. (1989). Biographical and critical works: *On Extended Wings: Wallace Stevens' Longer Poems,* Helen Vendler (1969).

Algernon Charles Swinburne (1837–1909)
Born in London. Educated at Eton and at Balliol College, Oxford, he was a friend of Dante Rossetti and his circle. His second book, *Atalanta in Cal-*

ydon (1865), revealed his mastery of form and won him great renown at an early age.

Selected publications: *Collected Poetical Works* (1917). Biographical and critical works: *Swinburne,* J. J. McGann (1972).

Sara Teasdale (1884–1933)

Born in St. Louis, educated privately, and became part of Harriet Monroe's *Poetry* magazine circle in Chicago. She won the Pulitzer Prize in 1918.

Selected publications: *Rivers to the Sea* (1915); *Love Songs* (1917); *Strange Victory* (1933). Biographical and critical works: *Sara Teasdale, Woman and Poet,* William Drake (1979).

Alfred, Lord Tennyson (1809–1892)

Born in Somersby, England, and educated at Cambridge. *Poems Chiefly Lyrical* was published in 1830. He began work on *In Memoriam* in 1833, following the death of his friend A. H. Hallam. He succeeded Wordsworth as Poet Laureate in 1850.

Selected publications: *Poems of Tennyson,* C. Ricks, ed. (1969). Biographical and critical works: *Tennyson the Unquiet Heart,* Robert Bernard Martin (1980); *Tennyson's Gift,* Lynn Truss (1996).

Dylan Thomas (1914–1953)

Born in Swansea, Wales. Published his first book, *18 Poems,* when he was nineteen. His elaborate lyrics were celebrated in his lifetime. He traveled and gave readings widely in the United States and died in a New York hospital.

Selected publications: *Collected Poems* (1952); *Collected Prose* (1969). Biographical and critical works: *The Life of Dylan Thomas,* Constantine Fitzgibbon (1965); *Dylan Thomas: His Life and Work,* John Ackerman (1996).

Edward Thomas (1878–1917)

Born in London. Educated at St. Paul's School and Oxford. A pivotal point in his life was his discovery of the poetry of Robert Frost. During World War I he enlisted in the British army and was killed in France.

Selected publications: *Collected Poems,* Walter de la Mare, ed. (1928). Biographical and critical works: *Edward Thomas: The Last Four Years,* Eleanor Farjeon (1997).

Henry Timrod (1828–1867)

Born in Charleston and attended Franklin College. Enlisted in the Southern army during the Civil War, and his poems of advocacy and elegy for that cause led to him being called "The laureate of the Confederacy."

Selected publications: *Uncollected Poems of Henry Timrod* (1942); *Collected Poems* (1965). Biographical and critical works: *Henry Timrod, E. W. Parks* (1964).

Jean Toomer (1894–1967)

Born in Washington, D.C. He attended five different colleges before opting for a literary career. The poems and prose pieces that are contained in his only book, *Cane* (1923), were first published in various magazines and were received with much interest in the literary community. He developed an interest in Gurdjieffian mysticism and became a teacher of that subject.

Selected publications: *Collected Poems of Jean Toomer* (1988). Biographical and critical works: *Cane: An Authoritative Text, Backgrounds, Criticism,* Darwin T. Turner, ed. (1988).

Mona Van Duyn (1921–   )

Born in Waterloo, Iowa. Educated at University of Northern Iowa and University of Iowa. She has taught at several universities and edited the literary journal *Perspective* in the late 1970s. She was awarded the Bollingen Prize, the Hart Crane Memorial Award, the Ruth Lilly Poetry Prize, the Loines Prize of the National Institute of Arts and Letters. She was appointed Poet Laureate of the United States in 1993.

Selected publications: *To See, To Take* (1970); *Near Changes* (1990); *If It Be Not I: Collected Poems 1959–1982* (1993); *Firefall* (1993). Biographical and critical works: *Discovery and Reminiscence: Essays on the Poetry of Mona Van Duyn,* Michael Burns, ed. (1998).

Derek Walcott (1930–   )

Born on the island of St. Lucia. Educated at the University of the West Indies, Jamaica. First collection, *Twenty-Five Poems,* was published in 1948. Actively involved in Caribbean theater. Taught for many years in the United States. Awarded the Nobel Prize for Literature in 1992.

Selected publications: *Collected Poems, 1948–1984* (1986); *Omeros* (1990); *The Bounty* (1997). Biographical and critical works: *Critical Perspectives on Derek Walcott,* Robert D. Hamner, ed. (1993).

Rosanna Warren (1953–   )

Born in Fairfield, Connecticut. *Stained Glass* (1993) won the James Laughlin Poetry Award from the Academy of American Poets. Her other awards include the Lavan Younger Poets Award, a Lila Wallace–Reader's Digest Award, the "Discovery"/*The Nation* Award, the Witter Bynner Prize from the American Academy of Arts and Letters, and a fellowship from the

Guggenheim Foundation. She teaches English and foreign language at Boston University and lives in Needham, Massachusetts.

Selected publications: *Snow Day* (1981); *Each Leaf Shines Separate* (1984).

Phillis Wheatley (c. 1754–1784)

Born in Africa. The exact place is unknown but may have been Senegal or Gambia. She was sold into slavery to a Boston merchant. She started to write English verse when she was thirteen. She published *Poems on Various Subjects: Religious and Moral* in 1776. After the death of her master and his wife, with whom she was a favorite, she was freed by his sons and married another freed slave. Two of her children died and the third died soon after her own early death.

Selected publications: *The Poems of Phillis Wheatley* (1989). Biographical and critical works: *Phillis Wheatley,* Merle Richmond (1987).

Walt Whitman (1819–1892)

Born on Long Island. Worked as a journalist and an editor. Helped the wounded during the Civil War. He published the first edition of *Leaves of Grass* in 1855. Subsequent editions were considerably enlarged. *Drum Taps,* a collection of poems on the Civil War, was published in 1865.

Selected publications: *Leaves of Grass* ("deathbed" edition, 1891). Biographical and critical works: *Walt Whitman,* Nancy Loewen (1995).

John Greenleaf Whittier (1807–1892)

Born into a Quaker family in Haverhill, Massachusetts, he was an outspoken abolitionist. His first book of poems, published in 1837, was about abolition. Became an editor of the *New England Review.*

Selected publications: *The Complete Poetical Works of John Greenleaf Whittier* (1873); *Complete Writings of John Greenleaf Whittier* (1969); *The Letters of John Greenleaf Whittier,* John B. Pickard, ed. (1975). Biographical and critical works: *John Greenleaf Whittier His Life and Work,* Georgina King (1972).

Richard Wilbur (1921–)

Born in New York City. Educated at Amherst College and Harvard. He served in the U.S. Army during World War II, then went on to take a degree at Harvard. He succeeded Robert Penn Warren as U.S. Poet Laureate. He is known not only for his poetry but for his translations from the French. Among his honors are the Aiken Taylor Award for Modern American Poetry, the Frost Medal, the Gold Medal for Poetry from the American Academy of Arts and Letters, and the Bollingen Prize. He has taught at Harvard, Wellesley, Wesleyan, and Smith.

Selected publications: *Things of This World* (1956); *Walking to Sleep: New Poems and Translations* (1969); *Opposites: Poems and Drawings* (1973); *The Beautiful Changes and Other Poems* (1997). Biographical and critical works: *Ecstasy within Discipline: The Poetry of Richard Wilbur,* John B. Hougen (1995).

Oscar Wilde (1854–1900)

Born in Dublin. Educated at Trinity College, Dublin, and at Oxford. Renowned for his plays—including *A Woman of No Importance* and *The Importance of Being Earnest.* Two of his more remarkable works, *The Ballad of Reading Gaol* and *De Profundis,* were the outcome of his imprisonment in 1895.

Selected publications: *Complete Works* (1966); *Some Early Poems and Fragments* (1974). Biographical and critical works: *Oscar Wilde,* Richard Ellmann (1988).

C. K. Williams (1936–)

Born Newark, New Jersey. Educated at Bucknell and the University of Pennsylvania. His fifth collection, *Flesh and Blood* (1987), was given the National Book Critics Circle Award. He also won the *Paris Review*'s Bernard F. Connor Prize. He established a program of poetry-therapy for the emotionally disturbed in Philadelphia. He teaches at Princeton.

Selected publications: *Poems 1963–1983* (1988); *A Dream of Mind* (1992); *Repair* (1999).

Miller Williams (1930–)

Born in Arkansas. Received a master's from the University of Arkansas. Has worked in Chile and at the University of Mexico. Wrote the Inaugural Poem for President Clinton's second term inauguration. Among his many honors are the Amy Lowell Award and the Prix de Rome for Literature from the American Academy of Arts and Letters. He teaches at University of Arkansas and is founding director of University of Arkansas Press.

Selected publications: *Adjusting to the Light: Poems* (1992); *Some Jazz a While* (1999). Biographical and critical works: *Miller Williams and the Poetry of the Particular,* Michael Burns, ed. (1991).

William Carlos Williams (1883–1963)

Born in Rutherford, New Jersey. Having attended a number of schools he was admitted to the medical school of the University of Pennsylvania. He published his first book, *Poems,* in 1909, studied pediatrics in Leipzig, then returned to Rutherford as a general practitioner and published many volumes of poetry and criticism.

Selected publications: *In the American Grain* (1925); *Paterson* (1946); *Autobiography* (1951); *Selected Essays* (1954); *Collected Poems,* A. Walton Citz and Christopher MacGovern, eds. (1986–88).

Yvor Winters (1900–1968)

Born in Chicago. Educated at the Universities of Chicago and Colorado, and Stanford, where he remained for the rest of his writing and teaching life. He was well-known as an essayist and critic; his criticism emphasized the moral content of art. His early books of poetry include *The Magpie's Shadow* (1922) and *The Bare Hills* (1927). His *Collected Poems* were published in 1952.

Selected publications: *Anatomy of Nonsense* (1943); *In Defense of Reason* (1947); *Early Poems of Yvor Winters* (1966). Biographical and critical works: *An Introduction to the Poetry of Yvor Winters,* Elizabeth Isaacs (1981).

Nellie Wong (1934–   )

Born in Oakland, California. Educated at San Francisco State University. She worked at the Bethlehem Steel Corporation as a secretary, which led to a life-long activism in the labor movement. She began writing poetry in the early 1970s and is one of the founding members of Unbound Feet, a writing collective of Chinese-American women. She was visiting professor in women's studies at University of Minnesota, Minneapolis. She is an affirmative action officer at University of California, San Francisco.

Selected publications: *Dreams in Harrison Railroad Park* (1977); *The Death of the Long Steam Lady* (1986); *Stolen Moments* (1997). Biographical and critical works: "Mitsuye & Nellie, Asian American Poets," (film) (1981).

William Wordsworth (1770–1850)

Born in Cockermouth, England, and educated at Cambridge. He visited France in 1790 and 1791 and was strongly influenced by the aftermath of the French Revolution. With Coleridge, he published *Lyrical Ballads* in 1798. In 1843 he succeeded Southey as Poet Laureate of Great Britain.

Selected publications: *Poetical Works* (1940–49). Biographical and critical works: *The Hidden Wordsworth: Poet, Lover, Rebel, Spy,* Kenneth R. Johnston (1998).

Charles Wright (1935–   )

Born in Pickwick Dam, Tennessee. Educated at Davidson College and the University of Iowa. His first collection, *The Grave of the Right Hand,* was published in 1970. *Halflife* is a collection of essays and interviews. His collection *Black Zodiac* (1997) won the Pulitzer Prize. He has also won the Ruth Lilly Poetry Prize and the National Book Award.

Selected publications: *Country Music: Selected Early Poems* (1983); *The World of the Ten Thousand Things: Poems 1980–1990* (1990); *Chickamauga* (1995); *Quarter Notes : Improvisations and Interviews* (1995); *Appalachia* (1998). Biographical and critical works: *The Muse of Abandonment: Origin, Identity, Mastery in Five American Poets,* Lee Upton (1998).

James Wright (1927–1980)

Born in Martin's Ferry, Ohio. Educated at Kenyon College, where he studied under John Crowe Ransom. Served with the U.S. Army in Japan then resumed his studies at the University of Washington. His *Collected Poems* (1971) was awarded the Pulitzer Prize.

Selected publications: *To a Blossoming Pear Tree* (1977); *This Journey* (1982); *Above the River: The Complete Poems* (1990). Biographical and critical works: *The Poetry of James Wright,* Andrew Elkins (1991).

Judith Wright (1915–   )

Born in Armidale, New South Wales, a remote part of Australia. She lived so far from the nearest school that she was educated via correspondence course until she was twelve. Later, she attended the University of Sydney. In addition to her poetry, she has written short stories, essays, and books for children. She has been active in both the anti-war and conservationist movements in Australia.

Selected publications: *Collected Poems* (1971); *The Double Tree: Selected Poems 1942–1976* (1978); *Phantom Dwelling* (1985); *Collected Poems 1942–1985* (1994). Biographical and critical works: *Judith Wright,* Jennifer Strauss (1995).

Mary Wroth (c. 1587–c. 1651)

Daughter of the Earl of Leicester. Niece of Mary Herbert, Countess of Pembroke. First Englishwoman to produce a full-length prose romance. The first also to compose a sonnet sequence.

Selected publications: *Poems of Lady Mary Wroth* (1983); *The Norton Anthology of Literature by Women: The Tradition in English,* Sandra Gilbert and Susan Gubar, eds. (1985). Biographical and critical works: *Love Sonnets of Lady Mary Wroth: A Critical Introduction,* May Nelson Paulissen (1982).

Thomas Wyatt (c. 1503–1542)

Born in Kent, England. Educated at Cambridge, he was Ambassador to Charles V from the court of Henry VIII. A student of foreign literature, he introduced the sonnet from Italy into England. His lyric poetry is of great quality.

Selected publications: *The Canon of Sir Thomas Wyatt's Poetry,* Richard C.

Harrier (1975). Biographical and critical works: *Life and Letters of Sir Thomas Wyatt,* Kenneth Muir (1963).

Elinor Wylie (1885–1928)

Born in Somerville, New Jersey, to a wealthy and prominent family. She was educated at home and moved in fashionable circles. Her most acclaimed volume was *Nets to Catch the Wind,* published in 1921.

Selected publications: *Collected Poems of Elinor Wylie* (1932). Biographical and critical works: *Elinor Wylie: A Life Apart,* Stanley Olson (1979); *The Life and Art of Elinor Wylie,* Judith Farr (1983).

W. B. Yeats (1865–1939)

Born in Ireland, and remained deeply involved in its destiny and development. Won the Nobel Prize in 1923 for his work in drama. Went from an early ornamental style to a commanding, complex, and late lyric achievement.

Selected publications: *Collected Poems* (1950); *The Letters of W. B. Yeats* (1954); *Uncollected Prose* (1970). Biographical and critical works: *Yeats: The Man and the Masks,* Richard Ellman (1949); *W. B. Yeats: A Life,* R. F. Foster (1997).

Suggested Reading

John Keats, Walter Jackson Bate
The Freedom of the Poet, John Berryman
Collected Prose, Elizabeth Bishop
Achievement in American Poetry: 1900–1950, Louise Bogan
Selected Prose, T. S. Eliot
Poetic Meter and Poetic Form, Paul Fussell
Proofs and Theories, Louise Glück
Can Poetry Matter?, Dana Gioia
Twentieth Century Pleasures, Robert Hass
Rhyme's Reason, John Hollander
Alone with America, Richard Howard
Poetry and the Age, Randall Jarrell
The Vintage Book of Contemporary American Poetry, ed. J. D.
 McClatchy
Rules for the Dance, Mary Oliver
The Teachers and Writers Handbook of Poetic Forms, Ron Padgett
The Sounds of Poetry, Robert Pinsky
On Lies, Secrets, and Silence, Adrienne Rich
Missing Measures, Timothy Steele
The Necessary Angel, Wallace Stevens

Credits

Ai, "The German Army, Russia, 1943" from *Killing Floor* (Houghton Mifflin, 1979). Reprinted by permission of the author.

John Ashbery, "Pantoum" from *Some Trees* by John Ashbery (Yale University Press, 1956). Copyright © 1956 by John Ashbery. Reprinted by permission of Georges Borchardt, Inc., on behalf of the author.

W. H. Auden, "In Memory of W. B. Yeats" from *W. H. Auden: Collected Poems* by W. H. Auden, edited by Edward Mendelson. Copyright © 1940 and renewed 1968 by W. H. Auden, and from *Collected Poems* by W. H. Auden (Faber and Faber Ltd). Reprinted by permission of Random House, Inc., and Faber and Faber Ltd.

George Barker, "Sonnet to My Mother" from *Collected Poems* (Faber and Faber). Reprinted by permission of Faber and Faber, Ltd.

John Berryman, "Dream Song 324: An Elegy for W.C.W., the lovely man" from *The Dream Songs* by John Berryman. Copyright © 1969 by John Berryman. Copyright renewed 1997 by Kate Donahue Berryman. Reprinted by permission of Farrar, Straus and Giroux, LLC, and by Faber and Faber Ltd.

John Betjeman, "Death in Leamington" from *Collected Poems* (London: John Murray Publishers Ltd., 1970). Reprinted by permission of John Murray (Publishers) Ltd.

Frank Bidart, "To the Dead" from *In the Western Night: Collected Poems 1965–1990* by Frank Bidart. Copyright © 1990 by Frank Bidart. Reprinted by permission of Farrar, Straus and Giroux, LLC, and Carcanet Press Limited.

Elizabeth Bishop, "One Art" from *The Complete Poems 1927–1979* by Elizabeth Bishop. Copyright © 1979, 1983 by Alice Helen Methfessel. Reprinted by permission of Farrar, Straus and Giroux, LLC.

Louise Bogan, "Tears in Sleep" from *The Blue Estuaries: Poems 1923–1968* by Louise Bogan. Copyright © 1968 by Louise Bogan. Copyright renewed 1996 by Ruth Limmer. Reprinted by permission of Farrar, Straus and Giroux, LLC.

Lucie Brock-Broido, "Of the Finished World." Reprinted by permission of the author.

Gwendolyn Brooks, "We Real Cool" from *Blacks* (Third World Press, 1987). Copyright © 1987 by Gwendolyn Brooks Blakely. Reprinted with permission of the author.

Sterling A. Brown, "Riverbank Blues" from *Southern Road* by Sterling A. Brown. Copyright 1932 by Harcourt, Brace, & Co. Copyright renewed 1960 by Sterling Brown. Included in *The Collected Poems of Sterling A. Brown,* selected by Michael S. Harper. Copyright © 1980 by Sterling A. Brown.

Hayden Carruth, "Saturday at the Border" from *Scrambled Eggs and Whiskey.* Copyright © 1996 by Hayden Carruth. Reprinted by permission of Copper Canyon Press.

Amy Clampitt, "Fog" from *The Collected Poems of Amy Clampitt* by Amy Clampitt. Copyright © 1997 by the Estate of Amy Clampitt, and from *Collected Poems* by Amy Clampitt (Faber and Faber Ltd). Reprinted by permission of Alfred A. Knopf, Inc., and by Faber and Faber Ltd.

Lucille Clifton, "move" from *The Book of Light.* Copyright © 1993 by Lucille Clifton. Reprinted by permission of Copper Canyon Press, Post Office Box 271, Port Townsend, WA 98368.

Henri Cole, "The Roman Baths at Nîmes" from *The Look of Things* by Henri Cole. Copyright © 1994 by Henri Cole. Reprinted by permission of Alfred A. Knopf, Inc.

Jane Cooper, "After the Bomb Tests" from *The Flashboat: Poems Collected and Reclaimed* by Jane Cooper. Copyright © 2000 by Jane Cooper. Reprinted by permission of W. W. Norton & Company, Inc.

Wendy Cope, "Reading Scheme" from *Making Cocoa for Kingsley Amis* (Faber and Faber Ltd., 1986). Reprinted by permission of Faber and Faber Ltd.

Alfred Corn, "A Walrus Tusk from Alaska." First published in *The Bread Loaf Anthology of Contemporary American Poetry,* Michael Collier and Stanley Plumly, editors (University Press of New England, 1999). Reprinted by permission of the author.

Hart Crane, "Proem: to Brooklyn Bridge" from *Complete Poems of Hart Crane,* edited by Marc Simon. Copyright © 1933, 1958, 1966 by Liveright Publishing Corporation. Copyright © 1986 by Marc Simon. Reprinted with the permission of Liveright Publishing Corporation.

Robert Frost, "Directive" from *The Poetry of Robert Frost,* edited by Edward Connery Lathem. Copyright © 1979. Reprinted by permission of Henry Holt & Co., LLC.

Allen Ginsberg, "America" from *Collected Poems 1947–1980* by Allen Ginsberg. Copyright © 1956, 1959 by Allen Ginsberg. Copyright renewed. Reprinted by permission of HarperCollins Publishers, Inc., Penguin UK, and The Wylie Agency.

Louise Glück, "Mock Orange" from *The Triumph of Achilles* from *The First Four Books of Poems* by Louise Glück. Copyright © 1968, 1971, 1973, 1975, 1976, 1977, 1978, 1979, 1980, 1985 by Louise Glück. Reprinted by permission of HarperCollins Publishers, Inc.

Jorie Graham, "Reading Plato" from *The Dream of the Unified Field: Poems 1974–1994* by Jorie Graham. Copyright © 1995 by Jorie Graham. Reprinted by permission of HarperCollins Publishers, Inc., and Carcanet Press Limited.

Thom Gunn, "The J Car" from *Collected Poems* by Thom Gunn. Copyright © 1994 by Thom Gunn. Reprinted by permission of Farrar, Straus and Giroux, LLC.

Ivor Gurney, "To His Love" from *Collected Poems of Ivor Gurney,* edited by P. J. Kavanagh. Reprinted by permission of Oxford University Press and Carcanet Press Limited.

Marilyn Hacker, "Villanelle" from *Selected Poems: 1965–1990* by Marilyn Hacker. Copyright © 1974 by Marilyn Hacker. Reprinted by permission of the author and W. W. Norton & Company, Inc.

Thomas Hardy, "The Convergence of the Twain" from *The Complete Poems of Thomas Hardy,* edited by James Gibson. Reprinted with the permission of Simon & Schuster. Copyright © 1978 by Macmillan London Ltd.

Joy Harjo, "Perhaps the World Ends Here" from *The Woman Who Fell From the Sky* by Joy Harjo. Copyright © 1994 by Joy Harjo. Reprinted by permission of W. W. Norton & Company, Inc.

Gwen Harwood, "A Game of Chess" from *Selected Poems* (ETT Imprint, Sydney, 1995).

Robert Hass, "Meditation at Lagunitas" from *Praise* by Robert Hass. Copyright © 1979 by Robert Hass. Reprinted by permission of Harper-Collins Publishers, Inc.

Denis Johnson, "Heat" from *The Throne of the Third Heaven of the Nations Millennium General Assembly* by Denis Johnson. (HarperCollins, 1995). Copyright © 1995 by Denis Johnson. Reprinted by permission of the author and HarperCollins Publishers, Inc.

Donald Justice, "Pantoum of the Great Depression" from *New and Selected Poems* by Donald Justice. Copyright © 1995 by Donald Justice. Reprinted by permission of Alfred A. Knopf, Inc.

Patrick Kavanagh, "Epic." Copyright by Devin-Adair, Publishers, Old Greenwich, Connecticut, 06870. Permission granted to reprint "Epic," Patrick Kavanagh, 1964. All rights reserved.

Weldon Kees, "After the Trial" from *The Collected Poems of Weldon Kees,* edited by Donald Justice. Reprinted by permission of the University of Nebraska Press. Copyright © 1975 by the University of Nebraska Press.

Jane Kenyon, "Let Evening Come" from *Otherwise: New and Selected Poems.* Copyright © 1996 by the Estate of Jane Kenyon. Reprinted with the permission of Graywolf Press, Saint Paul, Minnesota.

Galway Kinnell, "The Bear" from *Three Books* by Galway Kinnell. Copyright © 1993 by Galway Kinnell. Previously published in *Body Rags* (1965, 1966, 1967). Reprinted by permission of Houghton Mifflin Company. All rights reserved.

Thomas Kinsella, "Mirror in February" from *Collected Poems 1956–1994* (Oxford University Press, 1996). Reprinted by permission of the author.

Mary Kinzie, "An Engraving of Blake" from *Summers of Vietnam* (Sheep Meadow Press, 1990). By permission of the author.

Carolyn Kizer, "Parents' Pantoum" from *Harping On.* Copyright © 1996 by Carolyn Kizer. Reprinted by permission of Copper Canyon Press, Post Office Box 271, Port Townsend, WA 98368.

John Koethe, "From the Porch" from *Falling Water* by John Koethe. Copyright © 1997 by John Koethe. Reprinted by permission of HarperCollins Publishers, Inc.

Yusef Komunyakaa, "Starlight Scope Myopia." Copyright © 1988 by Yusef Komunyakaa and reprinted with the permission of Wesleyan University Press.

Philip Larkin, "The Explosion" from *Collected Poems* by Philip Larkin. Copyright © 1988, 1989 by the Estate of Philip Larkin. Reprinted by permission of Farrar, Straus and Giroux, LLC, and by Faber and Faber Ltd.

General Index

Index of Authors,
First Lines, and Titles

Authors are indexed in **bold type,** first lines in roman, and titles in *italics.*